OMAHA

OMAHA

Where Imagination Meets Opportunity

Friends share lively conversation at one of the charming outdoor cafés in midtown Omaha. Young professionals are among the people attracted by Destination Midtown's effort to showcase the area as a vibrant urban experience where residents are close to work, shops, restaurants, and entertainment.

OMAHA

Where Imagination Meets Opportunity

Editor ....Rob Levin

Publisher ....Barry Levin

Associate Publisher ....Bob Sadoski

Greater Omaha Chamber of Commerce Project Director ....Karla Ewert

Senior Project Director ....Renée Peyton

Project Director ....Cheryl Sadler

Senior Photo Editor ....Jill Dible

Project Coordinator ....Muriel Diguette

Senior Writer ....Rena Distasio

Writers ....Kimberly DeMeza, Grace Hawthorne, Amy Meadows,
Regina Roths, Nick Schinker

Book Design ....Compòz Design, LLC

Jacket Design ....Kevin Smith

Prepress ....Vickie Berdanis, Judith Pishnery

Photographers ....Thomas S. England, Eric Francis, David Gibb, Joe Guerriero
Doug Henderson, Jackson Hill, Scott Indermaur, Dennis Keim,
Rod Reilly, Mark Romesser, Alan S. Weiner

Published by Riverbend Books
An Imprint of Bookhouse Group, Inc.
818 Marietta Street, NW
Atlanta, Georgia 30318
www.riverbendbooks.net
404.885.9515

Copyright © 2005 by Bookhouse Group, Inc.

Printed and bound in Korea

ISBN: 1-883987-24-5

Omaha's beautiful Heartland of America Park was the scene for one of the most colorful events held during the 150! Omaha's Birthday Celebration in 2004: a rousing musical tribute to the city's history performed by the Omaha Symphony, followed by a spectacular fireworks display. Conceived by the City of Omaha and sponsored by First National Bank, Mayor Mike Fahey, and some of the city's most prominent corporations, including ConAgra Foods and Union Pacific Railroad, the July 16–18 celebrations included a concert by Omaha's own 311 rock band, a citywide Family Reunion Picnic, and the 150! Family Festival.

OMAHA
Where Imagination Meets Opportunity

would not have been possible without the support
of the following major sponsors.

Alegent Health
Apollo Building Corp
Blackwell Sanders Peper Martin LLP
Blue Cross Blue Shield of Nebraska
C&A Industries, Inc.
Certified Transmission
City of Omaha
Commercial Federal Bank
ConAgra Foods
Creighton University
Creighton University Medical Center
Crowne Plaza Omaha Old Mill
Curt Hofer Construction, Inc.
DLR Group
Durham Western Heritage Museum
First Data Corporation
First National Bank
First Westroads Bank
Greater Omaha Chamber of Commerce
Greater Omaha Convention and Visitors Bureau
HDR, Inc.
Hilton Omaha
Leo A Daly
Methodist Health System
Metropolitan Community College
Mutual of Omaha
Omaha Performing Arts Society
Omaha Print
Omaha Public Power District
Omaha's Henry Doorly Zoo
Oriental Trading Company, Inc.
Prudential Ambassador Real Estate
Qwest
Rotella's Italian Bakery
SAC Federal Credit Union
Sitel
The Nebraska Medical Center
The Peter Kiewit Institute/Scott Technology Center
Union Pacific Corporation
University of Nebraska at Omaha
University of Nebraska Foundation
University of Nebraska Medical Center
Werner Enterprises, Inc.
Westin Foods
Woodhouse Automotive Family

greater omaha
chamber of commerce

Alegent Health

 ConAgra Foods®

 **Certified Transmission** — The Job Done Right . . . at the Right Price

 APOLLO HOMES ▲ VILLAS TOWNHOMES

BLACKWELL SANDERS PEPER MARTIN
LLP

O! GREATER OMAHA CONVENTION & VISITORS BUREAU

 **CURT HOFER** CONSTRUCTION, INC. *Making Your Dream Home a Reality.*

 CITY OF OMAHA, NEBRASKA — INCORPORATED FEBRUARY 2, 1857

 **Commercial Federal® Bank**

 Creighton UNIVERSITY

 CROWNE PLAZA® OMAHA - OLD MILL — THE PLACE TO MEET.

 Creighton UNIVERSITY Medical Center

 First National Bank

LEO A DALY

METHODIST
HEALTH SYSTEM

University of Nebraska's
The PETER KIEWIT
INSTITUTE

INFORMATION
SCIENCE,
TECHNOLOGY
& ENGINEERING

Prudential

Ambassador
Real Estate

Rotella's
ITALIAN
BAKERY
Inc.

UNIVERSITY 1 OF
Nebraska
Medical Center

UNION
PACIFIC

BUILDING AMERICA®

your energy partner®
OPPD
Omaha Public Power District

SITEL

Mutual of Omaha

westin foods

WOODHOUSE
AUTO FAMILY
WOODHOUSE
BLAIR - OMAHA
BELLEVUE

Ensuring that quality educational opportunities exist throughout Greater Omaha is a goal shared by parents, educators, and civic and corporate leaders. Public and private schools work hard to provide a complete educational experience. At Brownell-Talbot School, physical setting inspires learning. From classrooms wired to the Internet to studying outdoors, more than 450 students thrive in Nebraska's only private, coeducational independent school. With an emphasis on a traditional liberal arts curriculum, Brownell-Talbot serves a diverse student body from preschool to twelfth grade. **O!**

The O! is the symbol of Greater Omaha's passion for progress and excitement about the future. The O! Campaign (www.ososurprising.com) is a partnership program of the City of Omaha, the Greater Omaha Convention and Visitors Bureau, the Peter Kiewit Foundation, and the Greater Omaha Chamber of Commerce. Developed in 2003 to help Omahans become more active participants in promoting the city, it unites tourism and economic development under one campaign. The O! has been utilized in many creative ways—at events like the Cox Classic golf tournament (shown here), in holiday parades and summer festivals, in useful gifts distributed to coworkers and friends, and in business promotions. You will see O! in some of the most clever and exciting places all around metropolitan Omaha. Watch for it. It will remind you. We're not just Omaha. We're O!

Photo by Timothy Keen

Table of Contents

One of the most striking pieces in a gallery full of surprises is the glass sculpture *Inside & Out* by Dale Chihuly on display at Joslyn Art Museum in Omaha. The *gorgeous sculpture features more than two thousand pieces of individually blown glass. It is approximately thirty-five feet high and weighs fifteen thousand pounds.*

Foreword

Visitors to Omaha step off the planes at Eppley Airfield to an amazing sight. Nearby sits a gleaming downtown skyline. There are towering corporate headquarters buildings. Stylish hotels and condominiums. A spacious, modern convention center and arena. An elegant performing arts center. It's easy to be immediately impressed.

When they take a closer look, they see more than just steel, bricks, and mortar. They see a city eager for the future.

Greater Omaha is impressive every day. The people here are warm, intelligent, hard-working, and determined. They are committed to achieving prosperity not only for themselves but for the entire community. It's an energy rarely seen anywhere else. People everywhere dream big. Omahans are taking their dreams and making them come true.

That kind of wholehearted team effort yields results. It yields jobs, business growth, and new opportunities. It also yields pride. Omahans are proud of the great things that have been accomplished in the city's first 150 years—and rightfully so. The progress has been astounding. But it doesn't stop there. Omahans are proud because the next 150 years look even better.

Newcomers quickly catch on to what our lifelong residents already know and feel. That's because Omaha welcomes everyone as a friend and neighbor. It doesn't take long to appreciate the area's top-notch schools, universities, and medical facilities; the vibrant lifestyle; its fine arts, entertainment, and world-class restaurants; and the ample recreation and sports venues. New arrival or native born, they're proud to call themselves Omahans!

This book is a marvelous testament to the wonders of Greater Omaha. It truly is a place Where Imagination Meets Opportunity!

David G. Brown
President and CEO
Greater Omaha Chamber of Commerce

Photo by Joe Guerriero

 greater omaha chamber of commerce

what a community

"*This is where we live. This is where we're going to make a difference.*"

Shannon Wallace, media director

"Omaha is led by a group of people that is so open-minded that when you come up with a good idea, they're willing to hear you out and support you, and then it's a big 'Why not?' It really draws people in because they see that a large impact can be made in a short amount of time."

Julia Kotsiopulos Hernandez, senior sales executive

"There are two types of people in this world . . . those who are from Omaha and those who wish they were. I guess that tells you how I feel about our community!"

Todd Malouf, corporate vice president

"I work with a lot of small business owners, many of whom I meet through the Greater Omaha Chamber of Commerce. I think Omaha is blessed with an exceptional level of awareness and cooperation among business owners who understand that everyone's success is enhanced when we help each other succeed."

Marty Smith, business coach

"What's really struck me is how passionate everyone in Omaha is about Omaha, and how excited they are about what it's becoming, and where it's headed in the future."

Lynn Beha, media account coordinator

"The thing I love most about Omaha is that it has big-city opportunities and activities with a small-town feel and atmosphere."

Ann O'Connor, family social service agency vice president

"Whenever I'm asked why I came back to Omaha, I tell people I never left. I discovered that living in Omaha, I could take a job anywhere in the country, yet still have my friends, family, even my own theater in a place where I don't have to deal with the headaches, traffic, and violence of cities that have outgrown themselves. Omaha is a place of comfort to me."

John Beasley, acclaimed television and film actor

"Everything that you could hope for, from a cultural standpoint ... an educational standpoint, from an 'opportunity to grow a family' standpoint—everything is already here. But Omaha isn't finished yet. Anybody who comes here has a chance to be a part of it, to make a difference and to write the next chapter in Omaha's history. I think that's exciting ... and it's an exciting time to live here."

Rick Jeffries, attorney

"In Omaha, I know my children are being raised with the kind of education and influences they will need to be successful in the world. They have a great opportunity to learn in their school system, and they're around so many interesting people from different backgrounds and different perspectives. Talk about well-rounded!"

Wendy Wiseman Gustafson, media agency vice president

"Omaha is a good blend of driven individuals from all over the country. Here they have found the unique opportunity to be mentored by some outstanding corporate and civic leaders. If you believe you have the entrepreneurial spirit, there is a lot to take advantage of here."

Brian Gubbels, corporate president

"I am so lucky to be in a profession where every day I see the amount of generosity that comes from our community to help educate our youth, fund the arts, and take care of those in need. We are a city that dedicates itself to philanthropy."

Melissa G. Steimer, performing arts organization vice president

Chapter One

O! ENJOY

Since 1921, the Omaha Symphony has been bringing music to the city. Its nine-month season includes a masterworks series, family concerts, a chamber orchestra, free neighborhood concerts, and other programs. Guest artists such as Sayaka Shoji, shown here, add to the glamour and excitement of performances. O!

Photo by Alan S. Weiner

There is a very good reason Omahans rank among the healthiest people in the nation. With so much to enjoy, we rarely slow down.

There are state parks, city parks, family entertainment parks, and water parks. Biking and jogging trails. Waterskiing and cross-country skiing. Tennis courts and championship golf courses.

Spectators have a field day with Omaha Royals AAA baseball, nationally ranked college sports teams, and professional and amateur hockey clubs. Qwest Center Omaha is the site of the 2008 U.S. Olympic Swimming Trials. Rosenblatt Stadium is home to the NCAA College World Series.

We have fireworks shows, fairs, outdoor markets, and festivals that celebrate every reason and season. Omaha's Henry Doorly Zoo logs more than a million guests each year. Beauty dwells at the Lauritzen Gardens, Omaha's Botanical Center near the Missouri River; at Memorial Park with its fabulous rose gardens; and at Zorinsky and Cunningham lakes in west Omaha.

When it comes to style, Greater Omaha doesn't follow the East Coast or the West. We have our own. In art and fashion, the city's galleries, museums, and shops at the historic Old Market, to the vibrant South 24th Street district, and west to innovative Village Pointe please every taste.

Speaking of taste, our more than one thousand restaurants range from four-star elegance to four-napkin barbeque. After dark, the city boasts many fine theater groups. Nationally recognized productions are staged at the Omaha Community Playhouse and the John Beasley Theater. Big-name performers thrill audiences at Qwest Center Omaha, the Orpheum Theater, and the Holland Performing Arts Center. The North Downtown residential, retail, and entertainment district adds to the exciting options. The city's bar and club scene offers live jazz, indie rock, and comedy.

Who has time to sit still? **O!**

Photo by Joe Guerriero

In a city whose residents love to go out to eat, the annual Taste of Omaha, a Festival of Great Foods and Entertainment, has naturally become a highly anticipated event. Held at Heartland of America Park and Lewis & Clark Landing over a three-day weekend each June, Taste of Omaha provides some of the area's best restaurants with a unique opportunity to strut their culinary stuff. And attendees get to sample it all, everything from Mediterranean to Asian, Continental to good ol' American. The festival is also noted for its live music shows by top local and national entertainers, cooking demonstrations, wine and beer gardens, amusement rides, and an entire stage devoted to activities for the kids. **O!**

Photo by Thomas S. England

Lauritzen Gardens, Omaha's Botanical Center, provides opportunities for plant and flower enthusiasts of all ages to experience nature up close. HDR, an architectural, engineering and consulting firm, and Christner, Inc. helped create an elegant and engaging facility that not only provides year-round opportunities to connect with the natural world, but also offers visitors the chance to experience culture with an outdoor festival area and indoor art exhibits. **O!**

Stepping into the Hitchcock-Kountze Victorian Garden is like walking into a scene right out of the English countryside. Elegant, colorful perennials and vibrant vines and shrubs border a serene reflecting pool, which is accented by architectural remnants salvaged from throughout metropolitan Omaha. The perennial garden is a favorite among garden visitors and a treasure to behold. ■

Lauritzen Gardens,
Omaha's Botanical Center

Amid the hustle and bustle that is Omaha, there is a place where residents and out-of-town visitors can go to slow down, breathe fresh air, and experience nature in living color. It is a must-see destination — a hidden sanctuary of beauty — that is as glorious as it is unexpected in the heart of this lively metropolis. It is a "pocket of peace," and its name is Lauritzen Gardens, Omaha's Botanical Center.

Bordered on the east by the Missouri River, Lauritzen Gardens comprises one hundred acres of gardening grandeur, with natural woods and rolling terraces accented by breathtaking displays of perennials, annuals, trees, shrubs, roses, wildflowers, and more. From the arrival garden to the woodland trail, the venue's dynamic offerings are at once distinctive and welcomingly familiar.

"When you come to the garden, it's peaceful, tranquil, and inspirational. You can sense a personal connection to the botanical world," observes Spencer Crews, executive director. "To enjoy the beauty of nature — it's one of those experiences that cannot be duplicated by many other experiences."

Photo by Dennis Keim

When the air loses its winter chill and lush green foliage permeates the landscape, Lauritzen Gardens celebrates May's renewal with the Spring into Spring Festival. Participation by area garden clubs, as well as performances by groups like The Living Garden®, a performance troupe that enchants vistitors by transforming itself into an animated fountain, rock, and grapevine, make the annual weekend event a celebration well worth waiting for. And while they enjoy the festivities, attendees have the opportunity to purchase beautiful flora at the highly anticipated plant sale. ■

Photo by Maria Watts

When you come to the garden, it's peaceful, tranquil, and inspirational. You can sense a personal connection to the botanical world.

No one knew this better than Helena Street, the former Omaha World-Herald garden columnist who conceived the idea for an Omaha botanical garden in 1982. Her proposal laid the foundation for the project, which was developed by dedicated volunteers and donors. Benefactors of the garden, the Lauritzen family has long played an influential role in the Omaha community and was instrumental in bringing Street's vision to life.

The garden has been open to the public as a major attraction since 2001. It welcomes one hundred thousand visitors annually and has more than four thousand members. Capital development is a continuous process at this living museum with the frequent addition of new gardens and amenities, such as the Sunpu gate at the site of the future Japanese garden. New in 2005, Kenefick Park introduces visitors to Centennial No. 6900 and Big Boy No. 4023, two of Union Pacific Railroad's greatest locomotives and the centerpieces of an informative display. Plans are also under way for a significant fifteen-thousand-square-foot conservatory featuring a captivating waterfall, tropical and temperate growing environments, and an overlook that offers magnificent views of the jungle floor twenty feet below. Also to be included are permanent plant collections including orchids, palms, and tropical water lilies — creating "gardens under glass."

Crews credits the quality of the garden to a talented, educated year-round staff and a legion of devoted volunteers. These individuals manage everything from planting and weeding displays to coordinating the garden's indoor floral shows, seasonal outdoor family festivals, and other events. Also offered is outstanding educational programming, held in the thirty-two-thousand-square-foot visitor and education center.

Lauritzen Gardens has become a true community jewel, an ever-changing model of environmental stewardship, and Crews looks forward to building on its success. "Our community is appreciative and engaged in the product that we're delivering," he says. "It makes you feel like the community has adopted you. We aim to educate and inspire every visitor by creating the finest botanical garden we can." ■

Photo by Mark Romesser

Photo by Mark Romesser

A Memorial Day Tribute Concert at the innovative Village Pointe retail and entertainment center attracted nearly four thousand people to help kick off the summer season. The free outdoor event featured a concert by the Omaha Symphony and a rousing performance by Buddy Holly impersonator Billy McGuigan. Before sitting down to enjoy some music under the summer stars, attendees received O! stickers, temporary tattoos, and balloons from volunteer Sara Zehnacker. It was a festive occasion enjoyed by all. **O!**

Photo by Mark Romesser

Photo by Village Pointe®

This student savors a short break between classes, lounging on a bench and enjoying a cold soda while taking advantage of Creighton University's peaceful campus setting. During the fall semester, the area is especially beautiful as leaves begin to give way to vibrant jeweled tones and a cool breeze replaces the warm winds of summer. With so much natural resplendence to bask in, it's easy to feel far away from Omaha's bustling downtown business district—even though it is only just around the corner. O!

Photo by Mark Romesser

Photo by Thomas S. England

Beautiful jogging and biking trails like this one that winds through stately Elmwood Park are just a segment of the programs and facilities maintained by the City of Omaha Parks, Recreation and Public Property Department. Walkers, joggers, bicyclists, and skaters regularly enjoy the eighty miles of interconnecting trails linking neighborhoods, schools, shopping areas, and businesses. This section of the Elmwood Park Connector Trail begins at 72nd and Pacific Streets and continues east to 67th Street. The huge elm trees prompted the original commissioners to give the park its name. O!

" *I love driving home in September, especially through midtown where I live. There is orange, red, and yellow everywhere.* "

Jason Gilbreath, financial manager

Photo by Mark Romesser

Photo by Mark Romesser

Whether it's a snowy morning or a cold, crisp winter day, there's something beautiful to discover while strolling through the Fontenelle Forest Nature Center in Bellevue. Featuring more than fourteen hundred acres and twenty-six miles of walking trails along the Missouri River south of Omaha, the forest is managed by the Fontenelle Nature Association. Bird watching is a popular activity, and those who venture out in winter are rewarded with the exhilarating sight of thousands of migrating birds and the arrival of cool-weather residents such as Juncos and Mallard ducks. In addition to its educational mission, the association is responsible for preserving the area's natural resources through ecologically sound practices that involve controlling the spread of invasive plant species, planting prairies on appropriate open sites, restoring bur oak savanna habitats, and managing the whitetail deer population. O!

City of
Omaha

By consciously planning for growth, fostering competitive economic development, and providing residents with effective and efficient city services, Omaha distinguishes itself as one of the country's best places to live, work, and play.

With vision and teamwork, Omaha, Nebraska, has become the envy of cities nationwide. A modern metropolitan area, Omaha boasts an economic climate where any business or citizen can succeed. (Just ask any of the four Fortune 500 companies that call Omaha home.) And its unique public/private partnerships ensure that Omaha continues its march to an even brighter future.

With a current metropolitan population of eight hundred thousand Omaha is a AAA-bonded economic leader in telecommunications, health services, transportation, and defense.

Most recently Omaha rebuilt its downtown and Missouri Riverfront with a $2 billion reinvestment. It's where Omaha took root more than 150 years ago. Omahans and visitors alike enjoy the transformation that

Mayor Mike Fahey and Martin Luther King III at the unveiling of the Dr. Martin Luther King Jr. sculpture outside the Douglas County Courthouse. The nine-foot-tall work by Littleton Alston was a project driven by Mayor Fahey with financial support from the Lozier Foundation. ■

Photo by Tess Fogarty

A modern metropolitan area, Omaha boasts an economic climate where any business or citizen can succeed.

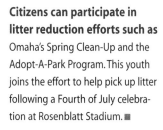

Citizens can participate in litter reduction efforts such as Omaha's Spring Clean-Up and the Adopt-A-Park Program. This youth joins the effort to help pick up litter following a Fourth of July celebration at Rosenblatt Stadium. ■

Photo by Eric Francis

includes the First National Bank Tower, Qwest Center Omaha Convention Center & Arena, Lewis & Clark Landing, The Holland Performing Arts Center, Gallup University, ConAgra Foods, and the National Park Service Midwest Regional Headquarters.

Soon a new urban neighborhood will offer waterfront residences, and a $25 million pedestrian bridge will cross the Missouri to connect Omaha with Council Bluffs, Iowa, and miles of biking and walking trails.

The city's outstanding parks and recreational system comprises 203 public parks and an eighty-five-mile interconnected walking and biking trail system which includes the highly acclaimed Lewis and Clark Riverfront Interpretive Trail. Additional opportunities include fourteen community/senior centers, adult basketball and volleyball teams, three ice arenas, a citywide swim program, eight public golf courses, a summer youth program, and wheelchair sports camp, just to name a few. The city also owns and operates Rosenblatt Stadium, Nebraska's premier baseball facility and home to the College World Series, and manages operations of the Qwest Center Omaha through the Metropolitan Entertainment & Convention Authority (MECA).

Recent administrations, exemplified by that of the highly effective and popular mayor Mike Fahey, have extended the revitalization efforts throughout the city. Current enhancement projects include the Neighborhood Parks and Library Renovation Plan that is renovating 70 of 120 neighborhood parks and five libraries, and the Mayor's Neighborhood Grant Program. Designed to empower neighborhood leaders with improvement tools, the grant program has been the catalyst for significant transformations citywide.

Urban design continues to set Omaha apart. As the largest initiative of its kind ever undertaken by a city in the United States, "Omaha By Design" is a comprehensive urban development program that ensures the city is built to

Continued on page 36

Continued from page 35

higher standards, promoting streetscapes, neighborhood preservation, pedestrian-friendly connectors and design guidelines.

Additionally, the City of Omaha has worked closely with neighborhood and business leaders to craft individual economic development plans for the revitalization of Omaha's smaller business districts. Among those are Destination Midtown, North Downtown, and work along the North and South 24th Street Business Corridors. The ultimate goal is to create destinations all across the city.

The city's commitment to a strong economic environment and livable residential communities is matched by its commitment to an educated, talented, and progressive citizenry. Omaha is

Thousands of Omahans turned out for a free concert in Memorial Park featuring Omaha's own 311 rock band, as part of Omaha's 150th birthday celebration in 2004. ■

Photo by Alterick Wilson

Photo by Andrew J. Baran

Part of the city's North 24th beautification project, this Littleton Alston sculpture and the newly created plaza in which it stands, Dreamland Plaza, pay tribute to North Omaha's rich jazz history. ■

Photo by Joe Guerriero

Protecting Omaha's citizens, families, and businesses is the mission of the city's team of well-trained, highly professional, and dedicated fire firefighters. ■

home to the University of Nebraska Omaha, Creighton University, Metropolitan Community College, University of Nebraska Medical Center, Creighton University Medical Center, and top-rated K-12 public education. Each contribute to Omaha's diverse and well-educated workforce and responds quickly to business training needs.

To ensure the community as a whole runs smoothly and efficiently, city government also supports scores of municipal services, a dozen different departments including public works, parks, tourism, police and fire, finance and workforce development, as well as a half dozen city-related agencies like the Douglas-Omaha Technology Commission, Keep Omaha Beautiful, and an Independent Public Safety Auditor.

In just over 150 years, Omaha has grown from a small ferry stop on the banks of the Missouri River into one of the most prosperous cities in America. Its success combines many factors, not the least of which is a long history of progressive public- and private-sector leaders who have embraced the promise of the city's future. ■

Photo by Mark Romesser

These youths prepare to cast their lines on a fishing trip as part of the City of Omaha's Sun Dawgs summer program for kids. The program provides fun, educational, and cultural activities for youth throughout the summer months. ■

U.S AIR FORCE

Underneath the massive glass and steel atrium of the Strategic Air and Space Museum is housed one of the world's most awesome military aircraft, the Lockheed SR-71 Blackbird. Established in 1959 at Offutt Air Force Base as the Strategic Aerospace Museum, in 1998 after a $33 million capital campaign, the museum moved to its present location in Ashland, just off I-80. With the change, the museum incorporated its tradition of preserving the history of the Strategic Air Command with permanent and traveling exhibits dedicated to the sciences, engineering, aviation, and space travel. The museum also offers an array of educational programming to teachers of all grade levels to help foster interest in aviation and aerospace studies. In addition to the glass atrium, the three-hundred-thousand-square-foot museum contains two aircraft display hangars, a traveling exhibit area, a children's interactive gallery, an aircraft restoration gallery, a two-hundred-seat theatre, and a museum store and snack bar. O!

Photo by Doug Henderson

Photo by Mark Romesser

Photo by Mark Romesser

Every summer from the middle of June to the beginning of August, kids from age four through eighth grade can discover the wonders of the natural world at the Fontenelle Nature Association's Nature Discovery Camps. Broken down into six different age/grade groups, with programs within each group, the camps are taught by Fontenelle Nature Association's year-round professional educators, college students, and local teachers, who use games, stories, art activities, and explorations of the Fontenelle Forest and surrounding waters to instruct their young charges in various natural science topics. Here, seventh- and eighth-graders participate in the Camping and Science Investigators' Camp Canoe Craze, a three-day adventure that teaches canoeing and water navigation skills and provides opportunities for wildlife viewing and exploration. O!

Photo by Mark Romesser

Photo by Mark Romesser

Famous
Dave's

The moment he sampled Famous Dave's barbecue, retired restaurateur Willy Theisen knew it was time to get cooking again. The "almost addictive" flavor, combined with Famous Dave's finely tuned operating plan, led Theisen to open his first franchise in Omaha. "If you want good barbecue served in a family-friendly, cheerful setting, Dave's is the place," explains Theisen.

Today, Theisen owns a half-dozen Famous Dave's in Nebraska and Kansas, part of a string of over one hundred such restaurants nationwide.

Taking the time to produce a consistent product is the key to the restaurant's popularity, says Theisen. "We start early in the morning, slow roasting all these meats, and all our side dishes are handmade from scratch. In fact, everything is made from a recipe, which makes it good every time."

Indeed, patiently seeking perfection is a company heritage, instilled by founder Dave Anderson, who

The Parker family enjoy a Famous Dave's Feast seated next to the restaurant's fireplace. A welcoming, downhome atmosphere adds that extra inviting touch to every meal at Dave's. ■

Photo by Alan S. Weiner

"If you want good barbecue served in a family-friendly, cheerful setting, Dave's is the place," explains Theisen.

Famous Dave Anderson enjoying a slab of our hickory-smoked ribs.

spent a quarter-century developing the right combination of meat, smoke, and sauce.

Growing up in Chicago, Anderson was raised on ribs purchased by his father from the city's street vendors. Determined to create the best barbecue to be found, Anderson spent years eating at restaurants and roadside joints, and countless hours cooking and tasting his own creations.

The result was the first of what would become a collection of six award-winning sauces, each representing a regional taste discovered during his travels.

From the original "Rich & Sassy" to the spicy "Devil's Spit," Famous Dave's sauces have netted acclaim far and wide. Slathered on slow-cooked ribs, brisket, chicken, or pork, and accompanied by mouthwatering sides like corn muffins or Wilbur beans (named after the company mascot) as well as legendary homemade desserts, you have a meal fit for a night out or on the run.

Truth is, the meals travel so well that takeout and catering are large portions of the company's daily net.

Still, menu is only a portion of the story.

Famous Dave's is a place that knows the meaning of a good time. With down-home décor, foot-stomping tunes, and friendly folks waiting to serve things up just right, every visit to Famous Dave's is a real treat.

It is an environment fostered by a belief in training, team building, and internal promotion—in short, treating people like kin. "We're not just trying to provide jobs, we want to provide a career," says Theisen. "And we do well with young people because we've got a great product and a hip place where they can make a good income. As a result, we've got some great people working for us, some who have been with us since the doors opened."

Food and fun in a place that feels like home—turns out Famous Dave's has found the perfect recipe for success. ■

Photo by Jackson Hill

It started small—actually out of the back of a station wagon—but since its inception in 1976, the Omaha Children's Museum has grown and grown and grown. Rather than delivering workshops and programs on wheels, today the museum is located in the former McFayden Ford building. Its most recent renovation opened the second floor, which has made the facility one of the largest children's museums in the country. Visitors, like Benjamin and his friend, have a great time at Rainbow Farm where they can "pick" corn and other vegetables, take them into the farmhouse kitchen, and "cook" them up for supper. In another part of the community, young Caleb, who was visiting with his grandparents, tries his hand at driving the big red fire truck. **O!**

LEARNING

EXPLORING

Photo by Jackson Hill

Photo by Jackson Hill

" *The kids love it here. They always have such a great time playing and learning.*"

Kerri Thompson, museum visitor and mother of five

Photo by Thomas S. England

Anderson Partners
Advertising

"Every facet of our new building was specifically designed to fulfill client needs and make Anderson Partners a better partner," Mark Lanham, chief creative officer, said.

Anderson Partners recently relocated its headquarters to a building at 70th and Dodge Streets, which the Omaha advertising agency bought and completely redesigned to create a state-of-the-art client service center.

"Every facet of our new building was specifically designed to fulfill client needs and make Anderson Partners a better partner," Mark Lanham, chief creative officer, said. "The location, technology, and layout were carefully chosen to help us deliver more value to our clients."

The building located on the southeast corner of 70th and Dodge Streets was chosen for its central location and for the opportunity to develop a facility specifically for an advertising agency.

A new open floor plan was designed by Holland Basham Architects and encourages even more collaboration and communication between agency departments.

"What makes Anderson Partners different," said CEO Scott Anderson, "is the depth of understanding of our clients' businesses and our ability to provide integrated solutions. The design of our new building reflects the value our clients place on collaboration and communication."

An expanded voice and data center supports enhanced communications and a completely digital conference room and presentation system.

According to Dan Hatfield, creative director, "The north face of our building offers us unique, billboard-sized panels which we will be using to promote ourselves and our clients to over eighty thousand vehicles a day." Hatfield said these unique panels will feature logos, campaigns, and promotional messages.

Anderson Partners is a full-service advertising, public relations, and marketing consulting company based in Omaha, Nebraska, which serves a broad range of national and local clients in the health-care, food, and retail industries. ∎

Photo by Rudy Smith

Photo by Neville Murray

Visiting jazz violinist Ken Ford conducts a Soul School Music workshop for young people at the Love's Jazz & Arts Center in Omaha. As an educational institution, the center attracts school groups from Omaha and surrounding areas for exhibits, workshops, performances, educational programs, and special activities rooted in the African American experience. O!

The Love's Jazz and Arts Center is a cultural gem set in the old Jewel Building in north Omaha. Named for the late Omaha jazz musician and alto saxophonist Preston Love, the eight-thousand-square-foot center features Love memorabilia, gallery space, performance areas, and classrooms. Executive director Neville Murray stands beside some of the center's artwork. O!

U.S. Air Force Heartland
of America Band

Photo by Eric Francis

Bringing great pride and joy to the city of Omaha is the United States Air Force Heartland of America Band, a sixty-member unit based out of Offutt Air Force Base. The band, which travels the country performing a broad range of music for both military and civilian audiences, is nationally recognized for "setting the standard for musical excellence in today's military." Established on February 1, 1943, as the 402nd Army Air Forces Band, the unit has evolved to encompass an impressive assortment of ensembles, from the popular forty-member Concert Band to the country and rock showcase band Night Wings, the jazz ensemble the Noteables, the Clarinet Quartet, the Offutt Brass, and the Winds of Freedom chamber group. Together, these entities boast a remarkable discography, as well as myriad accolades, such as four Air Force Outstanding Unit Awards and four Organization Excellence Awards, among many others—including being presented three times with the John Philip Sousa Foundation's Citation of Musical Excellence for Military Concert Bands. When the Heartland of America Band comes home to Omaha, particularly at the holidays, local citizens turn out in droves for a night of melodious magic. Here, the unit presents its annual holiday concert series, complete with beautiful music and singing, storytelling by Santa Claus, and greetings from Nebraska residents serving overseas. **O!**

Photo by Eric Francis

Greater Omaha
Chamber of Commerce

O maha's founders had a great vision when they incorporated the city more than 150 years ago. Today, that vision is reborn in excitement and exuberance sweeping the area. Development and expansion stretch from the Missouri riverfront west to the horizon and spread north to Washington County and south to Sarpy County, well beyond the city limits. New and expanded business parks. Retail development. New homes, schools, hospitals, and churches. New opportunities and promise for the future.

With one of the largest chamber memberships in the nation, the Greater Omaha Chamber of Commerce is dedicated to continuing this momentum. Its very mission statement—to increase business, investment, and employment in Greater Omaha—is a commitment to the entire metropolitan area and the state of Nebraska.

From major employers to small family-owned shops, the Chamber serves as a catalyst for growth. It is a united voice to lawmakers, a partner in community studies and planning, a source for education and workforce development, and a provider of business resources. The Chamber understands that what benefits its members will ultimately benefit everyone.

To increase business, investment, and employment in Greater Omaha is a commitment to the entire metropolitan area and the state of Nebraska.

News media and dignitaries crowd a room at the Tip-Top Apartments building as Mayor Mike Fahey, Greater Omaha Chamber of Commerce president and CEO David G. Brown, and HDR's Doug Bisson unveil the North Downtown Study and plans for the city's newest mixed-use urban neighborhood. ■

Photo by Mark Romesser

Attracting, retaining, and building business is the foundation of a strong community—and Omaha is a strong community. The city's longtime corporations read like a who's who of American business, including Fortune 500 headquarters for Berkshire Hathaway, ConAgra Foods, Mutual of Omaha, and Union Pacific. These companies recognize the advantages of the area's vibrant work ethic. They've set their roots here and continue to grow.

New businesses are constantly being added to the mix, thanks to the efforts of the Chamber's economic development team. Led by GO!—the Greater Omaha Economic Development Partnership—an investor base of two hundred companies has pledged nearly $20 million over five years to the initiative.

Taking its role as advocate to the state Capitol, the Chamber partnered with the governor and legislative leaders to champion the passage of a landmark incentive legislation package. Provisions for capital investment, tax exemptions, and credits for manufacturers, research and development, and micro-enterprises promise to make the state an even greater attraction for business in the years to come.

Omaha's strategic location, diverse economy, business-friendly incentives, and ample energy and telecommunications amenities make it easy to see why the city continues to draw a variety of young entrepreneurs and established multinational corporations. Once these companies and their employees experience the high quality of life, healthy economy, and energetic atmosphere, they realize they've made the choice of a lifetime.

For these and all its members, the Chamber provides a wealth of resources and activities designed to grow business. Each year, the Chamber coordinates more than one hundred networking events. Each day, there are opportunities for Chamber members to share leads, advice, and ideas.

The advantages are impressive. Education and research. Leadership and workforce development. Marketing and networking. Member rewards programs. Advocacy and support. Dedication and vision. Vital components of success made available through one source: the Greater Omaha Chamber of Commerce. ■

On a beautiful October day, Chamber president and CEO David G. Brown and his wife, Maggie, pass out treats from a 1927 Ford touring car. Every year since 1982, the annual Heritage Parade rolls down the streets of Omaha, celebrating the city's western and agricultural history. The Heritage Parade is one of the activities of the Knights of Ak-Sar-Ben annual River City Roundup. O!

Photo by Eric Francis

Photo by Eric Francis

Borsheim's Fine Jewelry
and Gifts

Few gifts evoke as many emotions and memories as jewelry. Intricately tied to people's personal relationships, a gift from Borsheim's is a constant reminder of the occasion that inspired the purchase.

For more than 130 years, Borsheim's has stood for quality, selection, and value. Founded in 1870 by Louis Borsheim, the company was purchased in 1947 by Louis Friedman and was shaped by his son, Ike Friedman, to become the phenomenon that it is today. The first small store, offering a wide variety of merchandise to customers, was located in downtown Omaha. In 1986, Borsheim's had outgrown its downtown facility, thus prompting a move to its current location in fashionable Regency Court. Borsheim's market expanded to include loyal customers in all fifty states, and in 1999, borsheims.com was launched, offering an extensive selection of products for online purchases. After a series of carefully planned expansions, today Borsheim's is a forty-five-thousand-square-foot enterprise poised for continued growth in the twenty-first century.

Borsheim's knows its customers want quality items for that special occasion, or simply just to express love or gratitude. ■

Photo by Thomas S. England

Borsheim's has distinguished itself among jewelers through its sales staff expertise, depth of product selection, and extraordinary Borsheim's prices. Within its forty-five thousand square feet of beautiful floor space, Borsheim's is able to offer customers over one hundred thousand pieces of inventory at an exceptional value. ■

Photo by Thomas S. England

"Our job is to listen well, offer our knowledge and experience, and help customers find exactly what they want."

In 1989, Borsheim's became part of the Berkshire Hathaway, Inc., family. Through a simple handshake, chairman and CEO Warren E. Buffett purchased the majority of Borsheim's stock from Ike Friedman. Buffett gave the management team straightforward directions: "Don't change a thing."

Borsheim's has distinguished itself among jewelers through its sales staff expertise, depth of product selection, and extraordinary Borsheim's price. Borsheim's sales staff consistently exceeds expectations. "Our job is to listen well, offer our knowledge and experience, and help customers find exactly what they want. I know I'm successful when they tell me, 'That's it, I love it,'" says Diane Bailey, one of Borsheim's senior sales associates.

Finding the perfect expression of a customer's love, gratitude, or respect isn't difficult at Borsheim's. By bringing together the company's renowned buying power and extremely low operating costs, Borsheim's is able to offer customers over one hundred thousand pieces of inventory at an exceptional value. To help newly engaged couples celebrate one of the most special times in their lives, Borsheim's provides an extensive selection of fine china settings, flatware, wonderful wedding gifts, and of course, wedding rings.

Talk to any one of the 375 Borsheim's sales associates, graduate gemologists, bench jewelers, and support staff, and it's clear that their job is not simply a job, but a passion. Among the keys to success at Borsheim's is the professional and exceptional customer service that each employee imparts to customers every day.

The opportunity to assist customers with a gift to celebrate the most memorable occasions is the cornerstone of Borsheim's business. Borsheim's legendary devotion to outstanding expertise, incomparable value, and world-renowned customer service is setting the stage for the company's growth for the next one hundred years. ■

Spotlight on
O!

150! And Counting

Photo by Scott Indermaur

Music. Dancing. A picnic. Fireworks along the riverfront. A family festival, and enough cake to feed 39,000 of our closest friends.

Sound like a party? That's precisely what we threw for our city in 2004 in celebration of Omaha's 150th birthday.

Dubbed 150! Omaha's Birthday Celebration, the festivities staged during a spectacular three-day weekend in July, along with other events sprinkled from Cinco de Mayo (May 5) through December, brought together Omahans and visitors from all over.

Nearly every ethnic background, age, and lifestyle took part. El Museo Latino and Native American dancers celebrated the rich mix that is the city's heritage. Living history and needlework presentations by the Douglas County Historical Society were part of a Family Reunion Picnic that attracted 3,000 people to historic Fort Omaha.

Photo by Scott Indermaur

Music was everywhere. The acclaimed rock, rap, and reggae band 311, whose members are originally from Omaha, gave a free performance that drew 35,000 people to Memorial Park. Among them was a group of teenagers who had driven fifteen hundred miles from Connecticut just for the show.

The Omaha Symphony and a stellar group of Omaha vocalists, performers, and musicians delighted a packed audience at Heartland of America Park. The

CELEBRATE

Photo by Scott Indermaur

Photo by Scott Indermaur

concert was followed by fireworks that dazzled a crowd estimated at 150,000 people.

The weather was glorious. The events were impressive. The crowds far exceeded organizers' expectations.

Did we mention the cake? It was huge—and delicious. To cap the weekend party, thousands came to the Qwest Center Omaha to sample the frosted masterpiece and join the Opera Omaha Chorus in singing its rendition of "Happy Birthday to You." **O!**

150 YEARS

Photo by Scott Indermaur

Photo by Scott Indermaur

Photo by Scott Indermaur

Omaha struck up the band in July 2004 during the city's highly anticipated 150th Birthday Festival, a five-month celebration that commemorated the sesquicentennial. Performing under the stars on a special stage constructed over the lagoon at Heartland of America Park, and led by conductor Ernest Richardson, the Omaha Symphony entertained thousands of Omaha residents with a poignant musical retrospective of memorable songs from the last 150 years. At the conclusion of the outdoor concert, the skies above the Missouri River lit up for miles with a luminous display of colorful fireworks—the largest in Omaha's history. The breathtaking event marked the opening of the city's new riverfront and heralded the next phase of Omaha's rich and distinguished history. O!

Omaha's
Birthday
Festival

Presented by:
① First National Bank
Mayor Mike Fahey

Sponsored by:
ConAgra Foods® ⊛ Kiewit

Media Sponsors:
KETV⑦ ⊂ ClearChannel

Produced by:
DOi

Photo by Scott Indermaur

Photo by Scott Indermaur

Over three days in July 2004, the city was abuzz with activity as Omaha celebrated its 150th birthday, culminating on Sunday, July 18, with the 150! Family Festival. Held in downtown Omaha, the festival kicked off with a ceremony led by Omaha Mayor Mike Fahey, followed by a day of Omaha-themed activities at some of the city's finest historic buildings, museums, libraries, and cultural centers. A major highlight was the cutting of a gigantic thirty-by-forty-five-foot birthday cake, baked and decorated by forty Hy-Vee employees. When completed, the prodigious pastry comprised 448 sheet cakes and twenty-three hundred pounds of frosting. Rich's, a major supplier of cake and icing products to retail bakeries nationwide, donated all the ingredients, and Qwest Center Omaha hosted the party.

Photo by Scott Indermaur

Photo by Scott Indermaur

Photo by Scott Indermaur

Photo by Scott Indermaur

And The Celebration

Omaha hosted a grand five-month birthday celebration in 2004 to mark the city's sesquicentennial. Beginning in May and continuing through December, 150! Omaha's Birthday Celebration included parades, picnics, riverfront fireworks, and concerts for all ages. Here, the rock, rap, and reggae band 311, whose members are from Omaha, plays at a free outdoor concert in Memorial Park. The band's reputation for great live performances attracts fans and fans-to-be whether on tour, on the road, or back home. The band's recordings feature chart-topping hits like the cover of the Cure's "Love Sick," which was included in the soundtrack for the movie, *50 First Dates.* **O!**

Photo by Scott Indermaur

Continues!

Mary Parizek, an Omaha Ambassador who volunteers at the downtown GOCVB Visitor Information Center, answers questions for a couple honeymooning in Omaha. More than one hundred local volunteers serve as Ambassadors across the city and welcome thousands of visitors each year by pointing out Omaha's many attractions, hotels, and shopping and dining experiences. ∎

Greater Omaha
Convention & Visitors Bureau

O maha is rapidly rising as a new and exciting destination for conventions, corporate meetings, group tours, and family reunions—thanks to the efforts of the Greater Omaha Convention & Visitors Bureau (GOCVB). As a division of the City of Omaha, the bureau promotes the city nationally as a sensational choice for business and trade events as well as personal travel.

"We package the many wonderful attributes of Omaha to position our city in the marketplace as a primary destination," says executive director Dana Markel. "It takes coordination and the cooperation of political, civic, business, and visitor-industry representatives to make certain the Omaha experience is memorable."

According to the Nebraska Department of Economic Development and the Travel Industry Association, a tremendous financial impact on the area accompanies this activity, as visitors pump more than $1 billion annually into the local economy.

Just follow the "O!" Tradeshow delegates always receive a friendly greeting from GOCVB staffers and Omaha hotel representatives eager to promote the city. The sales team focuses their efforts on shows attended by key meeting planners instrumental in delivering national conventions. ∎

Photo by Renze Display

Photo by Eric Francis

"We package the many wonderful attributes of Omaha to position our city in the marketplace as a primary destination," says executive director Dana Markel.

Whether a group is interested in bringing a small meeting to the city or renting the entire 240,000-square-foot Qwest Center Omaha convention center, the GOCVB is a valuable source of information.

Working with the Greater Omaha Chamber of Commerce and other entities, the bureau communicates with meeting and convention planners across the country to tout the city's special qualities. After an organization schedules a convention or meeting, the GOCVB's Convention Services department provides a variety of resources, including information on Omaha's seven thousand hotel rooms and scores of attractions to maps, brochures, and nametags.

The bureau has a seven-member advisory board composed of business and civic leaders. In addition to the bureau's staff, local residents known as Hometown Heroes help to attract business meetings and other events. "We want the citizens of Greater Omaha to act as salespeople for the city and bring business 'home,'" Markel says.

The GOCVB also promotes the city to group-tour planners by pitching ideas that draw dozens of motor coach tours each year. Out-of-town guests are welcomed at the Visitor Information Center at 10th & Farnam Streets downtown, which supplies directions and ideas along with maps and brochures. More than thirty Ambassadors volunteer at the center.

The bureau publishes a Visitors Guide that is distributed to more than 250,000 people annually. Its Web site, www.visitomaha.com, affords instant access to a wealth of information including accommodations, transportation, events, entertainment, and local media contacts. There are also fun facts, a listing of famous Omahans and sample trip itineraries, and a link to the Greater Omaha Film Commission.

The GOCVB wants everyone to know that not only is Omaha a great place to live, it's a terrific place to visit, too. ∎

Photo by Alan S. Weiner

Ice skating in all its forms is a popular pastime in Omaha, and one place to hit the ice is Motto McLean Arena, an indoor multipurpose facility in Hitchcock Park at 45th and P Streets. Named for E. H. "Motto" McLean, who with Jake Milford ran the state's first youth hockey camp in 1968, the facility offers a full menu of public skating sessions, Learn to Skate programs, intermediate and advanced hockey leagues, Stick and Puck and drop-in hockey sessions, and figure skating programs. It also serves as the training facility for the University of Nebraska at Omaha hockey team, an NCAA Division I squad. Pictured here, Allie Cunningham and Jeff McCollister spend an evening gliding together on the arena's two-hundred-by-eighty-five-foot rink, bundled up to stay cozy as they share the ice with other skaters. **O!**

Photo by Doug Henderson

Sailing, waterskiing, and other aquatic activities abound at the many lakes and state recreation areas in the Greater Omaha area. Here, sailing enthusiasts Pete and Paige Festersen race their Snipe sailboat during a Memorial Day regatta at 660-acre Lake Manawa east of Omaha in Council Bluffs. The Festersens are members of the Lake Manawa Sailing Association (LMSA), a local racing club associated with the Iowa-Nebraska Sailing Association. Every weekend from May through October, LMSA members, who represent nearly thirty member boats, take to the water for local races, as well as regional, national, and world competitions. And because Lake Manawa is only minutes from downtown Omaha, nestled in 1,500-acre Lake Manawa State Park, the area is also a popular spot for a wide array of outdoor recreation activities. O!

GIFT SHOP

One of the popular attractions at Durham Western Heritage Museum is the Main Waiting Room. It has ceilings made of sculptured plaster, with painted gold and silver leaf trim, and restored bronze, copper, and glass chandeliers that are thirteen feet high and five feet in diameter. ∎

Durham Western
Heritage Museum

Visitors at Durham Western Heritage Museum can eavesdrop on the lives of people who traveled through Omaha's Union Station in the 1930s, '40s, and '50s, as they view the lifelike sculptures designed by local artist John Lajba. ∎

Photo by Jackson Hill

"Education and entertainment are equally important, and a museum must have both to make a successful connection to the community," said Leo W. Smith II, executive director of Durham Western Heritage Museum.

This museum definitely has both. The only problem is that the educational programs are so entertaining and the entertainment programs are so educational, it is sometimes hard to tell which is which.

Take the facility itself. It is impossible to walk into the Main Waiting Room of what was originally Union Station and not be overwhelmed. Union Pacific Railroad had its headquarters in Omaha, and when the art deco building opened in 1931, it quickly became a showcase. In its heyday, sixty-four trains and ten thousand passengers passed through Union Station every day. That's history.

However, try taking in the grandeur of the 160-foot long hall, which is 72 feet wide, 65 feet high, with ten cathedral-like windows, a patterned terrazzo floor, columnettes of blue Belgian marble, plus six immense chandeliers. That's pure drama. It is hard to grasp that this is a hands-on, working history museum.

Or consider this. If you are a teacher who just completed one of the museum's many training sessions and then you wander into the old-fashioned soda fountain—where everything is made by hand—and treat yourself to a chocolate phosphate or a strawberry sundae, is that education or entertainment?

The riddle posed by these two museum functions seems to please the administration and staff. "In order to expand our mission 'to collect, preserve, interpret and exhibit historical and cultural artifacts relating to the history and development of the western region,' we are always advancing our reach. We have formed important partnerships with the Smithsonian Institution and the Library of Congress," said Smith. "The Smithsonian Institution's Teachers' Night, for instance, is an open house for educators all over the country. We were proud to be one of the few museums chosen to participate in this event."

Teachers' Night includes free educational resources; a tour of the museum's special and permanent exhibits; a meeting with museum educators; hands-on learning activities; a drawing for free field trips, memberships, and educational materials; discounts at the museum store; and refreshments. Again, a mixture of fun and facts.

"Our partnership with the Library of Congress enables us to offer institutes and workshops led by their staff and speakers," Smith explained. In a recent one-day free workshop, educators participated in a Library of Congress staff–led computer lab that focused on teaching teachers how to access primary

Continued on page 70

"Education and entertainment are equally important, and a museum must have both to make a successful connection to the community," said Leo W. Smith II, executive director of the Durham Western Heritage Museum.

Photo by Jackson Hill

Continued from page 69

sources at the Library of Congress. They also learned how to explore the vast resources housed there on every topic of American history. Lesson plan resources were discussed, and teachers had time to actually do some research with assistance from the Library of Congress staff.

In addition to these special programs, the museum regularly tailors programs for every age from preschool through high school. The museum can customize tours for visiting groups and ensure that each tour is both entertaining and educational.

But don't get the idea that educators are the only ones who benefit from the facilities. Residents and visitors look to the museum for elegant occasions. The museum's largest artifact, the building itself, is an extraordinary setting for

Who says education can't be fun? These young visitors to the authentic 1931 Soda Fountain in the Durham Western Heritage Museum are learning the fine points of sundaes, malts, phosphates, and banana splits hand-dipped and served the old-fashioned way. A history lesson not to be missed. ∎

Youngsters taking part in hands-on classes at Durham Western Heritage Museum will go home with their heads full of facts and figures. In its heyday, Union Station was the fourth largest railroad center in the United States. During World War II years, the station included a USO Club, dormitory, and bathing facilities. ∎

Photo by Jackson Hill

Photo by scholzimages@aol.com

Durham Western Heritage Museum provides countless opportunities to discover Omaha's history. Visitors can explore the museum's permanent galleries to learn about Omaha's history including the Trans-Mississippi Exposition, the Byron Reed Coin Collection, community development, family life, and more. ■

weddings, receptions, balls, and celebrations. The Main Waiting Room accommodates up to six hundred guests for a seated dinner or eight hundred for a stand-up reception. The Swanson Gallery, which serves as a ballroom, features six original murals illustrating the different stages of transportation. The walls are simulated Italian Travertine stone trimmed in silver leaf and imitation leather.

The Criss Conference Center combines the function of a boardroom with the beauty of the station. Along with other amenities, the Criss has a private entrance and a Bose audio sound system built in for speakers and background music.

And even this description just scratches the surface. There are still the Adah and Leon Millard Foundation's Library, the photo archives—with over four hundred thousand images—the Mutual of Omaha Theater, the Harriman Track Level, train cars, model trains, and nine separate galleries to explore. Plus (yes, there is still more) special seasonal and holiday events that provide entertainment—or is it education?—to the entire community.

As if that were not enough, the museum's long-range plan envisions a system for distance learning using the latest high-tech advancements to bring all this education and entertainment to outlying areas. ■

Located in the historic Union Station, a beautifully restored Art Deco landmark, Durham Western Heritage Museum boasts over sixty-five thousand square feet of exhibits. The museum is a Smithsonian Affiliate and houses temporary exhibitions throughout the year. ■

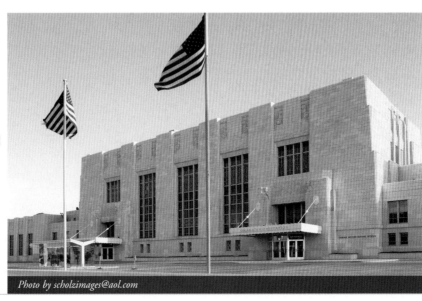

Photo by scholzimages@aol.com

When the weather warms, the players of Omaha head out to the diamond for some team action as part of Metro Omaha Softball, a competitive league coordinated by the City of Omaha Department of Parks, Recreation, and Public Property. The league offers team play in adult slow-pitch, men's and women's fast-pitch, and youth fast-pitch. Play happens at numerous area parks and runs throughout the week, with tournaments filling the weekend days. O!

Photo by Doug Henderson

Photo by Doug Henderson

Photo by Eric Francis

Who says exciting football action can only been seen on television during the NFL season? Some of the finest runs to the end zone take place on city fields courtesy of the Nebraska Midget Football League. Here, the Papio Jr. Monarchs and the OSSA Bulldawgs, which might just include a future Heisman Trophy winner or two, battle it out for bragging rights during an afternoon game. **O!**

Photo by Eric Francis

When Dan Matuszek (left) pays a visit to Rossi Clothiers, he looks forward to receiving the kind of personalized, one-on-one service that has become synonymous with Omaha's leading men's speciality store. Whether he needs a classic blue button-down, like the one he considers here, or a custom-made suit, this satisfied client knows that he can depend on Charles Rossi's (right) impeccable taste and advice. ■

Photo by David Gibb

Rossi
Clothiers

"The emphasis is on accommodating customers as much as possible to help them grow their wardrobes," Rossi says.

When Charles Rossi, proprietor of Rossi Clothiers, opened his fine men's clothing store in 1991, he had a goal in mind: to help customers acquire the same passion for clothing he possesses. Using his extensive experience from positions with Neiman Marcus and Suttons, he assembled an inventory of exclusive clothing lines that appeal to the most discerning clientele and created a comfortable, user-friendly environment in which to provide the highest level of customer service.

Today, a visit to Rossi Clothiers is more than just a trip to the store to choose some new garments. It is an experience. "The emphasis is on accommodating customers as much as possible to help them grow their wardrobes," Rossi says.

When clients walk through the door, they not only receive personalized attention as they peruse everything from tailored suits and handmade Gravati shoes to casual designer sportswear, but they also can relax with a cold beverage and catch a sporting event on television. The sociable setting, as well as Rossi's willingness to accommodate customers' busy schedules, has helped him build a rapport with his regular customers, who appreciate the incomparable taste and quality provided by Rossi and his wife, Karen, at this leading upscale shop.

"Most of my customers are very astute," he continues. "They know what they're looking for." And that's exactly why Omaha's professional men choose Rossi Clothiers as the place they go to develop their personal sense of style. ■

During a trip to Lauritzen Gardens, Omaha's Botanical Center, Carolyn, Matthew, and Elly Hoover find that there's a whole new world to discover and explore within Mother Nature's realm. And that's exactly what the staff at this illuminating venue want to impart to all young visitors—that "gardening and children go together naturally." That's why it places great emphasis on its children's educational programming, which offers everything from gardening and painting day camps to story hours and family-friendly festivals.

Junior League
of Omaha

With a mission to promote volunteerism, develop the potential of women, and improve communities through effective action and leadership, the Junior League of Omaha is a force for positive change both locally and throughout the region.

Affiliated with the Association of Junior Leagues International, the JLO was founded in 1919 by Harriet Smith Whiting, Rachel Kincade Gallagher, and Elizabeth Davis. Initially tasked with providing volunteers for the Visiting Nurses Association, the University of Nebraska Hospital dispensary, and the Salvation Army, the JLO went on to help start over a dozen local philanthropic organizations such as the Children's Crisis Center, Project Plus Literacy, and Women's Shelter Hope. Today, the JLO contributes volunteers and financial assistance to dozens more area fundraisers, organizations, and community projects.

Training is an important component of the JLO, which readies its members for charitable and educational work by providing them hands-on experience in fundraising, budgeting, program development, public relations, marketing, special events, and project coordination. Additionally, each year the JLO provides community assistance grants to deserving local causes and awards scholarships to high school seniors who have demonstrated a willingness to volunteer in the community. The league's Jumble Shop has served the community for over fifty years as an outlet for affordable clothing and household items.

Members of the Junior League discuss issues affecting the Omaha community at an Annual Luncheon celebrating their accomplishments. In the foreground, L-R: Julie Lyons, Lisa Russell, Cheryl Orlich, Eva Nunez, and Tracy Kempkes with son Dillon. ■

Photo by Dennis Keim

In the Ready Set Grow! Club at Girls Inc. of Omaha, JLO members teach children the basic skills of growing and enjoying their own fruits and vegetables. Ready Set Grow! is part of the League's Signature Program, HIP (Healthy Inspired & Proactive) Kids. ■

Photo by Doug Henderson

The Junior League of Omaha is a force for positive change both locally and throughout the region.

In 2001, the League's Signature Project Committee identified childhood hunger as an immediate and unmet community need in Omaha and immediately began what would become three years of intensive research into the issue. In May 2004, the JLO celebrated the kickoff of the resulting Signature Project, Healthy Inspired Proactive Kids (HIP Kids), which seeks to promote and provide healthy eating and activity choices for children and their parents.

But tackling hunger is just one aspect of HIP Kids.

Says current JLO president Sam Hohman: "What we found out in our research is while there are children who experience hunger, an even greater problem is that a lot of children, while fed, are nutritionally hungry. Once we realized this issue was bigger and broader than we thought, we knew one single program wasn't going to fit our needs."

Instead, HIP Kids focuses on a three-tier approach. Ready, Set, Grow! teaches children the basics of gardening and introduces them to the healthful and tasty benefits of fresh produce. Foodtastics brings parents into the equation, teaching them how to make healthful food choices as well as how to effectively plan, prepare, and budget their meals. Foodtastics programs like Family Nights, for instance, create fun, interactive programs that educate, not lecture, via live entertainment, informational booths, cooking instruction, sports activities, and hands-on demos.

Lastly, the HIP Kids Awareness and Advocacy component seeks to raise community awareness regarding the issues of childhood hunger, nutritional deficiencies, and the dangers of childhood obesity, and promotes community resources for parents and children.

By researching the community's most pressing needs and then implementing programs to address those needs, the Junior League of Omaha helps to change lives for the better, demonstrating that for a dedicated core of Omaha women, volunteerism isn't an obligation, it's a privilege. ■

With a flick of a switch by the mayor and a group of local children, the holiday season officially begins on Thanksgiving night. Thousands of lights at the Gene Leahy Mall provide the background for music, fun, and, for this couple, a little bit of private time for romance. The evening's celebration also includes a free ice show at Qwest Center Omaha.

The Pace Picante ProRodeo Challenge hosted by River City Roundup in September is one of the four major televised rodeos in the nation. Champions collide when ninety-six cowboys compete against the best animal athletes in the world. ∎

The Knights of
Ak-Sar-Ben Foundation

One of the country's most distinguished civic and philanthropic organizations, the Knights of Ak-Sar-Ben Foundation has its roots in an 1895 challenge that's straight out of the annals of the Old West. Dismayed by the State Fair's lack of family-style evening entertainment, the Fair Board challenged local business leaders to provide visitors options other than saloons, gambling houses, and honkytonks.

Soon thereafter, twelve of the city's most prominent businessmen decided to take charge of the festivities, with the suggestion they travel to New Orleans to secure for the fair all the floats that had appeared in the Mardi Gras parade. While there, these twelve men met up with the local civic group responsible for organizing Mardi Gras and were inspired to create a similar organization, the Knights of Ak-Sar-Ben Foundation.

Although its name is "Nebraska" spelled backwards, for over 110 years this organization has consistently moved toward the future, with a singular mission "to help build a more prosperous Heartland, where communities can flourish and every child can succeed." Since its inception, the Ak-Sar-Ben Foundation has

Honoring Heartland families dedicated to community service, the Ak-Sar-Ben Coronation and Ball tapped Dick Davidson, chairman and CEO of Union Pacific Corp., as the 108th King and Paige Dinsdale as Queen. To date, nearly $3 million in scholarship funds has been raised. ■

contributed more than $30 million throughout Nebraska and western Iowa toward projects in the area of community enhancement, youth enrichment, and heartland development.

Comprising a Board of Governors (company chairmen and CEOs), His Majesty's Council (company presidents or vice presidents), and a six-hundred-plus set of public volunteers known as the Ak-Sar-Ben Friends, the Foundation manages nearly a dozen volunteer awards and scholarship programs, including its signature event, River City Roundup. This annual celebration of the region's western heritage boasts three core events: the Ak-Sar-Ben 4-H Livestock Exposition, the Douglas County Fair, and the Pace Picante ProRodeo Challenge, which is aired by OLN and CBS television. Not only does the event draw more than 150,000 attendees, it raises scholarship funds for 4-H youth.

Most recently, the Ak-Sar-Ben Foundation partnered with the National Hockey League's Calgary Flames to bring American Hockey League competition back to Omaha for the first time in more than thirty years—a move, says current president Beth Greiner, in keeping with the Foundation's goals of always thinking in the long term.

"One of the unique characteristics of the Foundation is that our mission has remained the same since we were established," she explains. "We look at projects that are going to continue to make our community and state a viable place to live, work, play. Involvement opportunities can be anything, from business and education to the arts and culture. Certainly, sports entertainment and healthy living are part of community vitality. That's where our hockey partnership comes into play."

Additionally, the intent is to use proceeds from the sale of hockey tickets for charitable purposes.

The ability to give, says Greiner, is one of Omaha's most distinguishing features.

"Our volunteers do this because they truthfully want to do something for the community and for the state. It doesn't matter if they're a CEO or a mom, they're just as dedicated. I think Omaha has a wonderful spirit of giving. The more you're here, the more you see what a caring place it truly is." ■

This organization has consistently moved forward toward the future, with a singular mission to help build a more prosperous Heartland, where communities can flourish and every child can succeed.

Omaha JAZZIN' IT UP

The lively sounds of jazz and blues emanate from the shores of the Mighty Mo' during the annual Omaha Riverfront Jazz and Blues Festival. Held each July at Lewis & Clark Landing, the festival celebrates the diversity of people and music with smooth sounds of jazz and blues. National, regional, and local artists delight enthusiastic crowds who gather in celebration of the city's musical heritage. O!

Photo by Eric Francis

" The Riverfront Jazz and Blues Festival is becoming one of Omaha's premiere summer events. The diversity of the crowd and the riverfront venue combine to create a warm atmosphere for some very cool music."

Fern Spencer, marketing vice president

"The mission of Rotella's Italian Bakery, Inc., is to masterfully blend old-world skill and experience with modern efficiency to provide the very best in high-quality breads and rolls. This coupled with our dedication to strive for extraordinary service is what really completes our mission."

Louis Rotella Sr.

Rotella's
Italian Bakery, Inc.

Since the dawn of time, bread has been an essential part of our diets and our lives. We speak of the bread of life, of earning our daily bread, of casting bread upon the waters. It is even immortalized in poetry, "A loaf of bread, a jug of wine . . ." So it is not surprising to find a family-owned business that is proud of its long history of making this most basic of all foods.

Rotella's Italian Bakery, Inc., specializes in breads and rolls made from ingredients that ensure products superior in appearance and nutrition. In its state-of-the-art production facility, Rotella's strives to achieve a consistent product each and every time.

Rotella's has built its reputation on quality and service. Eighty-plus years experience in the wholesale bakery business has established Rotella's as one of the premier wholesale bakeries in the industry, providing breads and roll products nationwide.

Rotella's Italian Bakery has come a long way since the days in Calabria, Italy, when Domenico Rotella raised his own wheat, milled it into flour, baked it in a wood-fired oven, and delivered it in a horse-drawn wagon. The variety of breads and rolls may have changed, but the commitment to quality remains the same. ■

The fleet of Rotella's Italian Bakery trucks rolls out each day to distribute their precious cargo of bread loaves, dinner rolls, bread sticks, hoagies, hamburger buns, hotdog buns, brat buns, and specialty breads. Just like in the early days, the company's secrets for taste and texture are still baked into every loaf. ■

Photo by David Gibb

Rotella's Italian Bakery, Inc., specializes in breads and rolls made from ingredients that ensure products superior in appearance and nutrition.

True to its mission, unsurpassed product quality and careful attention to customer needs have served Rotella's Bakery well since 1921. The Rotella tradition, though, actually began in 1850 in Calabria, Italy, where Domenico Rotella raised his own wheat and milled it into flour, which he used to bake hearty bread that he sold to the villagers. Over time, Domenico's mastery of baking became second to none. He passed that knowledge on to his son, Alessandro, who immigrated to the United States in 1909.

Alessandro and his wife, Maria, settled in Omaha and opened Rotella's Italian Bakery in 1921. At first they baked bread in a wood-fired oven and delivered the fresh, hot loaves to their customers in a horse-drawn wagon. Over the years, Alessandro continued practicing his father's art and became a master baker himself.

Today, under the leadership of Alessandro's son Louis Senior, grandson

Continued on page 86

Five generations after this picture of Alessandro Rotella holding Louis Rotella Jr. outside their first bakery was taken, their family dedication has become an American success story. The first bakery was located at 2117 Pierce Street. ■

Experience the Flavor ...O

Rotella's Italian Bakery Inc. invites you to experience the flavor and variety on our all new website.

www.rotellasbakery.com

NEW FEATURES

History / Interactive Timeline •
Production Video Tour •
New Product Listing & Photos •
Taste and Texture Hi-lite •
Wholesale Section •
Family Favorite Recipes •
Sales Rep Locator •

You can almost smell the fresh-baked bread and rolls just by opening Rotella Bakery's website. It's no wonder they won the 2005 Addy Award from the Nebraska Advertising Foundation. Browsing this website is not only informative, it's fun. You even get favorite family recipes to try on your own. ■

Continued from page 85

Louis Junior, and other key family members including Jimmy Rotella, his son Rocky Rotella, Louis Senior's son-in-law Dean Jacobsen, and his son Dean Junior, the Rotella tradition continues with great-grandson Louis Rotella III.

Another step into the future is also a remembrance of the past. "We recently purchased a 'Ciabatta Line' from Italy which gives us the capability of producing an assortment of Artisan Breads," says Louis Junior. "These Old World–type products will be more rustic and hearty, with a heavy crust and porous texture."

The continued success of Rotella's builds on connections with both the past and the future. "We invite you to experience the 'flavor' and variety of our award-winning website," said Louis III. "In addition to the display of our products, there's a neat interactive timeline and a video production tour, which begins with some historic footage, then leads up to our present-day manufacturing facility. It's all

nline.

In 1950, Louis Rotella Sr., who is now the CEO and president of Rotella's Italian Bakery, stood proudly by his delivery truck. Today, a whole fleet of trucks delivers products in the Omaha area, and distribution centers make nationwide delivery possible. ■

Photo by David Gibb

Rotella's Italian Bakery produces a wide variety of specialty products, such as these diagonally split hoagies that are distributed throughout the United States. ■

Photo by Mark Chickinelli

absolutely real. My great-grandfather, Alessandro, shot the film on his last trip to Italy in 1958. Some of this exact footage is what you will see if you take the online tour of our facility." Rotella's invites you to view its website at www.rotellasbakery.com.

In closing, Louis III quoted his grandfather, "We wish you the very best, from the Rotella family." ■

Photo by Mark Romesser

Since 1958, Opera Omaha has made attending the opera a truly magical experience. Offering three or four superlative performances per season at the majestic Orpheum Theater, the organization has hosted some of the country's finest musical and artistic talent over the years, including opera legends like sopranos Beverly Sills and Renée Fleming. Performers like these bring moving productions to life on stage each year, such as Giuseppi Verdi's *La Traviata* (shown here). Opera Omaha found a permanent home in 1975 at the Orpheum Theater, a twenty-six-hundred-seat proscenium theater built in 1927 as a vaudeville house. Today, the facility's stage boasts not only operatic performances, but also touring Broadway musicals, Omaha Theater Ballet productions, and other popular entertainment.

Photo by Mark Romesser

Photo by Mark Romesser

Photo by Mark Romesser

Crowne Plaza
Hotel Omaha

"The Place to Meet" in Omaha is the Crowne Plaza Hotel Omaha. From its exceptional location in burgeoning West Omaha to its impressive 223 guest rooms, including 11 guest suites, this well-appointed property is one of Nebraska's finest. Yet what really makes the hotel stand out is the unsurpassed personalized attention that guests receive from the moment they walk through the door.

When a guest visits, the hotel staff prefers to think of them as a guest in their home. If the guest is new to the hotel, the staff strives to understand their needs and tries to help them achieve their goals for the visit. If the guest is one of many returning guests, they welcome them back and try to be that home away from home for them.

As the only Crowne Plaza in the state, the hotel is able to do this for all types of travelers by offering an incomparable collection of outstanding services, such as the unique Sleep Advantage program. The initiative

A melange of comfort and luxury is the theme when it comes to the Crowne Plaza Hotel Omaha's 223 guest rooms. Nowhere is this more apparent than in the hotel's 11 spacious guest suites, which boast elegant furnishings and decorations, deluxe king-size beds, and separate living room areas. Of course, every guest is treated to the property's unique "Sleep Advantage" program, which helps them get a good night's sleep thanks to duvet comforters, triple sheeting, sleep CDs, and more. ■

The hotel's ten-thousand square feet of banquet and meeting space make it an outstanding location for a wide range of events, including wedding receptions of all sizes. Here, one of the spacious ballrooms is set up to receive several hundred guests and is adorned with formal black and white decorations, which serve as the perfect backdrop for the centerpieces made of dazzling ruby red roses. ■

Photo by Mark Romesser

Photo by Mark Romesser

When guests visit, the hotel staff prefers to think of them as guests in their home.

is designed to help guests get a better night's sleep and includes deluxe features like duvet comforters, triple sheeting, sleep amenities, sleep CDs, and a number of additional services. While the hotel's renovation in 1999 was extensive, these types of continuous upgrades are what have brought the property back to the landmark status that it enjoyed in the late 1970s.

From floor to ceiling, guest room to meeting room, swimming pool area to restaurant, everything was changed during the 1999 renovation. Now guests have access to complimentary high-speed Internet access in every guest room and meeting room, a full-service business center, and an on-site health and fitness facility, as well as a beautiful oversized swimming pool and Jacuzzi, which offers one of the best views in Omaha.

Of course, visitors also have the opportunity to use the hotel's complimentary shuttle service, which will take them to many of the local restaurants, malls, or entertainment venues. And because the property is situated between the Old Mill and Miracle Hill business parks with proximity to Dodge Street and I-680, guests can get downtown or to any of the nearby attractions and developing West Omaha corridors very easily.

Furthermore, residents throughout the city, as well as visitors to Omaha, can take advantage of the Crowne Plaza Hotel's ten thousand square feet of flexible meeting space, divided between nine different rooms. Whether groups need a comfortable boardroom for twelve or a large ballroom that accommodates more than three hundred people, the hotel can handle this and everything in between. It also offers one of the most experienced banquet staffs and boasts of some of the area's best chefs.

Without a doubt, the Crowne Plaza's entire staff of more than one hundred people is dedicated not only to making every guest's stay comfortable, but also enjoyable. As soon as guests step in the door, it's easy to see that the

Continued on page 92

Photo by Rod Reilly

Continued from page 91

staff is having fun. This comes through in everything they do. Whether they are helping a local company put on a successful conference or cheering on the next College World Series Champs, they simply love being part of their guests' success.

The staff also applies this mind-set to the community the hotel calls home. "As our business continues to grow, we continually search for ways to give back to the community," reveals Jeff Bailey, general manager. Therefore, the Crowne Plaza teams with many local charities, including the Ronald McDonald House, the Juvenile Diabetes Research Foundation, and the American Cancer Society. "In addition to these charities, being part of this project is just one more way for us to say thanks," he continues. "It's something that we feel is important for Omaha." ■

Some of the best views of the city can be found poolside at the Crowne Plaza Hotel Omaha. Since its renovation in 1999, the indoor pool, with its controlled climate and sun-soaked outdoor deck, has been one of the property's most popular amenities among guests of all ages. ■

Breakfast is the most important meal of the day, and the hotel makes sure that its guests get the fuel they need for an active day in Omaha in its onsite restaurant, found on the first floor. Offering an impressive buffet each morning, as well as delightful lunch and dinner menus, the restaurant makes it easy for visitors to get a hearty and delectable meal at their convenience. ■

Photo by Mark Romesser

Photo by Thomas S. England

Room to run is a rare luxury in some cities, but in Omaha, room to run is the distinguishing feature of many public spaces, including Memorial Park.

The idea for the sixty-seven-acre open space was suggested in 1944 by local teashop owner Mrs. J. W. Broad as a way to formally honor the men and women of Douglas County's armed forces who died in World War II. Funded entirely by private donations, construction began in 1945. Three years later, Harry S. Truman delivered the dedication address. In addition to the memorial colonnade, the park is distinguished by an All-American Rose Society Garden, playground, baseball field, walking trails, and plentiful open space, enough for an impromptu weekend game of lacrosse. **O!**

FUN in the SUN!

Photo by Mark Romesser

Photo by Mark Romesser

A lighthouse in Nebraska? You bet. It's just one of the many fascinating and fun features of Linoma Beach Resort. Located on the Platte River, just south of Omaha, the resort offers a full day (or several days) of fun with a forty-acre lake, sandy public beach, and recreational vehicle park. The Lobster Inn Restaurant is the resort's place to eat with lobster tails, of course, as one of the main delights accompanied by a daily buffet, home-cooked entrées, and luscious desserts. **O!**

Papio–Missouri River
Natural Resources District

The Papio–Missouri River Natural Resources District is one of twenty-three NRDs in Nebraska responsible for soil and water conservation, flood control, recreation, wildlife habitat, tree planting, and more—a daunting task made successful by public and private partnerships. "Our NRD includes metro Omaha, and the counties of Sarpy, Douglas, Washington, Burt, Thurston, and Dakota. Three major rivers meet within our district, plus the Papillion Creek Watershed adds many more water resource challenges," said Steve Oltmans, NRD general manager. "Our goal is to create multipurpose projects that combine sound resources management with recreation and other quality-of-life benefits."

After devastating floods in 1964 and 1965 in the Omaha area, a plan was drawn to build twenty-one dams throughout the Papillion Creek Watershed. Only seven of the structures have been built. Recently completed Newport Landing Development near Bennington is a cooperative public/private partnership

The Papio–Missouri River Natural Resources District partners with other government and private groups to provide hiking/biking trails. Thousands of Omaha residents regularly ride bikes, walk, and run on the metro area's beautiful Paths of Discovery. ◼

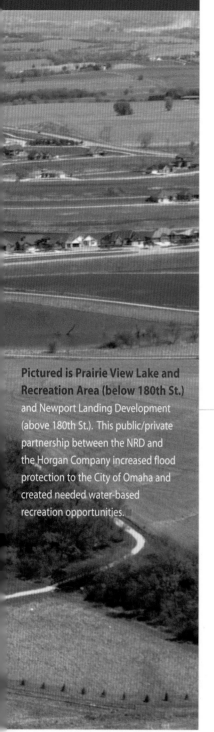

Pictured is Prairie View Lake and Recreation Area (below 180th St.) and Newport Landing Development (above 180th St.). This public/private partnership between the NRD and the Horgan Company increased flood protection to the City of Omaha and created needed water-based recreation opportunities.

Photo by Dennis Keim

Our goal is to create multipurpose projects that combine sound resources management with recreation and other quality-of-life benefits.

between the NRD and Horgan Development. "It's a win-win situation. The NRD maintains the dam, there's a great new lake community, and taxpayers get the same flood control at a fraction of the cost," said Robert Horgan, president of Horgan Development Company. Additionally, the flood control reservoir is surrounded by a public trail and offers a public fishing pier. Another public feature, Prairie View Lake and Recreation Area, was built by the NRD on land donated by the developer west of 180th Street. Flood Control Dam Site 13, near the northwest corner of 192nd and Dodge streets, is another partnership for recreation and flood control, this one between the NRD, the cities of Omaha and Elkhorn, and Dial Development.

Local meteorologist Jim Flowers, an avid fisherman, regularly takes advantage of area lakes and recreation areas. "I can take my kids out to any lake in the metro area and know they're going to have fun and catch fish. It's all right here. You can't beat it."

One of the most impressive achievements in decades for the Omaha metro area is its new Hiking/Biking Trails Network, a cooperative effort of the NRD and metro-area cities and counties. Nearly one hundred miles of trails attract thousands of walkers, runners, and bikers.

Ron Mortensen, past president of the Omaha Peddlers Bicycle Club, commented before heading out on a ride, "Our club has lots of different rides, some for exercise, some more social. It's one of the finest things that's happened in Omaha."

Larry Foster, Omaha director of parks, recreation, and public property, said, "We have the major elements in place for a trail linking Omaha and Lincoln. That's forty miles. Just shows we don't make small plans here."

There's more to come from the Natural Resources District. ◼

Photo by Eric Francis

Photo by Eric Francis

Mannheim Steamroller, Omaha's own Grammy Award–winning band, reinvented Christmas music with its 1984 blockbuster release "Mannheim Steamroller Christmas." Since then, both the band and founder/composer Chip Davis have rocketed to international acclaim for a unique style called "eighteenth-century rock-n-roll." More than 36 million albums later, Mannheim Steamroller has cemented its position as one of the best-selling bands of all time. Using Omaha as its base of operations, Mannheim Steamroller plays to sold-out crowds from coast to coast each holiday season. O!

Photo by Eric Francis

Photo by Eric Francis

Sand in the City™ puts corporate teams, local architects, and professional sand sculptors—along with 350 tons of sand— on Omaha's riverfront in a competition for top honors and a golden shovel. The public is invited to watch the massive sculptures being built and to vote on their favorites. The annual event benefits the Nebraska Children's Home, which provides care to children through a statewide adoption program, a foster-care program for medically fragile children, and day-care centers. O!

SAND
in the City

Photo by Eric Francis

Photo by Eric Francis

"*Our three children sing in many festivals, but we especially enjoy the Holiday Lights Festival downtown. We moved here so the kids could have something like this to be involved in, and in a safe, friendly, family atmosphere. That's why we live here.*"

Greg LeCleir,
corporate district manager

An artist from the Cincinnati-based Arctic Diamond ice carving team works on a large-scale sculpture for the 2004 ConAgra Foods Ice Sculpture Display and Demonstration on December 26. The six-member team turned one hundred blocks of ice weighing sixteen tons total into an intricate tribute to Lewis & Clark, featuring Corps of Discovery members as well as native plant and animal life. Held at ConAgra's downtown campus, the Ice Sculpture Display and Demonstration is one of nearly a dozen fun events that take place each year as part of Omaha's Holiday Lights Family Festival. Other popular events include museum tours, symphonic and choral performances, and a spectacular holiday lights display in and around downtown's Gene Leahy Mall. ConAgra also sponsors a fireworks display during the festival's New Year's Eve celebration. **O!**

Photo by Eric Francis

Photo by Eric Francis

Photo by Eric Francis

"I am as light as a feather,
I am as happy as an angel,
I am as merry as a school-boy.
I am as giddy as a drunken man.
A merry Christmas to everybody!
A happy New Year to all the world!
Hallo here! Whoop! Hallo!"
—Scrooge

The Omaha Community Playhouse, founded in 1925 by Dorothy Brando, mother of the legendary actor Marlon Brando, has staged *A Christmas Carol* every year since 1975. Actor Dick Boyd has played Scrooge since the play's debut and has never missed a performance—818 in all! The classic tale of a soul lost and found is one of the theater's most popular productions, and is sure to put the holiday spirit in the heart of any modern-day Scrooge. O!

The Walter and Suzanne Scott Kingdoms of the Seas Aquarium houses a variety of aquatic creatures, including Rockhopper, King, and Gentoo penguins. Viewing them is a real thrill, thanks to the sixty-foot-long, twenty-five-foot-high window that extends above and below the water. And to accommodate the arctic birds on land, the aquarium produces over twenty tons of manmade snow per day. ■

Omaha's Henry
Doorly Zoo®

S wimming with the fish in the ocean, observing the world's largest primates in their natural habitat: for many people these experiences are a far-off dream. But at Omaha's Henry Doorly Zoo, those dreams become reality.

As the world's largest indoor rainforest, the Lied Jungle allows visitors several vantage points from which to study its tropical plant and animal life—an ant's-eye view from the ground-level trail and a bird's-eye view from the canopy level. ■

Photo by Dennis Keim

Encompassing over 130 acres, nearly two dozen exhibits, a state-of-the-art IMAX® Theater, and a center for wildlife conservation and research, Henry Doorly Zoo has evolved from a small facility established in 1894 to one of the world's premier spots for wildlife viewing.

Known nationally and internationally for its state-of-the-art facilities, Henry Doorly Zoo accommodates close to 20,000 animals from among 855 species, including mammals, birds, reptiles, amphibians, fish, and invertebrates. The zoo also supports one of the country's largest wild cat populations, and serves as a major breeding facility for the animals.

The zoo is perhaps most famous for what the zoo's director, Dr. Lee G. Simmons, calls their thirteen "blockbuster, world-class exhibits." From its first large-scale project, re-creating the world's largest indoor tropical rainforest in the Lied Jungle, to Hubbard Gorilla Valley, where up to twenty-five of the world's largest primates will roam free, the zoo's goal has been to accommodate animals in as close to their natural environment as possible.

As Dr. Simmons points out, this approach benefits not only the animals, but also serves a vital educational function. "Our exhibits are like giant classrooms that transmit our conservation message through osmosis," he says. "You can shape public attitudes towards conservation so much more effectively by giving people an exciting and pleasant experience that they'll remember forever."

And that experience can be had year-round. Says Simmons: "I think the secret to our success is that we remain parklike with lots of open green space, and we put a number of our total immersion exhibits close to the main gates. That way visitors can come in on a hot summer or cold winter day and spend most of their time at our major exhibits without having to walk the entire 3.5-mile grounds outside."

Located close to the main gate are the Lied Jungle, the Desert Dome with its three desert ecosystems, the Kingdoms of the Night nocturnal exhibit, and Scott Kingdoms of the Seas Aquarium, featuring an 850,000-gallon coral reef/shark system and underwater tunnel. A walk farther through the park brings visitors to the Simmons Aviary, the second largest free-flight aviary in the world; the Cat Complex; and the Durham Family Bear Canyon, to name a few. The zoo also runs the off-site Lee G. Simmons Conservation Park and Wildlife Safari, featuring four miles of scenic prairies and wetlands filled with free roaming North American animals.

Omaha's Henry Doorly Zoo is also a recognized leader in animal conservation, research, and education, providing state-of-the-art capabilities in animal care and management, reproductive physiology, nutrition, genetics, and genome resource banking at its Bill and Berniece Grewcock Center

continued on page 106

"Known nationally and internationally for its state-of-the-art facilities, Henry Doorly Zoo accommodates close to 20,000 animals from among 855 species, including mammals, birds, reptiles, amphibians, fish, and invertebrates."

Photo by Dennis Keim

Ever wondered what bats are up to while the rest of us sleep? You'll find out at the Kingdoms of the Night nocturnal exhibit. With its wet cave, caverns, and indoor swamp, Kingdoms of the Night provides a rare glimpse into a world rarely seen by human eyes. ■

continued from page 105

for Conservation and Research. Additionally, millions of visitors each year enhance their knowledge of the natural world through real-life classroom experiences via school programs, on-site "Edzoocational" events, internships, adopt-an-animal sponsorships, and volunteer opportunities.

Offsite, Henry Doorly Zoo currently supports dozens of experts in the field who assist local and national governments in seven countries with conservation and reproductive work on a range of species, including large mammals, pachyderms, primates, and a number of rare plants.

Whether working at home or abroad, the mission at Henry Doorly Zoo is clear: provide a high-quality entertainment experience that benefits the zoo's resident animals and, ultimately, the world's wild animal and plant populations. ■

Photo by Dennis Keim

Total-immersion exhibits like the Desert Dome are what make the zoo one of the country's top attractions. Created with the utmost care in reproducing the environments of the Sonoran, Nambian, and Australian Red Center deserts, the exhibit is also notable for being contained beneath the world's largest glazed geodesic dome. ■

In Omaha, the arts community strives to be as child-friendly as possible, allowing our youth to enjoy the same rich cultural experiences as their parents.
An excellent example of this is found at the Rose Theater, part of the Rose Blumkin Performing Arts Center, a fully renovated 1927 movie palace. The center is named for the late Rose Blumkin, longtime Omaha resident and founder of Nebraska Furniture Mart. She purchased the historic building in 1981, deeded it to the Omaha Theater Company for Young People, and contributed the first $1 million toward the theater's renovation. Today, the theater company presents a wide array of productions for young audiences, such as *The Berenstain Bears On* Stage (shown here) and *Seussical the Musical.* O!

HDR architect Bruce Carpenter, Heritage Services president Susan Morris, and HDR CEO Richard R. Bell proudly anticipate the opening of the new Holland Performing Arts Center, downtown Omaha's newest destination. With a two-thousand-seat concert hall and acoustics to rival those found in Europe's finest venues, this facility will be a new landmark and cultural center for Omaha. ■

OMAHA
PERFORMING
ARTS
SOCIETY

Architects: HDR

POLSHEK PARTNERSHIP
ARCHITECTS LLP

Consultants: KIRKEGAARD
ASSOCIATES

FISHER DACHS
ASSOCIATES

Contractor: KIEWIT
CONSTRUCTION
COMPANY

HOLLA
Performing Arts

Photo by Joe Guerriero

HDR

Up to seventy-five thousand newspapers are printed per hour at the Freedom Center, the *Omaha World-Herald*'s production facility. HDR designed this facility, located downtown near the newspaper's existing headquarters, to house a seventeen-hundred-ton, German-made printing press. The five-story, 321,000-square-foot press hall is enclosed by glass walls to allow passers-by to watch the precise production of the statewide newspaper's five daily editions. ∎

Photo by Tom Kessler

"One great sustainable company" is not just a catch phrase at HDR. For this architectural, engineering, and consulting firm, it is a time-honored way of doing business. Headquartered in Omaha, HDR has a staff of forty-five hundred employee-owners in more than one hundred offices nationwide. Because HDR's professionals can provide solutions beyond the scope of traditional A/E/C firms, they have major projects in all fifty states and several countries.

"Whether we're designing a bridge or a building, restoring a fragile ecosystem, or finding innovative ways for medical professionals to spend more time with patients, we want to make communities better," said Richard R. Bell, chairman and CEO. "Our plan is to keep doing that for the next hundred years as a broad-based, employee-owned company."

Since its founding in 1917, HDR has built a reputation as the firm to turn to when the toughest, most complex projects come along.

When it came to relieving traffic congestion at Omaha's busiest intersection—114th Street and West Dodge Road—HDR was the choice. This five-year construction project will result in forty-foot-high, two-mile-long expressway bridges that will carry three lanes of traffic in both east and west directions.

When the Metropolitan Utilities District needed to design a treatment plant to meet the growing water needs of the metro area, HDR was the choice. The new facility is designed to address treatment requirements of future regulations, while being a good neighbor to anticipated residential development.

When Omaha wanted a landmark structure devoted to the performing arts for its revitalized downtown, HDR was the choice. The resulting Holland Performing Arts Center has a 2,000-seat concert hall and is a light-filled space modeled on the shoebox-shaped halls of Europe. HDR collaborated with another international architectural firm and theater consultants to create a facility that can accommodate various configurations, all with superb acoustics. A 450-seat chamber music hall and courtyard performance space complete the complex.

When government, business, education, healthcare, and neighborhood leaders wanted to define the future of Midtown, HDR was the choice. Destination Midtown is creating a new, vibrant commercial and residential community. HDR's plan will serve as a guide for continued growth and capital improvements.

Healthcare is another area where HDR shines. For example, the company was named the number-one healthcare design firm by *Modern Healthcare* magazine. "HDR has held that rank for two consecutive years on five different occasions, and our position is one of envy in the industry," said Bell. HDR consistently ranks in the "top" lists in a wide range of categories.

HDR designed the 118-bed Children's Hospital, which consolidates functions, allows expansion of essential services, and helps create new services by designing departments specifically geared to children. A glass atrium features

Continued on page 110

"Whether we're designing a bridge or a building, restoring a fragile ecosystem, or finding innovative ways for medical professionals to spend more time with patients, we want to make communities better," said Richard R. Bell, chairman and CEO.

Photo by Rod Reilly

HDR designed Children's Hospital in Omaha with its young patients in mind. For example, staff worked with area children to create artwork for the facility's public spaces. Through the use of warm colors, ambient light, natural elements, and whimsical artwork, patients and their families are welcomed and reassured. ■

Continued from page 109

a brook, trees, and two-story sunlit play space. Even from the outside, the design has a whimsical playfulness, and warm, inviting colors are used throughout the facility.

Another example is the Durham Research Center at the University of Nebraska Medical Center. Previously, the research facilities were dispersed throughout the campus. HDR consolidated them in a new facility providing multiple laboratories, an auditorium, offices, and classrooms. An enclosed pedestrian sky bridge links the research center with the rest of the campus.

And that's just the local tip of the iceberg. Notable among its national projects, HDR was awarded the engineering contract for the Hoover Dam Bypass project. This endeavor will feature a four-lane, divided highway just over three miles long, including two interchanges, a hard-

The University of Nebraska Medical Center now has a medical research facility that helps bring top researchers to Omaha. HDR designed the Durham Research Center to help facilitate the scientists' innovative research while encouraging professional interaction among staff, students, and researchers. ■

Photo by Tom Kessler

DURHAM RESEARCH CENTER

Destination Midtown is one of the largest and most proactive planning studies in the history of Omaha. HDR facilitated a unique partnership among neighborhoods, businesses, institutions, and the city that would establish a framework for Midtown's return to prominence. ■

Photo by Scott Dobry Pictures

rock tunnel, approximately two thousand feet of approach roadway bridges crossing several wildlife areas, and a two-thousand-foot bridge rising nine hundred feet above the Black Canyon of the Colorado River. The bypass, which crosses the river approximately fifteen hundred feet downstream of the dam, will redirect trucks and remove through traffic from the crest and the roadways leading to the dam.

HDR was part of a team responsible for renovating roughly 4 million square feet in Wedges 2-5 of the Pentagon, the world's largest office building. Removing 350 million pounds of debris, while keeping the offices fully operational for twenty thousand employees, was just one of the challenges on this project. HDR also designed a remote delivery facility that respected the Pentagon's historical significance. The facility garnered praise from *Washington Post* writer Benjamin Forgey, who said, "The new canopies for bus passengers, designed by HDR, are ingenious in concept, crisp in line, fluid in elevation—they're at once utilitarian and delightful."

To say that HDR's employee-owners excel on complex, challenging projects seems to be an understatement, but perhaps that's not so unusual for one great sustainable company. ■

West Dodge's new expressway, designed by HDR, will enhance traffic flow along Omaha's main east-west thoroughfare. With millions of square feet of development accessing West Dodge via cross-roads and frontage roads, keeping traffic moving throughout construction was a key part of the traffic control plan. This was particularly important at the intersection at 114th and Dodge, which is Omaha's busiest with more than 105,000 vehicles per day. ■

Hear ye! Hear ye! The Renaissance Faire of the Midlands is one of the Omaha area's most unique and highly anticipated events of the year! Held each June at the Westfair Fairgrounds east of Omaha in Council Bluffs, the three-day medieval extravaganza offers visitors a chance to travel back in time to the sixteenth century, when damsels in distress cheered for their knights in shining armor as they demonstrated their impressive skills on horseback during exhilarating royal jousting matches. During the festivities, faire performers, including premier jousting troupe New Riders of the Golden Age, treat attendees to entertaining shows, skits, singing, dancing, and much more on six stages, while costumed players amble through the fields and interact with guests of the court. In addition, merry visitors can participate in games of yesteryear, enjoy heart-pounding rides, and savor centuries-old cuisine and libations. And children have a kingdom of their own to explore in the Wee Folkes Glen, while older gents and ladies can stroll through the Artisans Market to find souvenirs that will remind them of their ancient adventure. It's family fun at its finest, as well as an event fit for a king (and queen). O!

Photo by Joe Guerriero

LEO A DALY

L EO A DALY's client list includes some of the world's most distinguished corporations; completed projects encompass fifty U.S. states and fifty countries; and its services range from architecture, planning, and engineering to interior design. World-renowned LEO A DALY remains very much rooted in America's heartland, following the values of excellence and service established by its founder over ninety years ago.

Founded in 1915 in Omaha by Leo A. Daly Sr., and in turn helmed by Daly's son Leo A. Daly Jr. and grandson Leo A. Daly III, today the firm ranks among the top ten planning, architecture, engineering, and interior design firms in the United States. Under the leadership of Leo A. Daly III, the firm has expanded its global presence, serving an international client roster that includes captains of industry, heads of state, and religious leaders including the late Pope John Paul II.

Located on the banks of the Missouri River, the Carl T. Curtis Midwest Regional Headquarters Building, National Park Service, U.S. Department of the Interior, is Nebraska's first LEED®-certified building. It received a Gold Level LEED® certification and features recycled materials, efficient heating and cooling systems, water-free landscaping, rainwater reclamation, and erosion control measures. ■

© *Tom Kessler Photography*

However diverse the project, each reflects the firm's unwavering dedication to the pursuit of excellence, innovation, and collaboration in the architectural process.

The high-rise corporate office headquarters for the First National Bank has become the signature landmark of the Omaha skyline. The forms gracefully build one on another until capped by the lantern terminus. The Tower has received numerous design awards and has attracted international praise. ■

© *Timothy Hursley*

The firm's first nationally recognized project, designing Omaha's historic Boys Town campus in the 1930s, set the tone for the future. A multidisciplinary firm with a staff of over one thousand in offices throughout the United States and in Hong Kong, LEO A DALY specializes in large-scale public and private projects for industries that include defense, aviation, high-tech, education, health-care, scientific, hospitality, retail, and commercial enterprises. Just a few of the firm's highly recognized projects include Washington D.C.'s Pope John Paul II Cultural Center, Ronald Reagan Washington National Airport, and the National World War II Memorial; the Cathedral of Our Lady of the Angels in Los Angeles; and Hong Kong's Cheung Kong Center. Some of the firm's most distinguished projects are located in Omaha and include the Woodmen Tower, Omaha Civic Auditorium, First Data Resources, Memorial Park and its World War II Memorial, numerous healthcare projects for The Nebraska Medical Center and Alegent Health, and award-winning projects such as the First National Tower, Carl T. Curtis National Park Service Headquarters, Lied Learning and Technology Center, Lied Transplant Center, and the Strategic Air & Space Museum.

Each project reflects the firm's unwavering dedication to the pursuit of excellence, innovation, and collaboration in the architectural process, while respecting the surrounding natural environment. Committed to the highest design quality, the firm's professionals continually refine and refresh their approach by combining ninety years of experience with the latest technologies, materials and controls, and management practices. Its Design Excellence

Continued on page 116

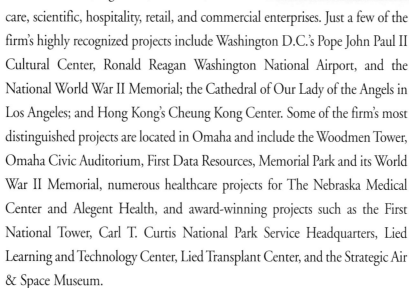

This unique project creates a link between research and transplant-related care by joining education and research spaces with patient "cooperative care" into one facility. The resulting center allows the University of Nebraska Medical Center and its hospital partner, The Nebraska Medical Center, to maintain its position as one of the leading transplant, research, and care centers in the country. ■

Continued from page 115

program, led by a committee of design directors from each office, helps reach these goals by creating and maintaining a set of uniformly high standards, while encouraging the sharing of innovative ideas.

LEO A DALY also knows there is more to a building than its design. The firm's work on large-scale, defense-related projects in the 1940s and 1950s led to continuing relationships with military and nonmilitary government agencies. LEO A DALY is recognized as a pioneer in the practice of multidisciplinary collaboration, bringing together architects, planners, engineers, and interior designers as permanent, in-house project teams. This unique team concept approach has allowed the firm to provide its clients with the broadest range of services and the highest possible level of expertise to achieve works that are unified in their aesthetics, functionality, durability, and environmental soundness.

However far its global reach, LEO A DALY is proud to call Omaha, Nebraska, its home. LEO A DALY lends constant, invaluable support to numerous local and regional organizations, initiatives, educational institutions, and services that strengthen the community at all levels.

To become a global leader in the design and construction of the built environment, LEO A DALY creates exemplary buildings and harnesses the power of architecture to enrich the human experience. ■

© *Paul Brokering.com*

Alegent Health is committed to architecture that is responsive to its mission of healing. Lakeside Hospital has set the Alegent standard for nurturing environments. Called Omaha's first "smart hospital," it accommodates the latest in medical digital technologies while promoting the patients' emotional, spiritual, social, and physical health. ■

© *Tom Kessler Photography*

Photo by Eric Francis

Photo by Dennis Keim

The view—and the company—can make an evening cruise on the *River City Star* three-and-a-half-deck riverboat a pleasurable trip indeed. Owned and operated by the Keystone Group in Omaha, the *River City Star* is the area's only passenger excursion vessel traveling along the premier Missouri riverfront development. Public trips include lunch, brunch, and dinner cruises, and the boat can be chartered for private parties and events. O!

Every Thursday night in July and August, Omahans enjoy live jazz on the east lawn of Joslyn Art Museum. Jazz on the Green is an eight-week free concert series that attracts notable jazz performers including Charlie Wood, Neal Davis, the Prairie Cats, and Bobby Watson. Since 1984, the series has become a very popular summertime event, treating thousands of music aficionados to some of the best mainstream, fusion, swing, big band, and Latin jazz around. Clearly, the music is working its magic on Connie McMillan of Omaha and Lee Taylor of Bellevue, who dance on the museum's Georgia Pink marble landing. O!

Photo by Eric Francis

Photo by Eric Francis

Photo by Eric Francis

UltraAir, LLC

When Omaha's corporations and upscale individuals want an especially high quality of charter air service, they turn to the company whose name says it all, UltraAir, LLC. "Air travel is serious business, so you owe it to yourself to fly with a company whose ownership understands what is necessary to provide the highest levels of safety and service," says president Scott Robertson. "Our clients are very successful businesspeople in their own right, and they have high expectations. Our mission is to exceed those expectations, and in every instance we have."

In fact, the desire to deliver an elevated level of customer service and safety is what led Scott and wife Gail to start UltraAir in 2002. Scott, a twenty-year manager of a major corporate flight department, had been looking for additional aircraft to supplement the airplanes owned by his employer.

When his search failed to locate an existing carrier that upheld his expected standards of training, experience, and customer service, he knew he had found a niche to fill. "We saw that large corporations and individuals were not getting the levels of service and safety that they expected and were paying for," says

In Omaha, delivering the highest quality of charter air service is a specialty of UltraAir. Corporations and successful professionals who turn to UltraAir know that their expectations will be exceeded with every trip. ■

Photo by Thomas S. England

Scott Robertson, president of UltraAir, in the cockpit of one of the charter company's aircraft. Having logged over nine thousand hours himself, Robertson knows what to look for in an experienced pilot and employs only those who also bring an ingrained sense of what customer service is all about. ■

Photo by Thomas S. England

"Air travel is serious business, so you owe it to yourself to fly with a company whose ownership understands what is necessary to provide the highest levels of safety and service."

Scott. "So we went out and started a company that does."

The couple spent five months looking for the right crew: pilots with the level of experience expected by corporations and who shared the founders' belief in making clients feel on top of the world. "Anybody can buy an airplane, anybody can hire pilots, but when it comes to customer service, you either know how to deliver it, or you don't," says Scott. "We don't train anyone in that area. We just hire the right people, those who know how to treat others. That's how we set ourselves apart."

UltraAir operates both jet and turboprop aircraft throughout North and South America and the Caribbean.

UltraAir also offers management and consulting services for clients operating, or considering the purchase of, their own aircraft. "This allows our customers to take advantage of our management expertise as well as our buying power for fuel, pilot training, insurance, maintenance, and other amenities," says Scott. "It also alleviates the day-to-day hassles and responsibilities of managing their own flight department."

While relatively new on the scene, UltraAir has made a tradition of community giving from the start. "Gail and I have both been heavily involved in the community for many years," says Scott, "and that's something we've continued since we started UltraAir. We think the community should benefit in some way from every business. We don't believe in taking from the community and not giving anything back; it's got to be a two-way street."

In addition to innumerable flights that provide transport for the speakers and guests of nonprofit organizations, the company auctions its services for charity, and its principals serve in leadership positions with a variety of area groups. It is a level of giving that mirrors the UltraAir standard of being "A Flight Above the Rest." ■

Spotlight on O!

A nyone who doubts that a diamond signifies a long-term commitment should take note of the baseball diamond at Omaha's Johnny Rosenblatt Stadium, home to the annual NCAA Men's College World Series (CWS) since 1950.

More than 5 million people have attended this national championship series. It has grown to the point that nearly twenty-five thousand fans crowd into the stadium for a single game—while millions more watch it on live television.

And while baseball may be the main draw, the festival atmosphere that accompanies the CWS each June has become a prime attraction. From the aroma of grilled Omaha Steaks sandwiches to the T-shirts, caps, and souvenirs hawked from sun-drenched booths lining nearby 13th Street, the action outside the stadium has a following of its own. For the hotels, restaurants, and others that serve the visiting throng, the CWS means big business—to the tune of an estimated $30 million boost to the area economy.

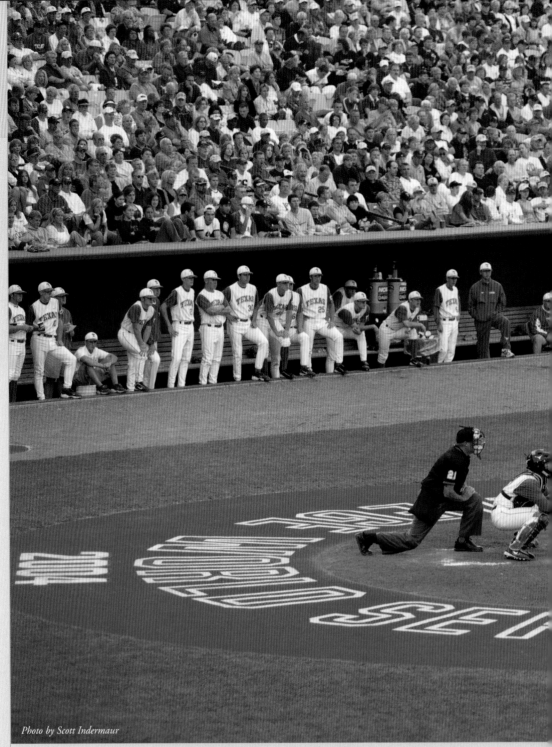

Photo by Scott Indermaur

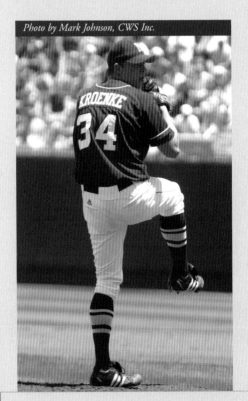

Photo by Mark Johnson, CWS Inc.

More than bucks and burgers, it's a great marketing event for the community, says Jack Diesing Jr., president of the nonprofit organizing committee, College World Series of Omaha, Inc. "It showcases who we are and what we can do."

The all-volunteer board of directors enlists support from businesses, government, civic organizations, and individuals. The board's executive committee meets monthly to develop plans that ensure the success and growth of every CWS.

College Wo

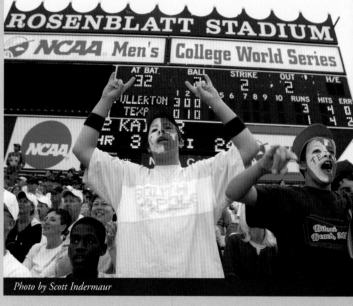

Photo by Scott Indermaur

Photo by Mark Johnson, CWS Inc.

For the teams and fans who travel the Road to Omaha and the local volunteers and businesses eager to welcome them, the CWS is a jewel to be treasured.

Perhaps ESPN commentator Mike Patrick best summarized the feelings of Omahans and baseball fans during a television broadcast of an action-packed CWS game. "Omaha is the best spot on earth for this event. I hope it stays here forever."

With endorsements like that, no matter who the home team is, Omaha always wins. O!

rld Series
The Road to Omaha

Photo by John Yochum

The star of the downtown riverfront redevelopment effort, Qwest Center Omaha is pulling in major attractions and conventions, and as a result, crowds from across the region. Omaha is now positioned as one of the Midwest's finest convention and entertainment destinations. ■

Qwest Center
Omaha

A revolutionary moment in Omaha's future happened when the citizens of Omaha overwhelmingly approved a ballot initiative to build a new convention center and arena. As a result, Qwest Center Omaha opened its doors in September 2003. With this facility, the city now finds itself on the A-list of the Midwest's premier meeting, sports, and entertainment destinations.

Qwest Center Omaha is the centerpiece of the city's $1.8 billion redevelopment plan along the Missouri River. Just five minutes from Omaha's primary airport, and in close proximity to Interstates 80 and 29, the facility is a state-of-the-art technology oasis in the heart of a charming shopping and restaurant district, the historic Old Market.

"With Qwest Center Omaha as the cornerstone to the riverfront redevelopment project, Omaha is now well on its way to being recognized as a modern and progressive city that has for too long been a hidden jewel in the middle of our country," said Roger Dixon, Qwest Center Omaha president/CEO. "Omaha's riverfront and downtown area place us next to no other city in revitalization. People continue to be amazed by this facility and are always commenting, 'I don't feel like I am in Omaha.' What a great testament to our community members who helped make this happen."

The convention center features 194,000 square feet of contiguous exhibit space divisible into three separate halls. In addition, there are sixteen meeting rooms and more than 32,000 square feet of meeting room prefunction space. The grand ballroom, often described as breathtaking, features thirty-foot-high ceilings and is elegantly finished with cherry wood accents. This 30,000-square-foot grand ballroom can effortlessly accommodate dining groups as large as several thousand, or as small as several hundred.

© scholzimages@aol.com

Adjacent to the convention center is a seventeen-thousand-seat arena. Because of its success, approximately fifteen hundred seats will be added in the summer of 2006. The arena attracts major touring artists that consistently produce record crowds. Qwest Center Omaha has continuously made Pollstar Magazine's list of top-twenty ticket-selling arenas in the world. Artists who once turned away from Omaha now make the city a must-stop on their tours. The arena is also home to the Creighton University men's basketball team and the University of Nebraska at Omaha men's hockey team. Qwest Center Omaha staff can transform the arena floor from a basketball court to a hockey rink to a concert floor in a matter of hours, allowing a wide variety of events to take place.

Accommodations are just as diverse and accessible. The 450-room Hilton Hotel is connected to the convention center via skywalk. A number of other nationally respected hotel facilities are located within minutes of downtown and the surrounding metro area, adding up to more than 10,000 available hotel rooms. Affordable, accessible, and accommodating, Omaha is a "triple A" host city, with Qwest Center Omaha as the Midwest's premier destination for conventions, meetings, tradeshows, concerts, and sporting events. ■

With this facility, the city now finds itself on the A-list of the Midwest's premier meeting, sports, and entertainment destinations.

Photo by David Gibb

The versatile Qwest Center Omaha can host a large exhibition, like the Metro Home Builders Show (above), a sales convention, or even a gala event. "If you can dream it, we can make it happen," says Roger Dixon, president/CEO. ■

No matter the generation, prom night means formal wear and what seems like hours of posing for the cameras. Moms and dads take dozens of shots looking for that perfect portrait as their sons and daughters move one step closer to adulthood. This group of girls was posing for their parents and friends at Heartland of America Park. O!

When local skateboarders and in-line skaters started talking about a place to call their own, the city listened. Actively incorporating the skaters' design ideas into their plans, the City of Omaha started work on its first skate park, a fourteen-thousand-square-foot facility to accommodate all skill levels, from novice to pro skater. Opened in October 1999, Roberts Skate Park includes all the latest in urban elements, including ramps, stairs, quarter pipes, a grinding block, fun box, and a flat area that opens up into four-foot and seven-foot bowls. **O!**

Photo by Jackson Hill

MING

WEST LANES 14 15 WEST LANES 16 17 WEST LANES 18 19

A night out to some people may mean dinner and a movie, but for bowlers it means a chance to meet up with friends, both old and new, and enjoy a little healthy competition participating in one of the nightly leagues. West Lanes, an Omaha icon for more than fifty years, has bowling leagues keeping the lanes hot from the end of August to the middle of April every year. Here, a parishioner from Holy Name Catholic Church enjoys bowling in the mixed league. There are also separate men's and women's leagues, as well as an instructional junior league for children ages four to nineteen. "Bowling is a sport for everyone," says Mary Phillips, West Lane's owner/manager. "The league, especially the mixed league, is a great way to have some fun and meet new people." O!

Photo by Jackson Hill

Described as a combination between shuffleboard, bocce, and bowling but with the strategy of chess, the sport of curling is rapidly gaining in popularity across the globe. In Omaha, enthusiasts have enjoyed the game for decades, formally establishing the Ak-Sar-Ben Curling Association in 1958. With a goal to promote the sport in the greater Omaha area and have fun doing so, today the league boasts close to sixty members, who play intramural games once a week from November to March at the Mid-America Center in Council Bluffs. Players of all ages and physical abilities are welcome. All that's required is a sense of sportsmanship and the desire to have fun. O!

As one of the nation's top catalog and Internet retailers, Oriental Trading Company markets toys, novelties, party supplies, and crafts to customers across the country. No matter what the item, from the initial creative concept to the finished product, the company focuses on fun. ∎

Oriental Trading
Company, Inc.

Oriental Trading Company (OTC) is in the business of fun. This dynamic direct marketer of value-priced toys, novelties, party supplies, crafts, and home décor has grown to become an industry leader, and ranks as one of the nation's top one hundred catalog and Internet retailers. From pink flamingos, yo-yos, and grass skirts to holiday decorations, scrapbooking, and crafts, OTC has something fun for everyone.

Oriental Trading Company offers more than twenty thousand products, and the list is as diverse as it is long. From pink flamingos to airplane gliders, Oriental Trading Company adds smiles to special occasions throughout the year. ■

"It's exciting to see our business expand as we develop new product categories and enter new markets," said Steve Frary, CEO. "But our mission remains the same—to provide our customers with an irresistible assortment of fun products for every occasion! Our customers are the real heroes—they bring smiles to others by using our products to celebrate holidays, special occasions, and events throughout the year."

"Our goal is to make the world more fun," Frary added, "and that will always be at the heart of our mission."

Evolution of OTC

Based in Omaha since its inception in 1932, Oriental Trading Company began as a wholesaler of value-priced novelties and gifts. The company became a major supplier to the U.S. carnival trade in the 1950s. The business experienced significant growth starting in the 1970s by using catalogs and direct marketing to target consumers, retailers, and businesses. In the 1980s, OTC introduced its first toll-free phone number and launched several seasonal catalogs that continued to drive growth. As the Internet grew in popularity in the late 1990s, OTC found a new channel to serve its ever-growing number of customers.

Today, the company continues to reach customers through colorful catalogs and the Internet. OTC offers more than twenty thousand products to meet the needs of consumers, teachers, schools, businesses, churches, and other not-for-profit organizations. Some of the most popular items include luau products, patriotic decorations, light-up items, and a wide variety of other novelties.

Oriental Trading Company's powerful Web presence is anchored by two easy-to-navigate sites: www.orientaltrading.com for toys, novelties, party supplies, crafts, and school supplies; and www.terrysvillage.com for home décor.

Continued on page 132

"For more than seventy years, our goal has been to make the world more fun, and that will always be at the heart of our mission."

OTC CEO Steve Frary

Oriental Trading Company catalogs showcase unique products that inspire parents, teachers, and party planners with creative concepts and ideas. ∎

Continued from page 131

Online sales now represent nearly half of OTC's business, which is testimony to the company's willingness to embrace new technologies in the interest of serving its customers.

Partnership with Omaha

Oriental Trading Company's success can be attributed to its long-standing Asian sourcing relationships, in-house product design capability, commitment to exceptional customer service, and dedicated employees. These factors, along with strong civic cooperation and pro-business policies of state and local governments, make Omaha a great place to do business.

"Omaha's central location provides access to major highways and railroad hubs, making it easy for us to serve our customers throughout the U.S.," Frary said. "The city also offers a high-quality workforce that's helped us assemble a talented, dedicated, and diverse team." In return, Oriental Trading Company has brought more than three thousand jobs to Omaha. The company is also active in Omaha through its support of various civic and charitable organizations.

Future Expansion

Oriental Trading Company has achieved uninterrupted growth for more than thirty years. To support this growth, OTC recently built one of Nebraska's largest buildings, a six-hundred-thousand-square-foot warehouse facility in the Omaha area.

"This facility will support our ambitious growth plans, help create new jobs in the Omaha region, and allow us to continue our long tradition of success," Frary added. ■

Oriental Trading Company's product offering includes many of the world's most recognized brands, including Disney, Nickelodeon, and Warner Bros. ■

Oriental Trading Company's new six-hundred-thousand-square- foot warehouse positions the company for further growth. The company ships millions of orders to customers each year, spreading fun and smiles across the country. ■

Since its inception in 1995, the Cox Classic presented by Chevrolet golf tournament has been an exciting way to spend the first week in August. For players, fans, and the legions of volunteers who assist the more than two hundred corporate sponsors, the tournament at the Champions Run in northwest Omaha has taken on a life of its own. National television coverage of the 2005 tournament on The Golf Channel presented a marketing opportunity that the Chamber and the Greater Omaha Convention and Visitors Bureau filled with two thirty-second commercials aired ninety-six times during the tournament, promoting Omaha as a great place to live, do business, and visit. The tournament followed its record-breaking tradition with 82,250 people watching the four-day event, and a purse of $625,000 handed out on championship Sunday. And the nightly party at the 19th Hole went on long after the sun had set. The tournament's success is also a boon to charities, which have benefited to the tune of more than $1 million. **O!**

Photo by Timothy Keen

Photo by Timothy Keen

Photo by Timothy Keen

"*Every August, Omaha comes alive with the Cox Classic golf tournament. From fantastic golf to free nightly concerts featuring the vast flavor of local bands, it's a 'can't miss' event that is the culmination of summer fun in the metro area.*"

Becky Phipps, auto club vice president/ regional director

Trenton B. Magid, president of Coldwell Banker Commercial World Group, and Jeff Beals, vice president of operations, inspect a construction site at The Thomsen Mile, a 145-acre, mixed-used development near 168th & West Maple Road in northwest Omaha. ■

Photo by Eric Francis

Coldwell Banker
Commercial World Group

> "When we take on a new client, our goal is to maintain a career-long relationship with him or her."

When Trenton Magid set out to establish a full-service commercial real estate firm in Omaha, he devised a twofold mission. Not only did he want to provide clients with an all-inclusive suite of unparalleled services, but he also wanted his company to become a dynamic community force, enhancing the local economy and environment by being an involved corporate citizen and civic contributor. Today, Coldwell Banker Commercial World Group (CBCWG) does all this—and more.

Since its 1997 founding, CBCWG has been firmly entrenched in every aspect of Omaha's vibrant market, from realty to charities to local politics. Started as World Group, LLC, the company became affiliated with Coldwell Banker Commercial in 2001 to boost its customer service and give clients access to expanded commercial real estate services.

Nowadays, the company offers seller and landlord representation, buyer and tenant representation, and property management services, directed by more than two dozen of the area's most talented and experienced real estate agents, professionally credentialed property managers, and staff members—all of whom make outstanding client service their first priority.

"When we take on a new client, our goal is to maintain a career-long relationship with him or her," says Magid, president. "We work very hard to earn a client's loyalty, and we never forget the role that client service plays in the success of our company."

From office, retail, and industrial sales and leasing to site selection, property management, and consulting services, CBCWG serves its clientele—and the community—comprehensively, remaining dedicated to helping Omaha thrive. ■

Playing to a packed house, with a variety show including original skits like *Romeo from Joliet*, the fourteen performers in this ten-week theatre program were certain to be a hit. Sponsored by the Region VI Developmental Disabilities Council, the Ollie Webb Center, the Circle Theatre, and Central Presbyterian Church, rehearsals and the performance helped the cast learn about listening, following directions, using their imaginations, and developing patience, tolerance, and self-confidence. Plans are under way for a return engagement. **O!**

Photo by Eric Francis

The Cornerstone
Mansion Inn

Historic charm meets modern convenience at The Cornerstone Mansion, a captivating fourteen-room guest inn located in the heart of downtown Omaha's celebrated Gold Coast area. Built in 1894 by famed architect Henry Ives Cobb for distinguished local residents Charles and Bertha Offutt, the fully renovated 10,200-square-foot Gothic Revival mansion has become a preferred location—and home away from home—for business travelers, couples, and families alike.

That's exactly what innkeepers Mark O'Leary and Julie Mierau wanted when they purchased the property in 1999. The mansion, known as the "Offutt House," had been transformed into a bed and breakfast in the mid-1980s, but these partners had a slightly different vision for the inn. They wanted to move beyond the conventional bed-and-breakfast concept and model the historic landmark after a New York boutique hotel, with a relaxed, stylish atmosphere accented by today's most sophisticated amenities. So they

The main floor library features a mahogany and pink onyx fireplace, original chandelier and beamed ceiling, all of which add to the room's warm, welcoming, homey ambiance. Pocket doors lead to the dining room and foyer, which are available for guests' use around the clock. ■

Photo by Thomas S. England

The fully renovated 10,200-square-foot Gothic Revival mansion has become a preferred location—and home away from home—for business travelers, couples, and families alike.

Built in 1894 for the Offutt family, the Cornerstone Mansion Inn offers guests an opportunity to relive the elegance of yesteryear with the conveniences of today. ■

Photo by Thomas S. England

refurbished the seven spacious guest rooms, two living rooms, dining room, and interior and exterior of the manor, bringing in new pieces of antique furniture, central air conditioning, wireless Internet access, and much more.

"We want our guests to feel comfortable and really feel like they can use the house," says O'Leary. "We don't want this to be a typical 'hotel' experience, but we want to give guests all of the hotel amenities they could want."

Striking that unique balance is what keeps the inn's guests coming back trip after trip. Even celebrities have taken advantage of The Cornerstone Mansion's well-appointed guest rooms and private baths, which are all different and boast features like ornate king- and queen-sized beds, fireplaces, oversized clawfoot tubs, and elegant decorations. One room even has a sunporch with an additional bed and loveseat. Furthermore, every room, including the mahogany library, has a fully stocked bookcase.

On weekday mornings, guests are treated to an expanded continental breakfast, complete with homemade muffins and pastries. Weekend visitors receive an added bonus: a gourmet breakfast presented in the formal dining room, which also doubles as a conference room with seating for twelve people. In fact, The Cornerstone Mansion hosts numerous meetings and corporate retreats, as well as luncheons, wine tastings, reunions, and other events. And thanks to the inn's beautiful gardens, gazebos, patios, and exclusive neighborhood surroundings, which include a forty-thousand-square-foot Scottish castle located directly across the street, it is also a perfect wedding venue.

A quick drive takes guests to a variety of attractions, like the zoo, the downtown Old Market area, and even Offutt Air Force Base, named for the Offutts' son, Jarvis. And with the airport only ten minutes away, the location could not be more ideal. Coupled with exceptional personalized service and an unparalleled blend of the past and the present, these coveted attributes make The Cornerstone Mansion Inn the best place to stay in Omaha. ■

Huntsman Mary Walker of the North Hills Hunt Club prepares to cast the hounds during a traditional fox hunt. Established in the early 1960s by Omahans Donovan Ketzler, Allan Mactier, and Dr. Irvin "Dutch" Blose, the club was recognized and reorganized by the Master of Foxhounds Association of America in 1965. Today, more than one hundred people are members of the North Hills Hunt Club, which hunts from October through April. Robyn Eden says members share a love of horses, hounds, and the beauty of the outdoors. "The joy comes from watching a finely bred, well-trained pack of hounds doing their job, trying to sort through a line in search of the quarry," she says. It is rare when the hounds are quick enough to catch their quarry, which varies from fox to coyote depending on the area. The club's written mission encourages the "humane and judicial treatment of all animals," and the promotion of conservation and preservation of all natural resources. **O!**

Whether they are riding the trail or competing in show, the members of the Nebraska Paint Horse Association are all about the beautiful horses they love. The Nebraska association has been going strong for over three decades and is but one example of the equestrian groups that exist in Greater Omaha. From trail rides and riding stables to formal shows and competitions, those who love horses, and those who love to watch the magnificent animals work and perform, enjoy many opportunities throughout the Omaha area. **O!**

Photo by Joe Guerriero

Photo by Scott Indermaur

BECOME A
FRIEND
&
CELEBRATE
SHAKESPEARE
in the
PARK
NOW
&
FOREVER

Photo by Scott Indermaur

**Every year, commoners, thespians, and the like gather on
the lush green spaces of Elmwood Park immediately south**
of the University of Nebraska at Omaha campus. They meet to
be enlightened and entertained by Shakespeare on the Green,
a world-class open-air theater. For two weeks in the early summer,
the Nebraska Shakespeare Festival presents a selection of two of
the Bard's best plays for the public to enjoy free of charge.
The plays are provided in cooperation with Creighton University,
the University of Nebraska at Omaha, and the City of Omaha. O!

Photo by Mark Romesser

Holland Performing Arts Center is recognized as a world-class center for arts and culture and as a landmark building on the Gene Leahy Mall in downtown Omaha. ∎

Omaha
Performing Arts

Formed in June 2000, Omaha Performing Arts is a nonprofit organization that's mission is to enrich the cultural lives of the citizens of Omaha and its surrounding communities through the presentation of the highest-quality local, national, and international artistic performances. Omaha Performing Arts is committed to the stewardship and management of the celebrated Orpheum Theater and the Holland Performing Arts Center; the presentation of a variety of the finest performing arts events; and education and community involvement efforts to support, enhance, and expand appreciation for the arts.

In 2002, Omaha Performing Arts assumed management of downtown Omaha's magnificent Orpheum Theater, built in 1927, as well as a new landmark structure, the Holland Performing Arts Center, which opened in fall of 2005.

Holland Performing Arts Center embodies Omaha's commitment to the performing arts. The building is named in recognition of local couple Richard and Mary Holland. The Hollands, along with many other members of the community, have generously supported the world-class building. Located downtown, the center features a 2,000-seat concert hall, a 450-seat recital hall, and an open-air courtyard. The Holland Center provides exceptional acoustics for a wide variety of performances by national and international touring artists offered by Omaha Performing Arts Presents. The Omaha Symphony and other local artists and organizations hold performances in this state-of-the-art facility.

Managed by Omaha Performing Arts, the Orpheum Theater and Holland Center are the perfect combination.

Built in the opulent vaudeville-house style of the 1920s, the 2,600-seat Orpheum Theater hosts a wide variety of theatrical presentations and entertainers. The Orpheum has a rich history of illustrious performances including Al Jolson, Bob Hope, and Lucille Ball. This tradition continues today with the very best in entertainment from Jerry Seinfeld to the leading touring Broadway shows, including The Producers and Disney's The Lion King. The Orpheum is the location for Omaha Performing Arts Presents touring artists, Broadway In Omaha, Opera Omaha, and a variety of other theatrical and dance events.

Omaha Performing Arts Presents reveals another of the organization's top priorities: to bring the very finest in touring artists to the metro area. Series offerings include the best in classical music, jazz, dance, popular entertainment, speakers/lecturers, contemporary, family, and children's programming, as well as Broadway In Omaha.

To ensure an outstanding customer experience from start to finish, Omaha Performing Arts established Ticket Omaha, a local ticketing service, providing outstanding customer service and ticket sales at the Holland Center's box office, over the phone, online at www.ticketomaha.org, via fax, or by mail.

Photo by Thomas S. England

Omaha's majestic Orpheum Theater, the site of performances by local, national, and international artists, has been providing audiences with memories since 1927. ■

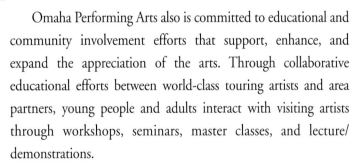

Photo by Rod Reilly

Omaha Performing Arts also is committed to educational and community involvement efforts that support, enhance, and expand the appreciation of the arts. Through collaborative educational efforts between world-class touring artists and area partners, young people and adults interact with visiting artists through workshops, seminars, master classes, and lecture/demonstrations.

By supporting and expanding cultural awareness, Omaha Performing Arts not only brings the community exceptional performing arts and entertainment, but also a greater understanding of how the arts play a vital and positive role in all our lives. ■

The Holland Performing Arts Center profile is generously supported by National Paper Company.

www.npaper.com

Through the Rose Theater, the lives of Omaha's families and youth are enriched with live performances, dance, and arts education. Housed in a former movie palace, a building of uniquely Moorish/Classical design, the Rose has been restored to a condition befitting its early days of splendor. Today, a nominal membership fee buys a family of four a host of discounts and amenities, including tickets to more than a half dozen shows like *Sleeping Beauty,* Tchaikovsky's magnificently scored version of the classic fairy tale. The Rose also offers for children and teens a variety of classes in the performing arts. O!

Let's DANCE!

Photo by Eric Francis

When Omaha's young professionals support a cause, they know how to fill the need in style—and have a whole lot of fun doing it! Take, for example, the annual Halloween costume party that not only brings out the alter ego in so many of the area's future community leaders, but also benefits the Siena-Francis House. Located in Omaha, the Siena-Francis House has been serving the metropolitan area since 1975 as part of the overall community effort to help the area's homeless population. O!

Photo by David Gibb

They came out in an even-numbered drove of three hundred to dance the night away at the Omaha Area Square Dance Council's fifty-fifth annual festival. With music spanning two decades, festival-goers had a great time. Organized in 1949, today more than a dozen square and round dance and clogging clubs make up the council. O!

Photo by Scott Indermaur

Photo by Scott Indermaur

Photo by Scott Indermaur

Photo by Scott Indermaur

As one of many arts and ethnic festivals and celebrations held throughout Greater Omaha, the Omaha Summer Arts Festival has drawn more than 1.5 million people downtown since its founding in 1975. Among the top festivals of its kind in the nation, the event stays true to its mission: to bring high-quality, diverse art to downtown. The heart of the Omaha Summer Arts Festival features the artists' market, where more than 135 exhibits display items that are available for purchase. O!

The Liberty Tavern Restaurant offers exquisite food in a casually elegant atmosphere. A private dining room for sixteen is also available for special occasions, and an outdoor patio offers open-air seating when weather permits. A sister venue, the Liberty Tavern Bar, offers casual dining and beverages. ∎

Hilton
Omaha

A great many things are happening in the heart of one of Nebraska's favorite cities, and anchoring much of the excitement is the Hilton Omaha.

Whether stopping in for a midday meal, taking part in an all-day meeting, or staying over for a week-long conference, the Hilton Omaha offers an unsurpassed level of elegance and comfort for visitors from all walks of life.

Opened in the spring of 2004 as an enhancement to the convention facilities of this world-class city, the Hilton Omaha has already become an attraction in its own right.

From the outside, the hotel is an impressive structure, connected via a glass-enclosed sky bridge to the Qwest Convention Center. Such architectural marvels make it a striking landmark in the city's center.

The Hilton Omaha commissioned dozens of area artists to create original works of art for its public spaces. The works chosen for display represent a sampling of both emerging young artists as well as some who have been creating pieces for more than forty years. Guests and locals alike enjoy the Hilton Omaha Gallery. ■

Photo by Alan S. Weiner

Photo by Alan S. Weiner

The Hilton Omaha offers an unsurpassed level of elegance and comfort for visitors from all walks of life.

But the Hilton Omaha is far more than a building of glass and steel, for within this property is an intentional focus on all that is Omaha, an institution determined, from the start, to bind itself wholeheartedly to its city.

From the beginning, builders of this hotel were committed to create a property worthy of both the renowned Hilton name and special place in the hearts of Omahans.

To ensure the success of its intent, the Hilton began, even before the hotel's opening, by recruiting some of the most qualified professionals in the business for its executive team, people who would focus on developing a place that represented a local flavor.

The result is a hotel that holds an intricate connection with the community, preserving the city's past while celebrating its future.

For example, in a nod to the city's rich history, the hotel's meeting rooms are named after properties that provided respite for travelers of yesteryear. From the simple log cabin that first sheltered guests to the upscale home of the renowned Reuben sandwich, Omaha's rich hotel past is celebrated in its newest entity. In addition, the hotel showcases Nebraska's beloved culture through the hundreds of works throughout its common areas created especially for the property by local artists.

Of course, features beyond the hotel's décor have forged its growing reputation for excellence. From its meeting rooms to fine dining options, the Hilton Omaha is a premier destination for business and leisure travelers as well as a popular spot for the locals.

Travelers staying in any of the hotel's 450 rooms will find themselves immersed in the best that Omaha has to offer, premium comfort with every feature needed for a restful night's stay. The hotel's accommodation choices also include executive-level rooms with private access, a private lounge with

Continued on page 152

The City of Omaha is proud to be the host city each year for the NCAA College World Series. The Hilton Omaha had the privilege of hosting the University of Nebraska team in 2005 and sent them off to each game with a energy packed pep rally. ■

Continued from page 151

complimentary breakfast and hors d'oeuvres, and upgraded room features.

The hotel's culinary venues make mealtime a pleasurable experience as well, whether dining in the Liberty Tavern Restaurant, relaxing in the Java Coast Coffee Emporium, or being seen in the lobby bar, a local hotspot.

Beyond its rooms and restaurants, the hotel provides travelers with extras such as extended room service, a twenty-four-hour business center, and a full-service health club complete with indoor pool, whirlpool, saunas, and spa/massage rooms.

Those traveling on business will find plenty of space for meetings of every size and subject matter. The hotel's thirty thousand square feet of flexible space encompasses a dazzling ten-thousand-square-foot ballroom, fifteen rooms of varying configurations, and sixty-eight hundred square feet of prefunction area.

For its superior standards of quality, appearance, and service, within only a few months of opening the Hilton Omaha was awarded the prestigious Four Diamond Award by the American Automobile Association (AAA).

The indoor swimming pool at the Hilton Omaha provides a place for a daily workout or a relaxing dip when traveling. The facilities also offer a patio area for sunbathers to catch a few rays. ■

Photo by Alan S. Weiner

Photo by Mark Romesser

It is a designation made possible, in part, by a staff of some three hundred employees who take pride in their positions and who carry that pride into a show of community spirit.

Backed by the hotel, Hilton employees support their community through a range of activities such as partnering with Omaha's newest educational institution, Liberty Elementary School. For the students of Liberty, the hotel and its people encourage academic excellence with programs like recognition for "green team" honor roll achievers, a designation corresponding to the Hilton self-rating system.

From the moment of inception, the Hilton Omaha has held a special place in the hearts of the city and its people, a bond it will continue to strengthen as it creates its own piece of history in the years to come. ■

The Hilton Omaha is the only hotel in Omaha with a full-service health club. The club's amenities include free weight and cardiovascular equipment, an indoor pool and whirlpool, two spa treatment rooms offering massages and facials, and men's and women's locker rooms, each equipped with a sauna. ■

Photo by Alan S. Weiner

Photo by Eric Francis

On Thanksgiving evening each year, Omaha
residents gather at Gene Leahy Mall to kick off the
holiday season with panache—otherwise known as the
Holiday Lights Festival. With the flick of a switch, the
downtown area from 10th to 14th Streets between Farnam
and Douglas Streets is illuminated with thousands of
twinkling holiday lights. Then families and holiday guests
head over to Qwest Center Omaha for Omaha's Holiday
Skating Extravaganza, a free ice-skating show produced and
directed by the coaches of the Blade & Edge Figure Skating
Club and the Figure Skating Club of Omaha. The production
features 119 of the area's finest figure skaters, including 6
who present solo holiday-themed performances for the
awed crowd. Afterward, the ice is opened for family skating
time, putting everyone in a proper holiday mood. O!

"Annie"

A chance to dress up, use their best manners, and sip tea from fine china—every little girl loves a tea

party. Blend that fun with the theater, and you've got the makings for a sunshine-filled day. These girls enjoy tea and the Broadway hit play *Annie*, the story of an orphan who always looks on the bright side. While these young ladies might not remember the late Henry Fonda, they might be interested to know that as a child actor Fonda took one of his first theatrical bows on stage at the Omaha Community Playhouse. **O!**

> **"** *The community theater in Omaha is like no other. We have a world class community playhouse, but also a lot of alternative venues showcasing unique plays and talent.*
>
> *Amanda Jedlicka, program manager*

Northwest of Omaha in Blair there's fun for all ages at the annual Gateway to the West Days in June. The three-day Washington County festival features parades, picnics, music, and Taste of Blair sampler plates provided by local restaurants. Other events include a car show, craft show, carnival, Fire Department water fight, and a street dance. O!

Bringing It Home. Lovgren Marketing focuses on strengthening the business behind the Omaha Royals team. Center: Doug Stewart, general manager and Casey with Linda Lovgren. From left: Nancy Petula, Sheri Johnson, Micki Pane, Bill Madden, Donna Maxey, Ann Eads. ■

Photo by Dennis Keim

Lovgren
Marketing Group

Photo by Joe Guerriero

S ince its founding in 1978, the client list of Lovgren Marketing Group reads like a who's who of Omaha's top businesses. With offices in Omaha and Colorado Springs, Colorado, the group is well versed in the creation of award-win-ning marketing strategies, advertising campaigns, major public-relations efforts, political campaigns, and special events. And along with all of the talent is their real specialty: building client relationships.

"Behind our greatest strength is the strategy and intellect of our work. It's not enough to design campaigns that WOW. Our efforts need to deliver the results clients expect," said Linda Lovgren, founder and president of Lovgren Marketing Group.

At Lovgren Marketing, the phenomenon is called ROI—Return On Ideas. It begins by assembling some of the most talented professionals in their individual specialties—creative, media, account service, production—and then giving them the tools they need to be successful.

"Our client's audiences are as diverse as the industries they represent. And they're not always confined to communicating with their own customers. Their relationships with other businesses, government leaders, and even the public at large can dramatically impact their ability to grow and expand," Lovgren said.

Lovgren is well versed in what it takes to build the community relationships that result in attracting more business and continue to foster economic development that generates greater opportunities for the people who live and work here.

Lovgren Marketing Group is a strong advocate of the community it calls home. "We all share the belief that what makes our clients successful makes us successful, too," she said.

As a team, Lovgren Marketing Group continues to drive the success of the clients it represents. Client focused and strategy driven, LMG continues to apply the principles of public relations, advertising, and marketing across a broad cross-section of industries. It's a strategy the company believes will continue to generate business success and value for its clients long into the future.■

"Our efforts need to deliver the results clients expect," said Linda Lovgren, founder and president of Lovgren Marketing Group.

From the Ground Up. Operating in a specialized business sector, defense company Northrop Grumman taps Lovgren to build relationships with business, government, and media, as it breaks ground on its new campus. Picture: Bob Hinson, Northrop Grumman, and Linda Lovgren. ■

Since its opening in 1931, Joslyn Art
Museum has been a cultural center for the
Omaha community. Built as a gift to the city from
Sarah Joslyn in memory of her husband George,
a prominent Omaha businessman, it is a monument
to their commitment to the arts. Here, visitors in one
of the museum's twenty galleries view nineteenth-
century art from Europe and America. The larger
painting is *Salome Dancing Before King Herod* by
Georges Rochegrosse. *O!*

KIEWIT GALLERY

From opening night when the Creighton women's soccer team shut out Northern Iowa and the men's soccer team defeated Vanderbilt, the five-thousand-seat Creighton University Morrison Stadium has been a great success. The structure was named in honor of the Rev. Michael G. Morrison, S.J.,who served as Creighton University's president from 1981 until 2000. The Rev. John P. Schlegel, S.J., who succeeded Morrison as president, said, "It's fitting that we name such a visible symbol of Creighton's campus expansion for the man who thousands of Omahans know fondly as 'Father Mike.'" "The design by DLR Group replicates European soccer stadiums with fan seating close to the field. The artificial playing surface provides unprecedented field usage for soccer as well as other outdoor gatherings. ∎

DLR
Group

apturing the essence of a nationwide company that employs 450 professionals and maintains fifteen offices might seem overwhelming. In the case of DLR Group, it can be done in six words found in their vision statement: "Client focused, design excellence, employee ownership."

"Everything we do comes back to our vision statement," said Dale Hallock, managing principal. "We start with clients and build a team to respond to their particular needs. We are not a general architectural and engineering firm. We match our specialized professional skills with the specific needs of our clients."

DLR Group is a firm that people look to for innovation and the design resources to produce premier facilities that have unique design characteristics. The Peter Kiewit Institute, Qwest Center Omaha, Creighton University Soccer Stadium, and Tecumseh State Correctional Institution are four prime examples.

Designed as a real-life, full-sized, hands-on lab, the Kiewit Institute incorporated innovative community partnerships in a building that took form in response to the educational curriculum. The Qwest Center is one

Photo by Jim Scholz

Photo by Tom Kessler

DLR Group is a firm that people look to for innovation and the design resources to produce premier facilities that have unique design characteristics.

of the few facilities in the country that combines into one event structure a convention center and an arena. Creighton University now has the first college stadium dedicated to soccer, and the Tecumseh State Correctional facility is the largest correctional institution in Nebraska using multibuilding, campus-style architecture.

"It's our responsibility to understand our clients' business," said Ken West, Omaha office director and principal. "It's part of our practice to bring additional knowledge to our clients. To build a highly specialized team, we hire or work with specialists (some are even former clients) who understand a building's operational requirements."

"Maintaining offices nationwide allows us to combine local presence with our national design expertise," said Hallock. DLR Group is dedicated to serving five types of clients: higher education, corporate/retail, justice, K-12 education, and sports/entertainment.

DLR Group's justice portfolio ranges from the Auckland Remand Prison design in New Zealand to more than ten county correctional facilities in Nebraska and Iowa. Recent corporate clients include Valmont, Blue Cross and Blue Shield of Nebraska, Streck Laboratories, The Boeing Corporation, and Ameritrade. The K-12 education portfolio ranges from new comprehensive high school designs in Arizona, New Jersey, Minnesota, California, Kansas, Wyoming, and Tennessee, to district wide improvements for Elkhorn, Gretna, Bennington, Ralston and Norris.

One of DLR Group's core values is to have fun both in the journey and the destination, an attitude that lends itself to creative design approaches.

DLR Group professionals join together with building owners in design charettes, an intensive, interactive, brainstorming workshop. Designers sketch as building owners and a wide range of user groups discuss project goals and respond to preliminary concept drawings. It is this level of interest in looking into new opportunities that brings clients back after years, even decades.

Continued on page 164

The Peter Kiewit Institute of Information Science, Technology, and Engineering is a hallmark DLR Group project and a prime example of technology and education in action. The challenge of this project was to provide laboratory, office, research, and computer lab spaces, as well as general-purpose classrooms and computer-user rooms all responding to the specific goals and objectives outlined by each college user group's academic plan. The infrastructure was designed for access and delivery of fully integrated, interactive voice, video, and data resources within and outside the building. The building as a lab concept was the key. ■

Another unique undertaking is the two-building Valmont Corporate campus designed by DLR Group. The facility is the corporate headquarters for Valmont's worldwide irrigation and pole operations. Using that as a starting point, DLR based the design on the circular imprint created by the Center Pivot Irrigation System, one of Valmont's main products. The entire project is built on a single radius point of 195.5 feet. A sixty-foot walkway connects the two buildings that comprise Valmont Plaza. State-of-the-art technology is employed throughout the facility, including video conferencing rooms with touch screen LCD displays, video cameras and projectors, a Network Operations Center (NOC), and an executive board room.

Photo by Jim Scholz

(Right) **People who live in glass houses have more fun. A mixed** metaphor, but in the case of the Qwest Center Omaha, it seems apt. The total redevelopment property span for this one-of-a-kind complex, designed by DLR Group, covers more than four hundred acres or approximately one hundred city blocks. The design features a glass wall running the entire length of the pre-function space, reaching seven stories high. It would take eighteen men standing on each other's shoulders to reach the top of the glass. Once inside this amazing structure, guests quickly see why the Qwest Center is Nebraska's premier convention, entertainment, and sports venue and the cornerstone of Omaha's $2 billion downtown riverfront revitalization. Whatever your passion, the chances are better than good that you will find something to your liking listed in the Center's calendar of events. ∎

Continued from page 163

Blue Cross and Blue Shield has been a returning client since the firm's start in 1966.

"Employees as owners, who pursue their work with energy, also bring clients back and attract new project categories. A primary example is the Kansas City International Speedway, NASCAR's recent addition to the race circuit," said Hallock. DLR Group's fan-friendly design has resulted in one of the most successful destination raceway locations in the country.

Through creative ideas and persistent effort, DLR Group success is guided by their vision: client focused, design excellence, and employee ownership. ∎

Photo by Doug Henderson

Photo by Rod Reilly

When guests staying at the Crowne Plaza Hotel Omaha walk through the door, staff members at the registration desk, situated in the hotel's spacious and luxurious lobby, welcome them with warm smiles and open arms. And after they've checked in and had a chance to behold their outstanding accommodations, visitors can head back down to the lobby to kick back and relax, converse with other guests, and have an evening cocktail. The area's inviting setting, complete with intricate woodwork and cozy chairs, is all part of the hotel's desire to make guests feel like they've found a real home away from home. O!

Photo by Alan S. Weiner

Photo by Alan S. Weiner

Photo by Alan S. Weiner

The Omaha Symphony welcomed a new era in 2005 with the addition of Thomas Wilkins as music director and a move from the historic Orpheum Theater to the new Holland Performing Arts Center. During his conducting career, Wilkins has been featured with orchestras including the Dallas Symphony, Cleveland Orchestra, Oregon Symphony in Portland, and Houston Symphony. He is a frequent guest conductor of the Baltimore Symphony, the Buffalo Philharmonic, and Washington D.C.'s National Symphony Orchestra. In addition to MasterWorks, Pops, Chamber Orchestra, Discovery Series, Light Classics, Family Series, radio broadcasts, and neighborhood concerts, the orchestra tours Nebraska and Iowa providing education, community concerts, and special events, reaching an estimated audience of three hundred thousand people annually. O!

Photo by Alan S. Weiner

The magnificently restored Orpheum Theater is the site for a rousing performance of the Broadway touring company production of *Fiddler on the Roof*. Known as Omaha's "Golden Palace," the Orpheum was built in 1927 as a vaudeville house, and for decades has hosted some of the world's most renowned performers. The Omaha Performing Arts Society, which manages the theater, in 2002 directed a $10 million renovation project that included improvements in seating, stage views, and acoustics. Of

Jack H. Jackson, president, in the lobby of the Omaha Public Power District Conference Center. Designed by Jackson-Jackson & Associates, Inc., the center serves as a multipurpose facility for one of the area's largest utility providers.

Jackson-Jackson
& Associates, Inc.

Grounded in the belief that architecture isn't just about building structures, it's about building communities, Jackson-Jackson & Associates, Inc., has made its mission to "Provide architecture that contributes to the human well-being."

Established in 1950 by Jack C. Jackson as a small commercial and residential design company, the firm has grown to become one of the leading providers of complete architectural design services for numerous multimillion-dollar projects throughout the Midwest. By focusing on projects for financial, educational, healthcare, religious, broadcasting, and industrial clients, Jackson-Jackson is able to contribute to the improvement of the built environment and to create beautiful, functional buildings that are also sound investments for the client and the community.

Such projects require balancing many elements—client need, budget, time constraints, the nature of the building site—and Jackson-Jackson integrates them all by focusing not just on the functionality of the space, but also on the surrounding environment, sustainability, access, linkage, and sociability. So too do clients

The firm has been nationally recognized for numerous award-winning school designs, including Druid Hill Elementary School for Omaha Public Schools. ■

Photo by Mark Romesser

Photo by Doug Henderson

Jackson-Jackson is able to contribute to the improvement of the built environment and to create beautiful, functional buildings that are also sound investments for the client and the community.

depend on Jackson-Jackson to work closely with them in a timely, economic manner throughout all phases of a project—from conception through construction and on to final acceptance. The firm's ability to work creatively and efficiently has won them many accolades, including Nebraska's Firm of the Year in 2004 by the Nebraska Chapter of the Construction Specification Institute for the development of outstanding construction documents, which help contractors build more efficiently and save the client money.

To complement their architectural design expertise, Jackson-Jackson's services also extend into master planning and programming, feasibility studies, needs assessment, site evaluation and selection, cost estimating, interior design, landscape planning, restoration, analysis of A.D.A. compliance, and bond issue campaign assistance.

Realizing that building doesn't stop with the structure itself, but extends outward into the landscape and community, Jackson-Jackson takes seriously its role as environmental stewards, developing projects that are energy efficient and building responsibly with sustainable and recyclable materials. For its efforts, Jackson-Jackson has received numerous City Beautification awards, and in 2004 was one of twenty-five firms in the United States recognized for innovative use of glass in the design of one of its school projects.

As a firm renowned for designing schools, banks, and churches, Jackson-Jackson naturally supports numerous educational and philanthropic efforts, including Presbyterian Outreach, the social ministry arm of the Presbyterian Church in Omaha. Company president Jack H. Jackson has served on the organization's Board of Directors for six years, three as president, and his staff serves numerous other religious organizations in the area by contributing time on their boards. Additionally, the Jackson family has enjoyed longtime membership in Kiwanis International, which serves various youth needs throughout the community and awards two one-thousand-dollar scholarships annually, each in tribute to company founder Jack C. Jackson.

With a firm commitment to building quality, lasting structures that reflect strong community values, Jackson-Jackson & Associates, Inc., will continue to contribute to the improvement of the built environment and the quality of life in the Midwest. ■

Photo by Dennis Keim

Photo by Dennis Keim

Cinco de Mayo celebrates the victory of forty-five hundred poorly armed Mexican soldiers who defeated sixty-five hundred well-outfitted French soldiers who were trying to capture Mexico City. In Omaha, where the Hispanic community is the fastest-growing segment of the population, Cinco de Mayo is celebrated with a parade, fiestas, Mariachi concerts, food, and games. In addition, El Museo Latino hosts an annual business community luncheon. An estimated twenty thousand people watched the 2005 parade as it passed along South 24th Street. O!

" *It's a before-school-starts tradition for my dad and me to spend a day at Fun Plex. We swim and do the rides. It almost makes going back to school something to look forward to. Almost.*"

Veronica Schinker, age eleven

The city of Papillion, named by the Frenchmen who originally came upon thousands of butterflies fluttering in the sunshine, today boasts a five-acre water park. Papio Bay is an outdoor recreation facility that includes a zero-depth swimming pool, two water slides, diving boards, sand volleyball courts, wading pools, a sand play area, concession stand, and, of course, a children's butterfly slide. Whether working on diving skills, hanging out with a friend, or just relaxing at the waterfall, from Memorial Day to Labor Day, Papio Bay is a great place to play. O!

Photo by Joe Guerriero

Photo by Joe Guerriero

Photo by Joe Guerriero

Thanks to Fun Plex, Nebraska's largest amusement and water park, kids—and their parents—have plenty of exciting things to do when the mercury rises. The water park features two five-story-tall Typhoon Waterslides, a wave pool, a kiddie pool, and the winding, relaxing Lazy River. The park also offers a host of electrifying rides and attractions, from the Tilt-A-Whirl and the Fun Plex Speedway to batting cages and an arcade. It's also a hot spot for corporate picnics, attracting hundreds of company events annually. **O!**

"Give me an M,"... or maybe it's a "C." Ollie, Mario Olive Company's official mascot, livens up the crowd at a Creighton University basketball game. The crowd is treated with Ollie bean bag toys, Mario T-shirts, and some pretty neat dance moves, courtesy of Ollie. ■

Westin
Foods

When he was six years old, Dick Westin had a chain of lemonade stands. He opened his first stand across from Jackson School in Omaha, and when a friend wanted to open one several blocks away, Dick offered to provide all the supplies and even write out the advertising signs. He diligently checked on the stands—there ended up being three of them—and delivered supplies in his little red wagon. It was the beginning of a great business adventure.

"He thought—and I guess he still does—that everything's negotiable," said his brother Click Westin. "One time he wanted to buy a pair of six-dollar roller skates, but he only had a quarter. So he talked the manager into letting him pay a quarter down and a quarter a week until he'd paid for the skates."

Negotiating wasn't Dick Westin's only skill. Throughout his life, he has been a superb athlete. "When I was in the fourth grade, we were playing another school, and I was taking shots and hogging the basketball.

Photo by Alan S. Weiner

"Dick built this company on a solid foundation, and we're continuing to build on his vision."

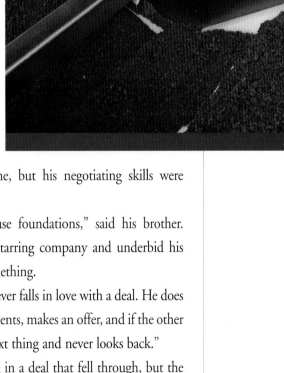

Bit by bit over the years, Feaster Foods has processed more than 2 million pounds of bacon in their Fairbury facility. The company recently expanded their production facility to include a state-of-the-art continuous cooking system, as well as a new flexible packaging system. ■

Photo by Rod Reilly

In the middle of the game, my coach, Frances Moriarty, pulled the rest of my team off the floor and told me if I wanted to play by myself, I could face the other team alone. I never forgot that. If you're going to succeed in anything, you need help from others."

Westin was a star athlete at Omaha Benson High School and went to the University of Nebraska on a football scholarship. He also won several gold medals in track and field, and everyone expected great things from him.

Then during a practice session his freshman year, he tore the ligaments in his knee, requiring the first of many surgeries. His breakaway speed was gone, but his negotiating skills were unharmed.

"In his college days, he tarred house foundations," said his brother. "Within a year, he had started his own tarring company and underbid his former employer. He was always into something.

"The secret of his success is that he never falls in love with a deal. He does his homework, studies the financial statements, makes an offer, and if the other fellow says 'No,' he just goes on to the next thing and never looks back."

"In the early '90s, Dick was involved in a deal that fell through, but the company was so impressed with him they offered him an olive processing plant in Spain, and Dick bought it sight unseen," said Scott Carlson, current

Continued on page 178

In an example of combining the best of both worlds, Mario Olives are harvested by hand in the province of Seville, Spain, and then processed in their modern facility which is recognized as the industry's most innovative. The Mario Olive Company is the largest olive and olive-related condiment company in the world. ■

Continued from page 177

president and CEO. Today, Mario Olives, a division of Westin Foods, is the largest importer of Spanish olives in the United States.

"Dick built this company on a solid foundation, and we're continuing to build on his vision," said Carlson. When asked if Dick Westin was still making deals, he smiled, "You can bet if he's involved, he's negotiating." ■

Tim Carlson, top, wrestles for Skutt Catholic High School at the 2005 Nebraska High School State Championships. Tim placed second in his weight class during the Championship round at Lincoln's Devaney Center. ■

Omaha is synonymous with great steaks, and with more than one thousand restaurants in the metropolitan area, finding a delicious dinner, whether it's steak, seafood, vegetarian, or specialty cuisine, is a task to be savored. From casual, family-style fare to formal, intimate dining, your choices start with Ahmad's Persian Restaurant in the Old Market and go on to Zio's New York Style Pizzeria in west Omaha. Since 1946, Cascio's Steak House, pictured here, has been a source of delicious steaks and Italian favorites. No matter what part of Omaha you visit, bring your appetite because there's a marvelous meal close by.

Photo by Doug Henderson

Finding a cool treat at a hot spot in the city is as easy as taking a trip to Omaha's Old Market. It's here at 1120 Jackson Street that Ted & Wally's Ice Cream shop serves up more than three hundred homemade flavors amid bright neon lights and funky décor in a renovated historic gas station. An Omaha tradition since 1986, Ted & Wally's is owned by brother-and-sister team Joe Pittack and Jeanne Ohira. The shop is a city favorite during special events and throughout the year, and serves as a gallery of sorts for local artists who showcase their work on a monthly basis. Local and touring musicians often play a few sets for customers as they enjoy their ice cream. Pittack also owns the 1930s-era Blake's Soda Fountain in Louisville, southwest of Omaha, where he serves Ted & Wally's fantastic flavors. O!

Photo by Eric Francis

When Matt and his father want to spend some quality time together, they take advantage of the City of Omaha Parks, Recreation and Public Property Department's outstanding facilities, which include more than two hundred family-friendly parks. Families and friends can easily find wide open spaces and recreational opportunities to suit their interests. Matt and his dad are enjoying a relaxing summer afternoon at Elmwood Park. O!

Wheeeeeeeeeeeeeeeee!

John Beasley

When in Omaha, one might see a surprisingly familiar face in that of actor and Omaha native John Beasley. Appearing on television shows including *Everwood*, *Judging Amy*, and *CSI: Crime Scene Investigation*, and in the movies *The Mighty Ducks*, *Rudy*, *Walking Tall*, and *The Sum of All Fears*, Beasley keeps pretty busy. Still, he's not too busy for his hometown where, in 2002, he founded the John Beasley Theater and Workshop. The 125-seat theater is home to educational programs and productions that inform, delight, and entertain audiences. O!

Photo by Dana Altma, North Sea Films.

Conor Oberst

When Los Angeles act Rilo Kiley sang "We'll go to Omaha to work and exploit the booming music scene," they did just that, releasing an album on local independent label Saddle Creek Records. Like Omaha's thriving music scene, Saddle Creek Records has flourished in recent years, becoming one of the most successful independent labels in the country with a roster that includes Bright Eyes, featuring Conor Oberst (pictured); Cursive; and The Faint. Saddle Creek's owners have turned down buyout offers from a number of major labels, choosing instead to invest further in our community by building new office space, and a live music venue, along with additional retail/residential space in the exciting north downtown area. O!

Photo by Rudy Smith

Johnny Rodgers, left, and Eric Crouch, are two of three University of Nebraska-
Lincoln football players who were honored as Heisman Trophy winners. Rodgers, who won the Heisman in 1972, and Crouch, who won in 2001, set and broke many records on their way to winning the most prestigious award in college football. Over the course of three years, Rodgers set offensive records as a wingback, many of which he still holds. In his senior season he scored seventeen touchdowns and ran more than two thousand all-purpose yards. Crouch holds multiple records as a quarterback for the renowned Cornhuskers, where he became the third NCAA Division I-A quarterback to garner a record three thousand yards rushing and four thousand yards passing. The third Cornhusker to win the Heisman, Mike Rozier, received his trophy in 1983. O!

Johnny Rodgers
Eric Crouch

Photo by Rudy Smith

Luigi Waites

One of the great musical talents of Omaha, Luigi Waites has a fifty-year legacy in the world of jazz.
A percussionist whose influences include legendary names like Buddy Rich, Max Roach, Joe Jones, and Louie Belson, Waites shares his own expertise and experiences through performances and seminars. Among those Waites has performed with or opened for are musical greats including Ella Fitzgerald, Dizzy Gillespie, Sarah Vaughan, and Jean Luc Ponty. Sunday nights, this "Nebraska Artist of the Year" and his Luigi Inc. group perform at Mr. Toad's in the Old Market, a tradition for more than twenty years. O!

Omaha
Print

Before the Pony Express, before the Civil War, before Nebraska became a state, and before Omaha had paved streets or automobiles, its sixteen hundred residents had the Nebraska Republican, one of the territory's most influential newspapers. Founded in 1858, the owners quickly saw a need and added job printing. By the 1890s, the Republican had gone out of business, but the printing side remained as the Omaha Printing Company.

"We're extremely proud of our long history," said Steve Hayes, president and CEO, "but that alone isn't enough. We have to prove ourselves every day. We have a simple business formula: produce a high-quality product at the lowest cost, and deliver it with unwavering reliability."

At the start, Omaha Print produced items such as proclamations, pamphlets, government publications, and church programs. Today their products fall into categories that include full-color catalogs,

A far cry from the days when type was set by hand, catalogs at Omaha Print are now printed at the rate of seventy thousand items per hour and shipped all over the country. ∎

Photo by Alan S. Weiner

The whir of smoothly running presses at Omaha Print brings a smile to the face of president and CEO Steve Hayes. ∎

Photo by Alan S. Weiner

We have a simple business formula: produce a high-quality product at the lowest cost, and deliver it with unwavering reliability.

magazines, booklets and marketing brochures, statement stuffers, newspaper inserts, and direct marketing materials.

Gone are the days of hand-set type and linotype production. "Speed and flexibility are the keys to success in today's high-end color printing business," explained Hayes. Omaha Print uses the industry's most advanced high-speed web and sheet-fed presses along with comparable finishing capabilities.

"Our entire internal process is computerized. This digital workflow means we can track any job at any point and any time. If a customer's schedule changes, we can respond to that almost instantly without hours of downtime.

"We're always looking for ways to improve, to find the right balance between investments in new equipment and meeting our clients' needs. It's quite a job. There have been more changes in the printing industry in the last 10 years than in the 150 years since we were founded. Pressmen used to be craftsmen, now they're technicians. We used to check color by eye and hand, and now an electronic eye reads color and automatically adjusts it while the press is running at two thousand feet a minute!"

It is all about seeing a need and supplying what is necessary. "We're focusing on catalogs, trade publications, collateral marketing materials, and direct mail segments for national clients. Digital technology makes this possible, plus we're in the geographic center of the country, so we can ensure simultaneous delivery of products or mail to locations coast to coast."

It is not only their customer base which is growing. Recently Omaha Print added twenty-six thousand square feet to their plant to make room for a new web press and additional support equipment. They have added new positions and opened sales offices in Kansas City and Dallas.

Continued on page 186

The Omaha Print building at the corner of 13th and Farnam, which for sixty years from 1914 to 1974 was the company headquarters, is decked out in patriotic celebration of Armistice Day. ■

Continued from page 185

Obviously their business strategy is working. For seven of the last eight years, Omaha Print has won a Top Management Award from the National Association for Printing Leadership. Closer to home, they received the 2004 Heritage Award presented by River City Roundup for contributing to the growth and development of their community, being a "good corporate" citizen, and playing an active role in matters affecting Omaha and the state.

When Gutenberg developed printing on paper with ink and movable type in the mid-1400s, it revolutionized the world. In the future, new technologies will continue to refine the process; as long as people continue to rely on the printed word, Omaha Print will, no doubt, incorporate those advances to serve their clients. ■

Photo by Alan S. Weiner

First-shift employees at Omaha Print have plenty of elbow room in the twenty-six-thousand-square-foot expansion recently added to make room for the new web press and support equipment. ■

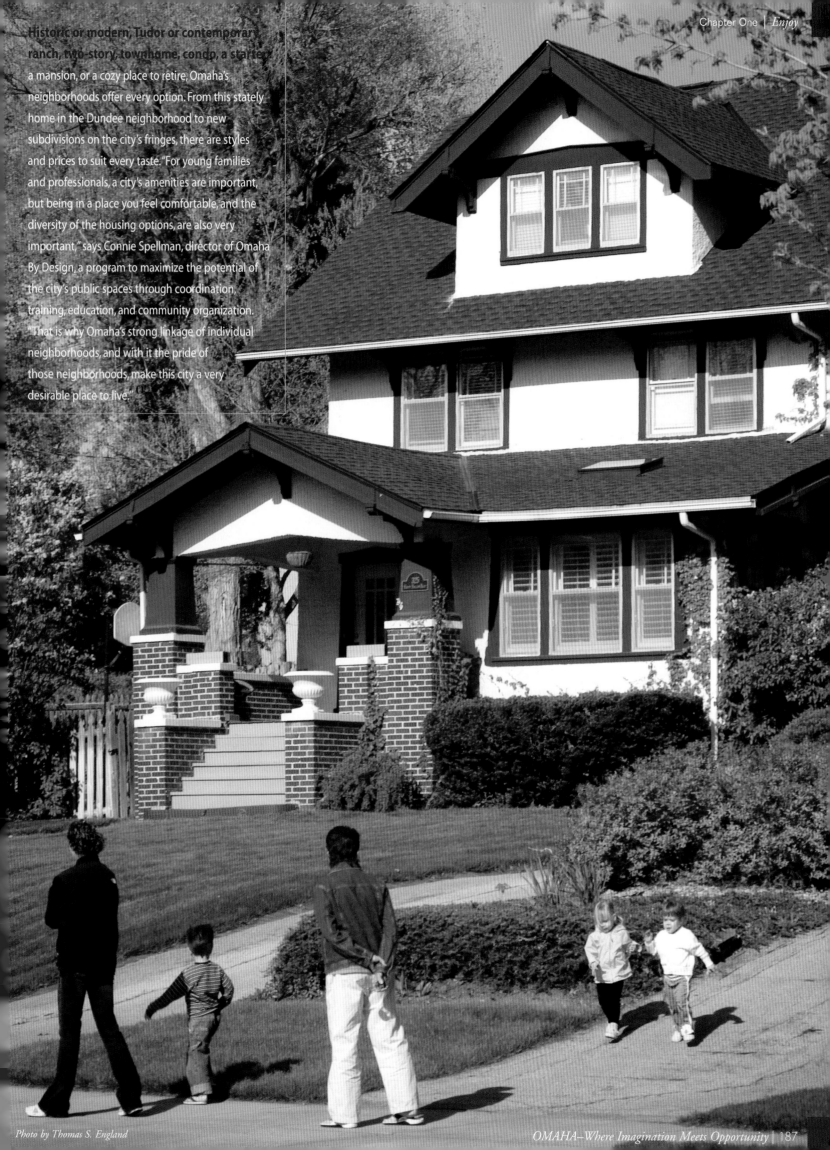

Historic or modern, Tudor or contemporary, ranch, two-story, townhome, condo, a starter, a mansion, or a cozy place to retire, Omaha's neighborhoods offer every option. From this stately home in the Dundee neighborhood to new subdivisions on the city's fringes, there are styles and prices to suit every taste. "For young families and professionals, a city's amenities are important, but being in a place you feel comfortable, and the diversity of the housing options, are also very important," says Connie Spellman, director of Omaha By Design, a program to maximize the potential of the city's public spaces through coordination, training, education, and community organization. "That is why Omaha's strong linkage of individual neighborhoods, and with it the pride of those neighborhoods, make this city a very desirable place to live."

Photo by Thomas S. England

Hot Fun in the City

Tyler Barry is a thirteen-year-old whose idea of hot fun is firing ceramics, blowing glass, and blacksmithing at the Hot Shops Art Center, a fabulous collection of art studios, showrooms, and gallery spaces catering to the Omaha art community.

At the heart of the Hot Shops are Bruning Sculpture, Loken Forge, Crystal Forge, and Wilson Custom Tile—four anchor shops whose forges, welders, and kilns give the ninety-two-thousand-square-foot art center its "heat."

The art center is situated in Omaha's north downtown district, an area that is generating a heat of its own. Positioned between the vibrant riverfront redevelopment, downtown, the Creighton University campus, and north Omaha, its vast potential as a pedestrian-oriented urban neighborhood has drawn a renewed interest from investors.

As a mixed-use district, north downtown is becoming a haven for creative talent, from visual artists to performing artists. It is the home of Saddle Creek Records—known internationally for its roster of indie bands and artists, including Conor Oberst and his band, Bright

Photo by Jackson Hill

HOT

Eyes. Young professionals are filling an expanding number of loft apartments and condos. Nightclubs and other entertainment venues are giving the district an exciting edge.

The Hot Shops is in a complex that formerly housed the Serta Mattress Co. factory. It was purchased in 1999 and converted into forty artist studios, the four anchor shops, three galleries, and a small café. The center has eighty studio artists and an artist residency program.

Omaha has welcomed the Hot Shops and its talent. The first Saturday of December, for example, the Crystal Forge glass studio has a holiday open house that draws hundreds of people for hand-blown Christmas tree ornaments and demonstrations of glass blowing.

Tyler got his start helping his father on various art projects, doing little more than lending a hand and moving things around. Gradually, his skills and responsibilities began to reflect his experience. Now, he works on projects of his own—much to the delight of visitors and the other Hot Shops artists. O!

SHOPS

Chapter Two

O! WORK

With its abstract geometric shapes, Sidney Buchanan's welded-steel sculpture *Mangonel II* is a fitting visual accompaniment to the modern architecture of Omaha's growing downtown skyline, which includes, left to right, the Woodmen of the World, First National Bank, Union Pacific, and Qwest buildings. The sculpture is one of several public art pieces that grace downtown's Gene Leahy Mall. It is one of two at the mall by Buchanan, an Omahan and a renowned creator of large-scale, welded-steel sculptures. O!

There has never been a better time to do business in Greater Omaha. New and expanding companies. More jobs. Billions of dollars in capital investment. Unprecedented partnerships between the public, private, and academic sectors. The metropolitan area is seeing businesses—both large and small—grow at a pace unlike any in its history.

There are at least a million reasons for this phenomenal growth—starting with the 1 million people who live within a fifty-minute radius of the city. They are hardworking, dedicated, and well-educated. The city's AAA bond rating, high quality of life, and comparatively stable economy appeal to companies, as do its central location and strong communications links. Tax incentives, job-training credits, and other benefits are in place that make the area and the state even more business-friendly.

Academic partners illustrate Greater Omaha's commitment to education and workforce development.

Together, it has resulted in a spirit of progress that is getting noticed.

New companies have come while others have expanded. The Pacific Life Insurance Co. regional business center. Northrop Grumman Corporation's operations facility in Bellevue, not far from Offutt Air Force Base, headquarters of U.S. Strategic Command, which includes U.S. Space Command. The AAA Auto Club Group's operations center. The Gallup Organization's university campus on the Missouri riverfront, which brings five thousand executives from around the world each year for training. First National Bank's spectacular forty-story tower. Union Pacific, one of Omaha's four Fortune 500 companies, and its grand corporate headquarters downtown that brought one thousand workers from St. Louis to Omaha.

Dynamic corporate leaders. Dedicated government officials. Valuable Chamber support. Easy access. Significant incentives. Proactive business and academic partnerships. An intelligent workforce. A united community spirit. More than a million reasons.

. Put simply, Omaha is hot. O!

Partnerships have been key to the phenomenal redevelopment in downtown Omaha and along the Missouri riverfront between Nebraska and Iowa. For more than thirty years, the Papio–Missouri River Natural Resources District (NRD) has worked to conserve, manage, and enhance the soil, water, wildlife, and forest resources within six counties along the Missouri River. As part of its efforts, the NRD has partnered with the City of Omaha and other public and private groups to establish "Back to the River," a revitalization effort to create and sustain an ecological corridor, while providing avenues for economic development through tourism, recreation, and cultural and historical interpretation. The program has been instrumental in revitalizing the riverfront, which has sparked more than $2 billion in new construction in the downtown area, from business capital investment to the addition of more than three thousand condominiums and apartments. The momentum of this downtown activity resulted in the North Downtown Redevelopment Study, designed to encourage complementary development in the area immediately north of downtown. This area has already attracted significant interest for mixed-use development—and is destined to attract more. O!

A Union Pacific coal train moves past the downtown city skyline, en route to serving the Omaha Public Power District's north plant. ■

Photo by Scott Dobry

Union Pacific

With the Pacific Railroad Act of 1862, President Abraham Lincoln directed the Union Pacific and Central Pacific railroads to connect the east and west coasts of America by rail. In 1869, the two railroads met, and a golden spike was driven to commemorate completion of the

Three of Union Pacific's top executives graduated from the University of Nebraska at Omaha. From left are Jack Koraleski, executive vice president, marketing and sales department; Jim Young, president and chief operating officer; and Dennis Duffy, executive vice president, operating department. ■

Photo by David Gibb

nation's first transcontinental railroad. Within a few decades, the railroad that helped link a nation also was helping to build it. By reducing the coast-to-coast journey from six months to ten days, Union Pacific had facilitated an unprecedented expansion of people, goods, and services into the American West.

More than 140 years later, Union Pacific remains the backbone of our nation's economy and continues to move the goods that build America.

As North America's largest railroad and one of the nation's leading transportation companies, Union Pacific moves a diversified mix of commodities—everything from food to automobiles, metals to minerals, and raw materials such as coal, lumber, and steel. Covering twenty-three states and thirty-three thousand miles of track, the railroad links every major West Coast and Gulf Coast port; provides service to the east through Chicago, St. Louis, Memphis, and New Orleans; and interchanges traffic with the Canadian rail system. Additionally, Union Pacific is the only railroad to serve the six major gateways to Mexico.

Innovation has been a cornerstone of the company from the start, and thinking "outside the boxcar" has allowed Union Pacific to thrive throughout the decades. Since the beginning, when standard time was adopted to accommodate the railroad's timetables, Union Pacific has worked diligently to increase the speed and efficiency of its service.

Today the railroad's forty-eight thousand employees use state-of-the art technologies such as Global Positioning Satellites to pinpoint the location of Union Pacific's seventy-seven hundred locomotives anywhere in North America. A massive computer network at the Harriman Dispatching Center in Omaha allows traffic control operators to manage the daily movement of about three thousand trains, while offering customers access to real-time information about shipments via the Internet.

Union Pacific's presence is strong in its hometown of Omaha. In June 2004, the company opened a new, $260 million downtown headquarters facility that can accommodate forty-one hundred employees. The nineteen-story, glass-enclosed structure occupies a full city block and features a full-height atrium, conference and learning center, fitness center, six-hundred-seat dining room, credit union, company merchandise shop, and television studio. Many of the amenities are open to the public, such as the dining room, which has earned a reputation for offering quality, healthy food that supports Union Pacific's culture of wellness and healthy lifestyles for its employees.

The family-friendly company, frequently recognized by *Working Mother* magazine, opened a child development center in 2005 near its downtown headquarters. The $5 million, twenty-thousand-square-

Continued on page 196

> More than 140 years after the driving of the golden spike, Union Pacific remains the backbone of our nation's economy.

BUILDING AMERICA®

Continued from page 195

foot facility can accommodate more than two hundred Union Pacific children. These two modern facilities make Union Pacific an integral part of Omaha's downtown redevelopment and underscore the company's commitment to the city and state of Nebraska.

Omaha's landscape also contains an impressive visual reminder of Union Pacific's historical presence—the world's largest steam and diesel locomotives. Looming over Interstate 80, the city's primary traffic artery, the 4000-class Big Boy steamer and the 6900-class Centennial diesel locomotive are on display at Kenefick Park on the grounds of the Lauritzen Botanical Gardens.

Union Pacific's $260 million headquarters building stands nineteen stories high and occupies an entire city block. The building's exterior and atrium comprise 315,000 square feet of glass (enough to cover six football fields), providing a light-filled environment for more than four thousand employees. ■

Photo by Doug Henderson

Union Pacific employees, spouses, and retirees enjoy free membership to the Health and Fitness Center. The nineteen-thousand-square-foot, state-of-the-art facility offers fifty strength training machines, fifty aerobic machines and a wide variety of fitness and health classes, directed by a staff certified by the American College of Sports Medicine. It is the largest corporate fitness center in Omaha and is a key component of Union Pacific's nationally recognized health and wellness program. ■

Photo by Jackson Hill

Union Pacific's role in building the transcontinental railroad helped establish seven thousand towns and cities throughout the west. Today, the railroad continues to support these communities through extensive charitable efforts. Since 1959, the Union Pacific Foundation has served as the company's philanthropic division, distributing funds for a variety of cultural, community, educational, and human service programs in the communities in which its employees live.

Union Pacific is one of the Omaha area's largest corporate donors to the United Way of the Midlands, with employees giving more than $1 million every year since 1996. In 2004, the company's longtime sponsorship of the Susan G. Komen Race for the Cure resulted in a team that was sixteen hundred employees strong, larger than all other Omaha-area corporate teams combined.

Additionally, employees are encouraged to enhance professional growth and community involvement through participation in company-sponsored clubs such as the Black Employees Network, Latino Employees Network and the women's initiative, LEAD (Lead, Educate, Achieve and Develop).

Thanks to its caring and innovative spirit, Union Pacific will no doubt remain the railroad that moves America, ever at the ready to assist our communities and economy by providing the means to grow our nation, now and into the future. ■

A sky-lit, 90- by 120-foot atrium is the focal point of the new Union Pacific Center, Nebraska's largest office building. Its architectural highlights include a ten-story copper wall accent, a black granite stone floor, and a 37- by 16-foot high-definition video wall located just outside the railroad's virtual television studio. ■

Photo by Jackson Hill

BUSINESS ON THE GREEN

Whether it's Coffee & Contacts in the morning, an afternoon of golf, or Rush Hour Connections after work, Greater Omaha Chamber of Commerce events and programs provide more than one hundred opportunities each year to network and market your business. The Chamber's annual golf tournament, Business on the Green, held at Tiburon Golf Course in southwest Omaha, gives members a chance to improve their contact list and their swing. At the 2005 tournament, Chamber president and CEO David G. Brown shares a golf cart with John K. Boyer, Chamber board chairman and Fraser Stryker law partner. Meanwhile, Steve Bruckner, also of Fraser Stryker, swings toward the green. O!

Photo by Mark Romesser

Over the years, the team at Bass & Associates has perfected the art of long-term relationship building. Here, vice president of operations Bruce Peterson (left) and president and CEO Deb Bass (right) spend some much-appreciated face-to-face time with client John Hayes, information services manager with Mutual of Omaha (middle), to discuss his renowned company's information technology needs. ■

Photo by Alan S. Weiner

Bass & Associates, Inc.

> Bass & Associates is recognized as Omaha's most significant and growing employer of highly educated and experienced IT industry professionals.

Since 1993, Bass & Associates, Inc., has been the Omaha business community's one-stop resource for consummate information technology consulting. Offering a wide array of business and technical services, from strategic planning to systems implementation, the award-winning firm is the perfect partner for companies that want to thrive in today's competitive business environment.

According to President and CEO Deborah Bass, long-term relationship building is one of Bass & Associates' keys to delivering tangible results. "We've had clients with us for more than ten years," she explains, "and they trust us with their innermost systems and operations because we have gained that kind of comfort level with them."

Bass & Associates is recognized as Omaha's most significant and growing employer of highly educated and experienced IT industry professionals. Potential team members go through a strict ten-step hiring process that includes educational and background checks, technical interviews, references, and more. This value-added effort allows the company to identify talented individuals who can work across all technical platforms and applications and implement customized solutions in a timely manner. And their work is followed up by rigorous quality assurance procedures to ensure client satisfaction.

As a local organization, Bass & Associates, Inc., also boasts enthusiastic community involvement, supporting organizations like the United Way, Heartland Family Service, and the American Heart Association, and presenting educational seminars for the public. For the Bass & Associates team, it's just another way to champion its business and community peers. ■

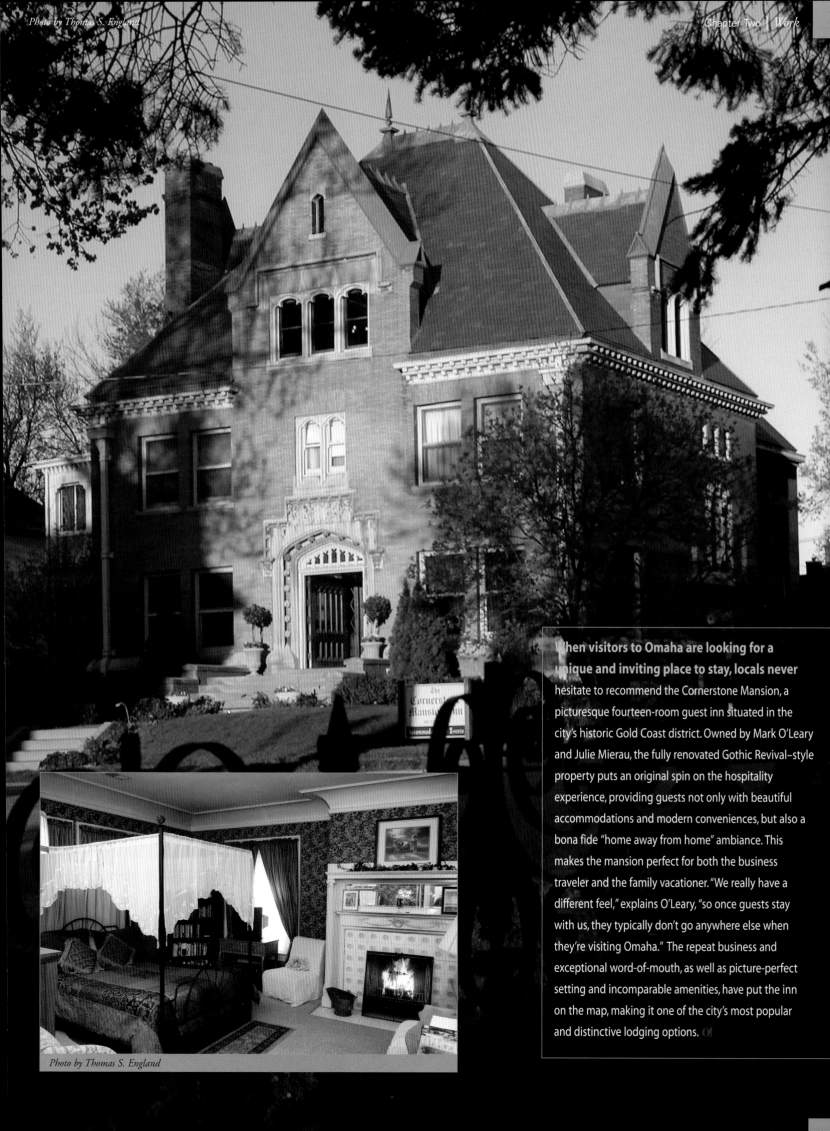

Photo by Thomas S. England

When visitors to Omaha are looking for a unique and inviting place to stay, locals never hesitate to recommend the Cornerstone Mansion, a picturesque fourteen-room guest inn situated in the city's historic Gold Coast district. Owned by Mark O'Leary and Julie Mierau, the fully renovated Gothic Revival–style property puts an original spin on the hospitality experience, providing guests not only with beautiful accommodations and modern conveniences, but also a bona fide "home away from home" ambiance. This makes the mansion perfect for both the business traveler and the family vacationer. "We really have a different feel," explains O'Leary, "so once guests stay with us, they typically don't go anywhere else when they're visiting Omaha." The repeat business and exceptional word-of-mouth, as well as picture-perfect setting and incomparable amenities, have put the inn on the map, making it one of the city's most popular and distinctive lodging options.

Photo by Thomas S. England

First Westroads
Bank

Times have changed since 1965 when First Westroads Bank was founded, but one thing has remained the same: the bank's commitment to fostering personalized relationships with its customers.

With fifty employees and two locations, First Westroads Bank operates not unlike many of the businesses it serves, believing that what customers need most from a banker is commitment to growth and the ability to deliver exemplary service in a timely fashion.

Specializing in serving individual, business, and entrepreneurial customers in the greater Omaha metro area, First Westroads assigns each of its customers a banking officer empowered with the ability to make decisions on behalf of specific client needs—on premises and usually within twenty-four hours.

"When a customer has a loan need, we respond immediately," says chairman and CEO Chris Murphy. "Once we have the information, we provide an answer. We don't tell our customers we have to meet with a

Success at First Westroads Bank is a team effort, led by the dedicated chairman and CEO Chris J. Murphy (middle), president Stephen F. Robinson (left) and CFO and executive vice president Wayne Pavlicek (right). ■

Photo by Dennis Keim

"People don't want to hear about your process; they want to hear you're going to help them."

Completed in 2005, First Westroads' new fifty-thousand-square-foot, three-story headquarters at 15750 West Dodge Road exemplifies its continued commitment to growth—both as a top employer in the community and as a provider of superior banking products, services, and technology. ■

loan committee and we'll get back to them next week. People don't want to hear about your process; they want to hear you're going to help them."

And save them time and money as well. To that end, First Westroads offers an innovative array of services, such as MobileConnect, which provides business clients with bonded and insured bank courier pickups on a daily, weekly, and monthly basis. Additionally, the bank's Internet Funds Management service allows commercial clients to access updated account information and perform financial services from the comfort of their own offices. And all customers benefit from the bank's CheckConnect Visa debit card, which provides customers account access at over 14 million locations worldwide, and Internet bill pay services that allow customers to pay their bills anytime, day or night.

First Westroads' ongoing emphasis on building customer loyalty over the last half century has established the bank as a significant player in the development of Western Omaha. Its peers in the industry have consistently recognized First Westroads for these achievements. For the past five years, the American Bankers Association's *ABA Banking Journal* magazine has recognized First Westroads as one of the top performers out of fourteen hundred community banks throughout the country.

"When we speak about relationships, we mean it," says Murphy. "We are a community bank that has strong customer service expectations, and we deliver on them."

So too does the bank deliver on its commitment to active and widespread civic involvement. From senior management on down, First Westroads professionals support numerous philanthropic and business organizations, including the Greater Omaha Chamber of Commerce, for which it serves as a major sponsor of that organization's Small Business Awards.

Says Murphy, "We feel strongly that to be part of the community and for us to grow as a business, we must be a part of organizations that allow business as a whole to grow." ■

Photo by Scott Indermaur

Of the many farmers markets available throughout the area, the Omaha Farmers Market at the Old Market downtown is a unique urban shopping experience. On Saturdays from May through October and Wednesdays from June through September, shoppers adore the abundance of farm-fresh fruits and vegetables, bedding plants, fresh-cut flowers, and crafts as well as specialty items such as honey, baked goods, and herbs. The Omaha Farmers Market offers fresh foods, and provides a colorful, bustling outdoor environment. It's a treat for you— and those at your dinner table.

"The Farmers Market—it's not just about the fabulous produce selection, it's about the energy that's generated when people of all ages and backgrounds come together. It's everything I like about other places I visit, only it's right here in our own city!"

Renee Franklin,
social services organization executive director

Photo by Scott Indermaur

Photo by Dennis Keim

Left to right: Partners John Katelman and Joyce Dixon with office managing partner Tom Dahlk at the riverfront campus of Gallup University, the Omaha research and training facility of client Gallup, Inc. ∎

Photo by Dennis Keim

Blackwell Sanders
Peper Martin LLP

Partner David Gardels at Opera Omaha. David is the immediate past chairman of Opera Omaha's Board of Directors. ■

Photo by Mark Romesser

I n response to today's fast-paced global business environment, Blackwell Sanders Peper Martin has emerged as one of the Midwest's leading commercial law firms, providing legal strategies and innovative solutions that meet the business and regulatory challenges of clients.

Founded in 1916, Blackwell Sanders, the international commercial law firm, moved into the Omaha market in 1995. Today the firm has offices in Omaha; Kansas City, St. Louis, and Springfield, Missouri; Washington, D.C.; and London, England.

Following a long tradition of hiring lawyers not only for their legal knowledge and academic excellence but also for their distinctive leadership and experiences, Blackwell Sanders is consistently recognized as one of the top law firms in the country. *Chambers USA* 2003–2004 and 2004–2005 named Blackwell Sanders among the top law firms in Nebraska and Missouri. In addition, thirty-nine of the firm's attorneys are listed in *The Best Lawyers in America* publication.

Anchored in a client-first philosophy and solution-driven approach, Blackwell Sanders has earned the trust of Fortune 500, multinational, and middle-market public companies, and some of the largest privately held companies in the United States. Multidisciplined as well as geographically diverse, Blackwell Sanders offers these clients over forty areas of expertise, including energy, health care, banking, securities, retail, and agribusiness.

Office managing partner Tom Dahlk believes this depth and breadth of knowledge distinguish his firm. "Our Omaha attorneys have access to the expertise of the entire firm," he says. "For instance, when a large Omaha client needed help defending its name worldwide, we tapped into the expertise of Blackwell's group of over twenty IP attorneys."

A strong focus for Blackwell in Omaha is assisting emerging businesses with everything from seeking venture capital funding, public offerings, or global alliances, to establishing vendor relationships with government agencies. Partner Todd Richardson, who helped launch the Midlands Venture Forum, says the goal is to help budding entrepreneurs and seasoned business veterans converge and foster new business growth. "It gives us the opportunity to network with people outside our own practice who can help our clients achieve their goals."

In addition to its global reach, the firm demonstrates a strong commitment to its local communities, with partners and associates involved in various community projects at the corporate, cultural, social, and political levels. In addition to financial contributions to such organizations as United Way, Opera Omaha, the Omaha Symphony, the Omaha Bar Association, Joslyn Art Museum, Habitat for Humanity of Omaha, and the Boys and Girls Clubs of Omaha, to name a few, many of the firm's partners and associates distinguish themselves in community leadership roles by serving in president, chair, executive board member,

Continued on page 208

Anchored in a client-first philosophy and solution-driven approach, Blackwell Sanders has earned the trust of Fortune 500,.multinational, and middle-market public companies.

Left to right: Blackwell securities
lawyers Todd Richardson,
Jisella Veath, and Jim Creigh at the
corporate headquarters of client
West Corporation. ■

Photo by Dennis Keim

Photo by Dennis Keim

Continued from page 207

committee member, and volunteer positions for these and other organizations.

In 2003, the firm relocated its Omaha office in support of the city's downtown revitalization project, a move that reflects the firm's progressive outlook. "We continue to grow our Omaha office, with new attorneys, new areas of practice, and the size of our practice areas," Dahlk says. "We represent Omaha's biggest and best corporations, and we aim to continue to be the leading corporate law firm for Omaha." ■

Left to right: Partners
Nicole Theophilus and
Howard F. Hahn with client
William S. Dinsmoor, chief
financial officer, the Nebraska
Medical Center. ■

Photo by Village Pointe®

The beautiful Village Pointe is Nebraska's new lifestyle center, home to an ever-growing and eclectic mix of retail shops, service stores, restaurants, and entertainment venues. The center's open-air design, reminiscent of the days when stores lined the streets of a city's downtown, features walkways, lush landscaping, distinctive architecture, and doorside parking. An outdoor amphitheatre and fireplaces welcome visitors to enjoy the center as a gathering place as well. O!

ConAgra Foods executive chefs work in the newly renovated, world-class Product Quality and Development building located at 6 ConAgra Drive. ∎

ConAgra
Foods

In this day and age, the answer to the question, "What's for dinner?" has never been so varied. Perhaps the only constant during mealtimes is that consumers want more foods that meet their individual preferences for quality and taste.

ConAgra Foods is there to satisfy those needs. Since selling its first bag of flour in 1867, ConAgra Foods has grown from a small Nebraska operation into one of North America's largest packaged food companies. Check the refrigerator or pantry of any family in America, and in over 95 percent you'll find a ConAgra Foods product, everything from Hunt's® tomatoes, to Chef Boyardee® pasta, Orville Redenbacher's® Gourmet® Microwave popcorn, Butterball® turkey, Hebrew National® hot dogs, Swiss Miss® cocoa, or Reddi-wip® topping. Even most of America's top restaurant chains use ConAgra Foods products.

But ConAgra Foods doesn't measure success based on the kind of food it makes. Instead, the company concentrates on meeting the varied tastes and nutritional needs of every type of consumer, at every stage of

ConAgra Foods products are found in virtually every aisle of the grocery store. ConAgra Foods has the products for any eating occasion and for every member of the family. ∎

life. When it comes to food trends, ConAgra Foods doesn't follow them, but anticipates them, emerging as a leader in shaping what America eats.

The company operates three business segments: ConAgra Foods Retail Products, ConAgra Foodservice, and ConAgra Food Ingredients. Each segment provides strength to the other.

ConAgra Foods Retail Products provides the brands people know and love, sold through grocery, convenience, and super stores. ConAgra Foodservice and ConAgra Food Ingredients offer innovative solutions to the restaurant and foodservice industries. Combining insights in consumer behavior and tastes with an insider's knowledge of its customers' businesses means ConAgra Foods is more than just a vendor; it's an invaluable partner that provides customers with the edge needed to succeed in today's competitive food industry.

Whether counting calories, fats, or carbs, consumers across the country rely on ConAgra Foods to provide a variety of nutritious and tasty foods, everything from Healthy Choice® frozen meals and PAM® cooking sprays to high-protein Egg Beaters®. The company even produces a line of meatless, soy-based vegetarian products under the Lightlife® label.

"The company concentrates on meeting the varied tastes and nutritional needs of every type of consumer, at every stage of life."

ConAgra Foods campus at 10th and Farnam— view of the clocktower. ∎

Continued on page 212

Continued from page 211

ConAgra Foods also brings that same level of dedication and innovation to improving the communities in which its employees live and work. Starting with the company's own operations, thousands of ConAgra Foods employees work to promote environmental stewardship and profitable growth through the company's Sustainable Development Program. Here, the goal is to improve production processes by introducing new technologies that reduce waste and conserve energy and water. As a result of various Sustainable Development efforts, the company has cut operating costs and reduced its consumption of natural resources.

A customer service representative responds to customer requests from across the country from ConAgra Foods' Omaha location. ∎

Likewise, the company's charitable division, the ConAgra Foods Foundation, assists dozens of projects around the country, from disaster relief to food safety education. One of its signature programs, Feeding Children Better, specifically targets child hunger in the United States through a partnership with America's Second Harvest. Today, Feeding Children Better is the nation's largest corporate initiative dedicated to eliminating childhood hunger.

In Omaha, the ConAgra Foods Foundation funds cultural, environmental, and educational projects. Through its support of the Iain Nicolson Audubon Center at Rowe Sanctuary on the Platte River Valley, the Foundation is helping restore and conserve vital habitat for Sandhill cranes and other wildlife along the Platte, as well as educating children and adults about the importance of this vital ecosystem. Additionally, the Foundation's funding of the Nature Conservancy has proved vital to conservation efforts along the Platte, helping establish farming practices that keep the land in production with minimal impact on the river's health.

ConAgra Foods also serves as presenting sponsor of some of the area's best-known events, including the Holiday Lights Festival and New Year's Eve fireworks held on the ConAgra Foods campus, the holiday ice sculpture display, and the Race for the Kids one-mile run/walk promoting physical fitness for children.

Whether providing the foods that help keep consumers happy and healthy, or the energy and funds that sustain our land and our communities, ConAgra Foods embodies the philosophy of "Doing well by doing good" —the only way the company believes in doing business. ∎

ConAgra Foods headquarters campus at 10th and Farnam is home to corporate, retail, foodservice, food ingredients, and product quality and development. ∎

When it comes time to harvest the nearly 18 million acres of crops grown in Nebraska each year, the choice for many producers, like Larry Coleman (left), conferring with CLAAS representative Rod Nelson, is a LEXION 500 series combine. The LEXIONs are assembled at CLAAS Omaha and delivered to farms throughout the United States, Mexico, Canada, and Australia. A division of German-based CLAAS, the world's leading manufacturer of farming machinery, CLAAS Omaha is North America's most modern combine facility, with over two hundred thousand square feet of manufacturing and office space; a theater, showroom, and a Ride-and-Drive demonstration barn. Not only does CLAAS Omaha assemble some of the best machines, it also assembles some of the largest. On the August 2, 2005, episode of the History Channel's *Modern Marvels*, the LEXION 590 was featured as one of the four largest machines in the agricultural, mining, and cutting industries in the world today. O!

Kutak Rock partners Michael Fahey, David Jacobson, and Patricia Peterson are pictured in the atrium of the Omaha Building, the historic downtown building owned by the Omaha-based, national law firm. Mr. Jacobson is chairman of the firm.

Photo by Alan S. Weiner

Kutak Rock has achieved consistent success by delivering extraordinary client service and by responding to difficult legal problems with inventive strategies.

KUTAK ROCK LLP

Established in Omaha in 1965, Kutak Rock LLP provides legal services to a wide variety of clients across a broad spectrum of businesses. Firm attorneys practice in three principal spheres—corporate, litigation, and finance—that contain many areas of specialization. Approximately 125 Kutak Rock lawyers practice in the Omaha location, the administrative center for the firm's network of sixteen offices.

Kutak Rock has achieved consistent success by delivering extraordinary client service and by responding to difficult legal problems with inventive strategies. The firm strives to achieve excellence through accessibility, efficiency, high-quality work product, and adherence to the client's timetable.

Community outreach is a priority of Kutak Rock, and firm lawyers sit on boards of charitable and cultural organizations and provide pro bono legal services to such institutions. The firm is an active participant in adopt-a-school programs for Omaha Public Schools, and firm members mentor students.

Kutak Rock strongly believes in the mission of Legal Aid of Nebraska and provides it with monetary support. The firm also provides financial support to The Robert J. Kutak Foundation, an institution that distributes grants and makes other forms of monetary assistance available to further its charitable, cultural, and educational priorities. ∎

Berkshire Hathaway chairman Warren Buffett and vice-chairman Charlie Munger enjoy a snack with Berkshire shareholders during their annual Omaha meeting, held in 2005 at Qwest Center Omaha.

Omaha's Good Fortune

Spotlight on O!

Omaha is home to a billionaire named Warren Buffett and the headquarters of four Fortune 500 companies: the Buffet-led Berkshire-Hathaway, ConAgra Foods, Union Pacific Corp., and Mutual of Omaha—a list that's the envy of cities twice our size. In addition, recent Fortune 500 company Peter Kiewit Sons' Inc. continues to be the most profitable construction company in its category.

With our "Fortune Four" as cornerstones, nearly eleven-thousand other companies act as the building blocks of Greater Omaha's business community. From small shops to large corporations, they manufacture, record, cook, build, tabulate, fabricate, sell, and ship the goods and services that satisfy the nation's consumers.

Their diversity is a testament to the area's many positive features. An intelligent workforce. High quality of life. Easy access to roads, rail transportation and Omaha's Eppley Airfield. Room to grow.

For decades, Omaha's government officials and business leaders have reached out across the world to tell the city's story. Today, sister cities in Japan, Germany, Lithuania, Ireland, and Mexico bear witness to Omaha's unique advantages by eagerly spreading our good news.

The rest of the world is listening. O!

Blue Cross and Blue Shield
of Nebraska

To many consumers, the value of their health care insurance company is defined simply as a means to cover the cost of a doctor's visit, a medical procedure, or a hospital stay. Generally, consumers don't think about their health care plan until a need arises. However, Blue Cross and Blue Shield of Nebraska (BCBSNE) is working to modify the way consumers and businesses think about their insurer, and health care as a whole. The Nebraska-based independent mutual insurance company believes the prescription for better health and, in turn, a better health care system, calls for a strategic focus on wellness. Through collaborative initiatives between consumers, businesses, health care providers, and insurers, consumers will be empowered to take a far more active role in their well-being.

"**Everything we do must come from the perspective of the consumer.** It's not just about lowering costs; it's about people getting quality health care." ■

—*Steven S. Martin,*
president & CEO, BCBSNE

Photo by Omaha World-Herald

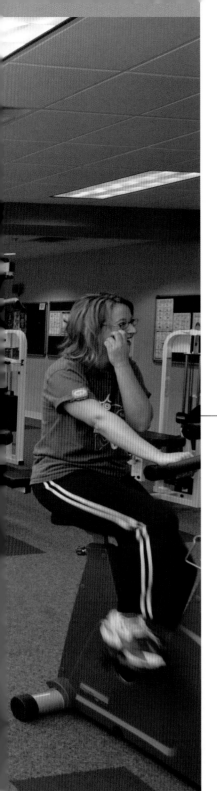

Photo by Alan S. Weiner

"Our mission is to be the company that offers health benefits that people value most," says Martin.

In the next ten years, one baby boomer will turn fifty years old every eight seconds. For employers, an aging population means the need to pick up a bigger share of health care costs. For employees, this translates to a bigger bite from the paycheck. As a result, the consumer is caught in the middle with little apparent control. "Unlike any other area of our economy, consumers have very little impact on rising health costs, other than the fact that they use the system," explains Steven S. Martin, BCBSNE's president and chief executive officer. Focusing on wellness, Martin says, is proactive. "We believe that wellness is a form of individual responsibility. It's an avenue for people to begin to understand their risks and what they can do about them, not only from what we typically think of in terms of lifestyle, but also in terms of those inevitable chronic diseases that we will all have one or more of as we age," he explains. "We can be far more capable of managing those elements as a system by working together."

A consumer-based health care plan is one of the ways in which to do so. Presently, many of these plans have higher deductibles and individual savings account features. However, BCBSNE is leading the way to structure their plans to offer participants the necessary tools to manage their health. When individuals can control, or perhaps even prevent a disease, they ultimately have the power to minimize the impact the disease has on their daily lives. Martin adds, "That's the direction we're moving. Today much of it is behind the scenes; but in the next few years it will unfold toward the individual consumer."

From the company's inception in 1939, BCBSNE has provided health care coverage primarily in the form of employer group plans and nongroup individual plans. "Our mission is to be the company that offers health benefits that people value most," says Martin. In addition, BCBSNE's not-for-profit

Continued on page 220

Photo by Alan S. Weiner

Blue Cross and Blue Shield of Nebraska communications specialist Melissa Cruickshank reads with her Conestoga Magnet School mentoring student, third-grader Jashonna Oliver. ∎

Continued from page 219

structure allows the company to reinvest in state-of-the-art technology, innovative products, and quality customer service, with the ultimate goal of benefiting both employer groups and individuals. "Everything we do must come from the perspective of the consumers. They want us to be there to pay their bill efficiently. We want them to get the care they need at the lowest possible price, but at a price that delivers enough revenue to keep good caregivers in the market," he explains. "It's not just about lowering costs; it's about people getting quality health care." And for the more than 560,000 Nebraskans who receive health care coverage or benefit administration from Blue Cross and Blue Shield of Nebraska, that's "the value of Blue." ∎

The Mobile Screening Unit is a valuable benefit for all Nebraskans. Each year, thousands of people are screened for diabetes, hypertension, and vision and hearing disorders. Blue Cross and Blue Shield of Nebraska has been a corporate sponsor of the Mobile Screening Unit since 1989. ∎

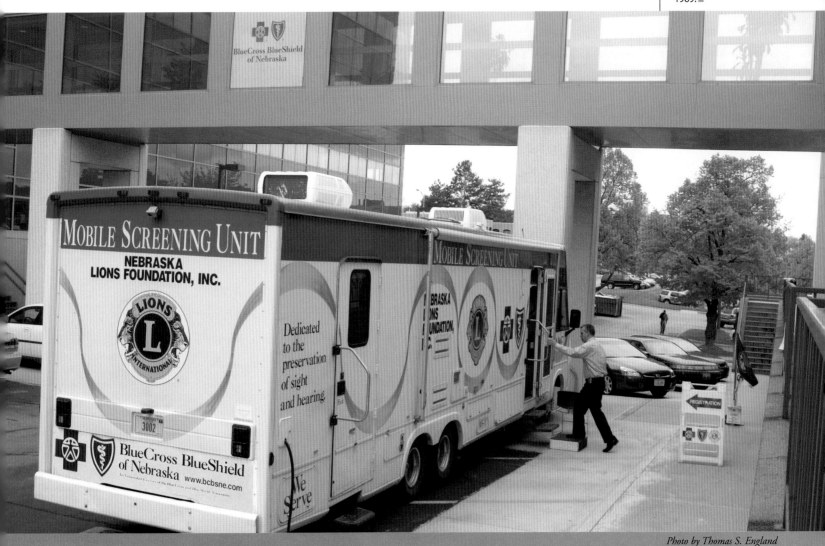

Photo by Thomas S. England

Photo by David Gibb

What was once a scrap-metal yard has been transformed into the vital and elegant seventy-five-acre university campus of the Gallup Organization. The lobby of the main building features glass walls and striking black-and-white photographic reproductions of moments in the Gallup corporate history. Completed in 2003, the campus was one of the initial projects that helped fuel momentum for redevelopment along the Missouri riverfront and downtown Omaha. O!

LEO A DALY assisted in the fund-raising efforts for the Saint Cecilia Cathedral building project by providing an architectural model of the existing structure and proposed enhancements envisioned for the future. Steve Laughlin, AIA, project architect, and Anne Franco, architect-in-training, place finishing touches on a model of the Cathedral, parish complex improvements, and local community development features. The Cathedral, a focal point in the Destination Midtown area, was designed by Thomas Rogers Kimball in the early 1900s, and is one of Omaha's many stunning landmarks. O!

Photo by Joe Guerriero

The Hilton Omaha hotel, Nebraska's only AAA four-diamond property, is a treasure within walking distance of many attractions, from Qwest Center Omaha across the street to the historic Old Market a few blocks away. Minutes from Omaha's Eppley Airfield, the hotel is but one example of the excellent quality accommodations—and seven thousand rooms—that await Omaha's visitors. They are perfect fits, no matter the season, or the occasion. O!

Woodmen Tower, the nerve center of the Woodmen of the World Life Insurance Society, is a true reflection of how Omaha has evolved over the years. Constructed in the late 1960s, its presence in the downtown business district is a testament to how far the city has come, attracting new enterprises over the years and becoming one of the country's most inviting locations for corporate headquarters. To this day, the tower stands tall and proud as one of Omaha's most recognizable landmarks.

Koley Jessen's team of professionals in front of Rosenblatt Stadium during the opening week of the College World Series. Koley Jessen serves as legal counsel to the College World Series of Omaha, Inc. ■

Koley Jessen P.C.
A Limited Liability Organization

A t Koley Jessen P.C., "clients first" is far more than an operating policy; it is the foundation on which this law firm is built. Koley Jessen makes serving its clients the top priority. This guiding principle has earned it an ever-expanding client base, as well as local, regional, and even national recognition for the highest quality of legal services.

In fact, so many have turned to Koley Jessen that the firm, formed in 1988 with seven attorneys, has become one of the five largest Nebraska-based law firms, with highly qualified attorneys, paraprofessionals, and staff that allow Koley Jessen to cover a full spectrum of practice areas.

The firm's practice encompasses such diverse areas as estate and business succession planning, employee benefits and executive compensation, mergers and acquisitions, securities and finance, creditors' rights, real

Paul Jessen and Omaha
World-Herald Company
chairman and CEO
John Gottschalk inside
the World-Herald's
Freedom Center. ■

Photo by Jackson Hill

Photo by Mark Romesser

Koley Jessen
strives to be an
integral part of
the client's team,
with a focus on
achieving results.

estate and construction, education, health care, environmental, occupational safety, media, intellectual property, litigation, workers' compensation, and employment. This range of services stems from a culture that is consistently looking to add new skills to an already talented group.

Koley Jessen strives to be an integral part of the client's team, with a focus on achieving results. The firm views itself as a partner to its clients. This often means working seamlessly with its clients' other advisors and business partners to help them reach their goals. This cooperative working relationship is an essential component of the "clients first" approach at Koley Jessen. In addition, such a level of involvement provides for more cost-effective legal work which is an important factor to those who are turning to the firm in greater numbers.

Koley Jessen's standards of high quality in the practice of law extend into its dedication to community as well. The firm and its attorneys know that contributing to the quality of life in the community and region requires integral participation at both the professional and civic levels. Not only does the firm provide support for area causes, its people also serve as leaders and hands-on members of charities and organizations that touch the community on many levels.

It is this emphasis on putting clients first, providing quality and diverse legal services, and a commitment to its community that has made Koley Jessen the firm that it is today. ■

Photo by Mark Romesser

Get Moving!

Photo by Mark Romesser

Students from Liberty Elementary School prepare to "Get Moving" in May 2005 as part of ACT!vate Omaha's eight-week media campaign kickoff. Sponsored in part by the Robert Wood Johnson Foundation's Active Living by Design physical fitness advocacy program and an Alegent Community Benefit Trust Fund grant, the campaign used television, radio, billboard, and poster ads to promote the message that physical fitness is fun and easy. More than three hundred people attended the event, including Mayor Mike Fahey, Alegent Health's Wayne Sensor, Blue Cross and Blue Shield of Nebraska's Steve Martin, City of Omaha employees, and staff from the Greater Omaha Chamber of Commerce. ACT!vate Omaha provides information on exercise programs; encourages the use of bike trails, parks, walking paths, and skate parks for daily physical fitness; and promotes ways to make neighborhoods walking and biking friendly. O!

West Corporation, headquartered in Omaha, is one of the top employers in the area. West offers diverse career opportunities, competitive compensation and benefits, and the opportunity to grow and make a difference with one of the top companies in the industry.

West Corporation

For years, premier companies across the nation have turned to West Corporation to provide them with the individualized customer care solutions that make the difference between simple contact and effective communication.

Since the company's founding in 1986, West Corporation has grown to become one of the world's leading providers of integrated customer contact solutions. Based in Omaha and with locations throughout North America, Europe, and Asia, West excels in helping companies communicate more effectively, maximize the value of their customer relationships, and derive greater revenue from each transaction.

West's integrated suite of customized solutions includes customer acquisition, customer care, and retention services, as well as conferencing and receivables management services.

West customizes every solution to meet the complexity and scope of each client's needs. Their unique ability to blend traditional call center agents, home agents, and automated solutions—with domestic, near-shore, and offshore facilities—helps West deliver the optimum customer contact solution to companies across a wide array of industries.

West's innovative customer contact services bridge the gap between contact and communication. Whether companies choose West for a comprehensive solution or select certain components, they will discover a level of expertise that is unmatched in the industry. ■

West excels in helping the nation's leading companies communicate more effectively, maximize the value of their customer relationships, and reach a higher level of success.

Photo by Thomas S. England

The sun sets on the Desert Dome at Omaha's Henry Doorly Zoo, the world's largest indoor desert. The dome houses an exhibit that represents the Namib Desert of southern Africa, the Red Center of Australia, and the Sonoran Desert of the U.S. and Mexico. The building features a thirty-foot-tall sand dune, a hummingbird canyon, a fifty-five-foot-tall central mountain, and live animals that inhabit deserts around the globe. Too much sunshine? Step beneath the Desert Dome to the Kingdoms of the Night exhibit, where day and night cycles are reversed, allowing visitors to see live nocturnal creatures hunt and play. O!

Whether they are at the bank serving as a wealth-building partner or in the community walking for a special cause, the people of American National Bank know how to make "American dreams come true." ∎

American
National Bank

Through great leadership, extraordinary customer loyalty, and a focus on relationship banking, American National Bank has grown into one of the largest locally owned billion-dollar-plus business banks in the Midwest. Commercial and real estate lending, cash management, and private banking are at the core of its wealth-building mission. It is also a midwestern leader in supplying indirect auto loans to car dealers as well as a major residential lender.

The bank was chartered in 1964 and is locally owned, including executive management ownership, within the Omaha/Council Bluffs area. "We enjoy a great reputation for safety and soundness; we have a great record to uphold," according to Margie Heller, executive vice president and chief financial officer. The

Photo by Dennis Keim

organization has acquired other banks and savings and loans with foundations dating back to 1887. In 2001, Peoples National Bank, Council Bluffs, Iowa, combined with American National. Doug Goodman, president of Peoples National Bank, notes that the bank combination "increases our lending capacity in the rapidly developing Council Bluffs market."

There are a number of reasons for the success of American National Bank/Peoples National Bank. Prominent among these is the bank's ability to forge strong relationships with customers who believe in the bank as a trusted advocate, advisor, and wealth-building partner.

The bank is known for assisting small businesses, charitable organizations, and some of the region's fast-growing companies and real estate developers. "The bank was named 'Lender of the Year' by the Nebraska Economic Development Corporation for 2004, which recognizes American National Bank's leadership statewide in SBA 7A and 504 lending," states Tod Ellis, executive vice president. Metro Leasing, a division of the bank, provides a lease option that "completes the business package," reports Mike Hall, senior vice president and manager of Metro Leasing.

"This is all part of making American dreams come true," according to president Jeff Schmid. "We believe that businesses value having the attention of a banker who can know and understand them and who can be an advocate and advisor for them as they grow."

Making "American Dreams Come True" actually states the bank's commitment to make every effort to fulfill a request of its customers and promote the customer's best interests. "We know our customers and include them in civic and bank events," indicated Mike Homa, executive vice president.

Cash management is also a major business tool. "We believe our customers deserve a cash management solution that is specifically tailored to them and which benefits them; nothing here is just 'off-the-shelf,'" according to Lorie Lewis, senior vice president and manager of the Cash Management Department.

For those clients with the additional means, American National offers a more personal touch through Premiere Banking and wealth-building services.

American National Bank is actively involved in giving back to its communities through the volunteering of its officers on local boards and projects, which is a prerequisite for officer status, and in donating to many area charities in its communities. ■

American National Bank's executive officers and shareholders from left to right: Margie Heller, Ed Kelleher, Tod Ellis, Len Olsen, Jeff Schmid, Lorie Lewis, Jim Burns, John Kotouc, Mike Homa, Mike Hall, Brad Konen, Jeff Holmberg, and Doug Goodman. ■

"We enjoy a great reputation for safety and soundness; we have a great record to uphold," according to Margie Heller, executive vice president and chief financial officer.

Spotlight on O!

The global role of the U.S. Strategic Command (USSTRATCOM)—headquartered at Offutt Air Force Base south of Omaha—is important to all who value a free America. The social and economic impact of Offutt and other military units here is also far-reaching and impressive.

Besides USSTRATCOM, Offutt is home to the "Fightin'" 55th Wing of the Air Combat Command. The four-thousand-acre base employs more than 10,500 military and civilian personnel, making it the largest employer in Greater Omaha. Offutt's annual economic impact upon the community is estimated at more than $2 billion.

Built in 1896 as Fort Crook, it was dedicated Offutt Field in 1924 in memory of Omaha's first air casualty in World War I, Lt. Jarvis J. Offutt. During World War II, the north side of the base held the Glenn L. Martin Co. Bomber

Plant, which produced 531 B-29 Superfortresses and 1,585 B-26 Marauders.

It was renamed Offutt Air Force Base in January 1948. Eleven months later, it became home to the Strategic Air Command (SAC).

In 1992, President George H. W. Bush established a new unified command, USSTRATCOM. For the first time in the nation's history, the planning, targeting, and wartime

Defending

Photo by Mark Romesser

Commerce has pledged to work to attract and retain the people and companies necessary to support the missions of the base and other local military units.

Today, USSTRATCOM provides intelligence, planning, space, and information operations expertise to U.S. forces and allies around the globe, defending America's freedom by making the world a safer place. **O!**

employment of strategic forces came under the control of a single commander.

A decade later, U.S. Space Command was merged with USSTRATCOM, bringing together a rich history that spans both the interrelated strategic and space communities.

The merger has enhanced Omaha's ability to recruit defense contractors and space-related industries to the area. To build upon this unique opportunity, the Greater Omaha Chamber of

Freedom

Photo by Mark Romesser

Certified Transmission is the realization of a childhood dream for Peter Fink, owner and president. Standing in the company's centralized, 106,000-square-foot, state-of-the-art remanufacturing facility in Omaha, he knows that he has achieved his ultimate goal—the establishment of a plant that provides a consistent level of high-quality service on all product levels for all Certified customers. ∎

Certified
Transmission

Growing up in Omaha, Peter Fink liked working on cars, particularly transmissions. Little did he know that when he opened Certified Transmission in an old service station in 1979, he would one day be the president of the largest remanufactured transmission supplier in the Midwest. With an innovative concept, an instinctive entrepreneurial spirit, and a keen understanding of customers' needs, Fink developed a company that has taken the automotive industry by storm, selling twenty-five thousand remanufactured transmissions to more than six thousand customers each year.

It all began with the unique way that Certified Transmission provides transmissions to its customers. "We have them available for exchange," relates Fink. "When you go to an auto parts store and you need an alternator or a starter, you buy one and pay a core charge. Then you can bring the core back later and get a refund on it. We did the exact same thing with transmissions, making them available immediately instead of

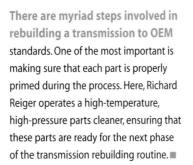

There are myriad steps involved in rebuilding a transmission to OEM standards. One of the most important is making sure that each part is properly primed during the process. Here, Richard Reiger operates a high-temperature, high-pressure parts cleaner, ensuring that these parts are ready for the next phase of the transmission rebuilding routine. ■

Photo by Eric Francis

Photo by Eric Francis

Vehicle owners discovered they could get their cars back promptly, but they also could get "the job done right . . . at the right price."

having to wait three, four, or five days until the transmissions were rebuilt. Nobody had done that before."

That simple idea made Certified Transmission extremely popular with the motoring public. Vehicle owners discovered they could get their cars back promptly, but they also could get "the job done right . . . at the right price." The demand for the company's transmissions grew quickly, and Fink soon recognized the opportunity to expand. Today, Certified operates fifteen repair centers in Nebraska, Iowa, Kansas, and Missouri. Two centralized remanufacturing plants support the shops, with the 106,000-square-foot main Omaha plant serving as the company's remanufacturing and corporate headquarters. Together, these facilities employ 275 of the most experienced technicians in the business.

"We have quality associates who push to build the absolute best transmission for the customer," Fink says. To help the technicians maintain this excellence, employees are encouraged to become certified by the National Institute of Automotive Service Excellence. Certified offers an extensive, paid thirteen- to twenty-six-week training program, which allows employees to specialize in remanufacturing a few specific types of transmissions to assure that they know those units upside-down and inside-out. It also teaches employees everything they need to know about doing things the Certified Transmission way. By making the remanufacturing process centralized and ensuring that each builder can apply a precise set of standards to the transmissions in which they specialize, Fink can guarantee the quality products that have become synonymous with his organization.

Another reason for Certified's distinction is the fact that the company keeps $1.5 million worth of parts on hand at all times. This stock allows builders and machinists to concentrate on the complex process of rebuilding

Continued on page 236

Photo by Rod Reilly

Anthony Fielding stays completely focused as he operates a dynometer, which pretests each transmission before it is installed into a vehicle. It's this strict attention to detail that allows Certified Transmission to ensure that its products not only function well, but also keep customers safe when they make their way onto the road. ■

Continued from page 235

transmissions to comply with QS9000 quality standards, using state-of-the-art OEM tools and equipment. Then, each transmission is rigorously tested twice to ensure its quality. Certified Transmission follows up with comprehensive and reliable one-, two-, and five-year warranties.

Additionally, Certified's pioneering ID system, which allows customers to select just the right transmission from its catalog, is an integral part of the company's burgeoning business-to-business division. Since the mid-1990s, general repair facilities have been turning to Certified Transmission for an array of remanufactured transmissions. The transmissions give owners of small shops the ability to serve their own customers comprehensively. "It gives them a new alternative," explains Fink. "They can grow their business by offering this service. We supply a transmission as a finished product, so the businesses don't have to have the technical expertise in how to rebuild a transmission. They just have to know how to install it." Now Certified is building a national network of distributors that will bring its products to customers around the country.

In the Machine Shop, Jonathon Alexander performs a final inspection on a machined part. He is able to perform this task at his absolute best thanks to the comprehensive training he received as part of Certified Transmission's paid training program. By investing in its associates and their talents, the company now boasts some of the most skilled technicians in the country. ■

Photo by Eric Francis

Isaiah Nielson, one of Certified Transmission's sixty-five specialized technicians, is working with hundreds of parts from the transmission he is remanufacturing to OEM specifications. If he happens to need an additional part while he's working, he can access it without delay thanks to the company's reserve of more than $1 million worth of stocked parts. ■

Photo by Rod Reilly

Certified's many endeavors have been documented nationwide. The company has been recognized seven times as one of Omaha's twenty-five fastest-growing companies, and it received the Better Business Bureau's National Torch Award for outstanding business ethics, among many other honors. Of course, these tributes are treasured, but Fink actually draws his greatest pleasure from giving back to his community.

In addition to working closely with the area's trade schools and supporting programs like Easter Seals, Make-A-Wish Foundation, and Heartland Family Services, Certified is actively involved with Teen Challenge Omaha, which helps at-risk individuals turn their lives around. The company often employs program members as apprentices and sets them on an exciting career path. For Fink, it's a privilege to help these people—and all of his employees—realize their potential. It's something he was able to do himself, and Certified Transmission's success is proof of his commitment to personal and professional excellence. ■

Photo by Rod Reilly

Mark Bohnenkamp, shown here in the torque converter department, is welding a converter together after it has been remanufactured. Highly technical work like this must be done right the first time to ensure the customer's total satisfaction, which is why all Certified Transmission employees go through extensive training to understand every aspect of the remanufacturing process. ■

Photo by Rod Reilly

Photo by Rod Reilly

Skilled hands at the Dehner Co. have crafted high-quality law enforcement, military, and equestrian boots—even boots for the NASA space program and Shuttle astronauts—since the company moved to Omaha in 1929. Many famous people have bought their boots from Dehner, including the late President Ronald Reagan, whose last pair of Dehner boots were mounted on Reagan's horse for the funeral procession in Washington, D.C. Here, Jeff Ketzler, the president and fourth-generation owner, carefully measures Omaha police officer Gary Shields to ensure the final product will be a perfect fit. O!

Photo by Rod Reilly

Karen F. Smith, RN, assists patient Jose R. Rodriguez using the HomeMed Monitoring System, a two-part setup that includes a home-based device measuring patient data that is connected to a central station monitored by health-care providers. The system is offered solely by the Visiting Nurse Association (VNA), an organization that has been providing home health services to Nebraskans for more than one hundred years. In addition to a comprehensive array of home health-care programs and services, the VNA provides hospice and palliative care as well as a host of community programs that reach out to both children and adults. O!

Mutual of Omaha

Since 1909, Mutual of Omaha has fulfilled a basic mission: to provide financial security and care in difficult times. Whether helping families protect their loved ones and build financial security, developing innovative employee benefit plans for businesses of all sizes or serving the communities in which it does business, Mutual of Omaha stands ready to help.

With a nationwide network of offices and sales representatives, Mutual of Omaha is a leading provider of insurance and financial services. For individuals and families, Mutual offers an extensive portfolio of life, Medicare supplement, long-term care, disability, critical illness, and hospital income insurance as well as annuities and investment products. Mutual of Omaha's experienced representatives can help customers with solutions that help prepare for life's planned events as well as its surprises.

Mutual of Omaha also provides businesses with benefit plans that help keep their employees healthy, engaged, and productive, offering a full portfolio of employee benefit solutions, including life, disability,

Photo by Mark Romesser

Mutual of Omaha's experienced representatives can help customers with solutions that help prepare for life's planned events as well as its surprises.

Mutual of Omaha employees make a community connection with Habitat for Humanity. Employees were given the opportunity to help build a Mutual of Omaha–sponsored home. Habitat for Humanity is one of the numerous community organizations supported by Mutual of Omaha. ■

health, and dental insurance as well as retirement plans and special coverages.

A Fortune 500 company with more than $18.5 billion in assets, Mutual of Omaha also has the financial strength to keep the promises it makes to its customers. The company's solid financial foundation, strong management, and competitive portfolio of products and services has consistently earned it high marks from the leading rating agencies, including A.M. Best, Moody's Investors Service, and Standard and Poor's.

The company also is committed to providing caring and professional customer service and consistently ranks in the top quartile of industry customer service ratings.

Mutual of Omaha is one of America's best-known and most-respected brands. The company was a television pioneer with its *Mutual of Omaha's Wild Kingdom* series, which premiered on network television in 1963 and remained in production through the mid-1980s. A modern, all-new *Mutual of Omaha's Wild Kingdom* is back on the air on the Animal Planet network. Using cutting-edge technology, the new *Wild Kingdom* takes viewers to the wildest places on earth to experience never-before-seen animal adventures. In addition, the best episodes of the original *Wild Kingdom* are now available on DVD at retailers nationwide.

But Mutual of Omaha's commitment to the natural world doesn't end there. The company also sponsors the Mutual of Omaha's Wild Kingdom Kids' Summit on Conservation. A nationwide essay contest, the Kids' Summit encourages young people to brainstorm creative ways to help save threatened and endangered species. One young conservationist from each state is chosen to attend the Wild Kingdom Kids' Summit on Conservation.

Mutual of Omaha is also an official sponsor of USA Swimming and is proud to present the Mutual of Omaha Duel in the Pool, a head-to-head swim

Continued on page 242

Continued from page 241

meet between the world's two best national teams: the USA and Australia. Held each summer, the Duel in the Pool is broadcast on NBC. In addition, Mutual of Omaha sponsors numerous local swim clubs across the country.

For young golfers and their parents, the company sponsors the Mutual of Omaha Drive, Chip, and Putt Junior Challenge, a nationwide series of golf skills events.

Mutual of Omaha's reputation for strength and integrity have made it the company of choice for those seeking careers in the insurance industry. With approximately five thousand employees at its midtown Omaha headquarters, Mutual of Omaha is one of the top-ten largest private employers in Nebraska and ranks among the top-five largest in Omaha.

Consistently recognized as an employer of choice, the company is the recipient of such distinguished awards as "100 Best Companies for Working Mothers," "100 Best Companies for IT Professionals," *Omaha Magazine's* "Best Employer Award," and the Wellness Council of the Midlands' "Gold Well Workplace Award."

As a sponsor of USA Swimming, Mutual of Omaha reaches out to its employees and local swim clubs with special events. In January 2005, Mutual sponsored Swim Stars Live!, an event for area swim clubs, which featured several Olympic gold medalists. ■

Photo by Alan S. Weiner

Mutual of Omaha's annual Take Your Child to Work Day gives employees' twelve- year-old children a chance to learn about the career opportunities available throughout the company. Participants also learn about the company's conservation heritage and meet *Mutual of Omaha's Wild Kingdom* co-host Jim Fowler. ■

Photo by Thomas S. England

Photo by Eric Francis

Mutual of Omaha also takes seriously its responsibility as a corporate citizen. The company's philanthropic efforts include grants, in-kind donations, and the talent of associates who enthusiastically volunteer to assist in the company's four areas of focus: education, community betterment, health and wellness, and arts and culture. Examples of this commitment include making the largest private donation to the Senior Health Foundation's assisted-living facility for Alzheimer's patients in Omaha as well as record-setting contributions to the Omaha Food Bank, the Salvation Army's school supplies and toy drive campaigns, and Toys for Tots. Through its innovative "HALO" program, associates contribute each payday to help the needy, culminating each November in Thanksgiving Baskets that provide groceries to more than 250 families in the Omaha metro area.

By staying true to a nearly one-hundred-year-old legacy of financial strength, customer-focused care, and community philanthropy, Mutual of Omaha continues to provide its customers and neighbors with financial security, and care in difficult times. ▪

Photo by Doug Henderson

An indoor cycling room, along with a beautiful fourteen-thousand-square-foot Wellness Center, is one of the many on-site programs Mutual of Omaha offers its employees. It helps them live happier, healthier, and more productive lives both at work and at home. ▪

Photo by David Gibb

Our hats are off to Herb Gindulis and the Great Plains Hat Company in Bellevue. "I run this place as a not-for-profit business, and if there is money available at the end of the year, I buy more authentic hat-making equipment from the 1800s." Herb searched the Great Plains area for equipment, and each piece has its own story, like one collection that had been sitting in a van in a pasture since the 1960s. If you drop by, prepare to stay a while. There is a lot to see and learn. O!

HATS OFF

Photo by Jackson Hill

Nebraska's beef cattle industry adds $4 billion to $5 billion in sales each year to the state's economy. According to the Nebraska Cattlemen's Association, one in every five steaks sold in this country comes from Nebraska. Jay Volk, his father, and his brother are kept busy during calving season, which starts in January and runs through March. Cattlemen and Omaha, home to the top stockyards in the nation during the 1960s after surpassing Chicago's Union Stockyards, have a long history together. In the mid-1880s cattle freely grazed the grasslands, and most of the prairie was undisturbed. Today, cattlemen have implemented practices to help preserve the native prairie while protecting and conserving the health of their cattle. **O!**

Grubb & Ellis
Pacific Realty

Photo by Thomas S. England

Members from various disciplines throughout the company come together to maximize the value of their clients' assets. The positive contributions made by their teamwork are reflected across the communities they serve. ■

"Grubb & Ellis/Pacific Realty doesn't just put together great deals, it builds valuable relationships."

When it comes to assisting clients with critical real estate decisions, Grubb & Ellis/Pacific Realty doesn't just put together great deals, it builds valuable relationships.

The company's origins go back to 1987, with the establishment of Omaha's Pacific Realty Group, Inc. In 1997, this successful real estate advisory company formed an affiliation with one of the nation's largest commercial real estate firms, Grubb & Ellis.

Today, with offices in Omaha, Lincoln, and Des Moines, Grubb & Ellis/Pacific Realty offers local, regional, and national clients throughout Nebraska and Iowa a variety of consultation, development, and advisory services, including investment sales, property development, construction management, brokerage services, tax consultation, market research, and landlord and tenant representation.

In Omaha alone, the company's brokerage services cover over 4 million square feet of office, retail, and industrial properties for major clients such as First National Bank of Omaha, Qwest Communications, Mutual of Omaha, and Magnum Resources, Inc.

Grubb & Ellis understands that in the retail industry, time is of the essence. In the retail discipline, this couldn't be more true than when securing new locations. Thanks to the firm's research and negotiating skills, companies such as top bakery Panera Bread and the successful retail chain Gordmans are able to secure prime retail locations for their operations, as well as meet their expansion goals.

For these and hundreds of other companies throughout Nebraska and Iowa, the real estate partnerships brokered by Grubb & Ellis/Pacific Realty translate into productive and prosperous relationships for everyone involved. ■

Photo by Doug Henderson

Canada geese taking flight are but one small part of Kent Ullberg's noted *Spirit of Nebraska's Wilderness* sculpture, developed for First National Bank's downtown corporate campus. The sculpture incorporates a mature bison, a mother bison and her calf, and a granite fountain from which fifty-eight geese take flight. A second location, between 14th and 15th Streets and Capitol Avenue, is home to more bison and bronze sculptures depicting two pioneer families with their covered wagons making their way west. **O!**

Fraser Stryker

Since its founding in 1898, Fraser Stryker has grown from a small group of lawyers representing the businesses that fueled Omaha's growth to a nationally recognized law firm known for its experience, breadth, and vision, and its relentless innovation to resolve client needs. The firm's commercial practice encompasses the full scope of services, from business start-up to mergers and acquisitions, for regional, national, and international corporations. Fraser Stryker has an active energy and environmental law practice and has represented Nebraska's largest electric utility since its formation in the 1940s.

Litigation has been a cornerstone of Fraser Stryker's practice. The firm has a talented group of trial lawyers with extensive litigation experience covering a broad range of complex cases. Fraser Stryker lawyers try cases throughout the country, bringing clients favorable results. The firm has been hired to bring and defend nationwide class-action lawsuits in the fields of environmental law, telecommunications, insurance, and employment discrimination, among others. Fraser Stryker offers the experience and resources of a much larger firm at an attractive Midwest cost structure.

Fraser Stryker attorneys Bob Freeman (right) and Sarah Yale (center) with Roger Dixon, president and CEO of the Metropolitan Entertainment and Convention Authority (MECA), in front of Qwest Center Omaha, which MECA manages. Fraser Stryker has represented MECA since its inception. ■

Photo by Thomas S. England

Photo by Thomas S. England

Ever on the cutting edge, Fraser Stryker represents technology companies in start-up, capitalization, product protection, and sales and licensing. The firm is nationally known in the telecommunications area, providing comprehensive legal services in support of operations ranging from the installation of an international fiber optic network to the development of franchise, interconnection, and Internet technology services. In these rapidly evolving segments of the economy, the firm maintains a visionary outlook that results in the highest level of client service.

A recognized leader in the constantly changing field of labor and employment law, Fraser Stryker knows that prevention and client education provide the best defense. In addition to representing clients before federal and state courts and administrative agencies, Fraser Stryker provides in-depth counsel to guide clients in the day-to-day administration of employment practices.

Fraser Stryker attorneys have garnered industry-wide recognition. Several of the firm's attorneys have been elected to membership in the American College of Trial Lawyers, the International Society of Barristers, and the College of Labor and Employment Lawyers. Several are also listed, by peer selection, in the Woodward and White publication *Best Lawyers in America*.

This dedication to excellence extends to the firm's support of community activities. In addition to pro bono representation for a diverse group of regional causes, including many focused on the needs of area youth, members of the firm provide leadership to local organizations. Fraser Stryker has long been involved in the development of Omaha's world-class Henry Doorly Zoo, ranked the Best Zoo in America in the May 2004 issue of *Reader's Digest*. The firm's commitment to its city is visually embodied in the new Qwest Center Omaha downtown arena and convention center, a crown jewel that the firm helped bring to fruition. Fraser Stryker attorneys have worked closely with community leaders to bring to Omaha the state-of-the-art Holland Performing Arts Center.

As it forges into its second century of serving Omaha, Fraser Stryker will continue to bring to its clients and the greater community the innovative legal skills needed to fuel the growth of a twenty-first-century city. ■

" In these rapidly evolving segments of the economy, the firm maintains a visionary outlook that results in the highest level of client service. "

Avaunt Garde Domini

Keeping the United States safe is the primary objective of the men and women at the U.S. Strategic Command. Established in 1992 by President George H. W. Bush and headquartered at Offutt Air Force Base outside Omaha, USSTRATCOM is charged with providing early warnings of and defense against nuclear missile and long-range conventional attacks. Since September 11, 2001, USSTRATCOM is also responsible for deterring and defending against the worldwide proliferation of weapons of mass destruction.

First Data
Corporation

irst Data Corporation keeps business humming. With a simple swipe of a credit card or keystrokes of a PIN number, the financial transactions of merchants and consumers are seamlessly linked in seconds. First Data Corporation is the company behind the business —the company that makes it possible for money to move electronically and the global marketplace to run smoothly.

Every second of every day, millions of people and businesses around the world engage in all types of transactions. From purchases at the retail register or the gas pump, to electronic bill payments, to withdrawal or transfer of funds, people and businesses move their money faster, more simply, and more securely largely in part to First Data Corp. "We want to lead with our brands, to process any payment, from any device, at any time, to any account," says Charlie Fote, chairman & CEO, First Data Corp.

While hardly a household name, homegrown First Data is the pioneer in the transaction processing industry. Its origins date back to 1971 when a small start-up company called First Data Resources was

Operating twenty-four hours a day, seven days a week, the Omaha Command Center is responsible for monitoring and maintaining multiple processing platforms to provide issue management and customer service to a diverse client base worldwide. ■

Photo by Doug Henderson

The origins of this electronic commerce leader can be traced back to Omaha in 1971, when a small company named First Data Resources was created to provide card-processing services to an association of seven Midwest banks. Now, First Data Corporation is a leader in the payments industry worldwide. The First Data Technology Campus, at 72nd and Pacific Streets in Omaha, plays an integral role in the company's global transaction card-processing operations. ■

Photo by Doug Henderson

From application to swipe through settlement, consumers and businesses rely on us to make buying, selling, and life easier.

created to provide credit-card processing services to an association of seven midwestern banks. Five years later the company became the first to process both Visa and MasterCard transactions. Today, the Omaha-based First Data Card Issuing Services group is a key business unit of Denver-based First Data Corporation (NYSE: FDC). Chances are strong that any given American consumer transaction purchase has passed through one of First Data's operations centers. Like an interstate highway, with Omaha at its center, First Data facilitates the efficient movement of commerce.

"First Data is the leader in the payments industry," says Fote. "From application to swipe through settlement, consumers and businesses rely on us to make buying, selling, and life easier. As the world continues to shift from paper to electronic transactions, First Data is uniquely positioned to encompass the entire value chain."

First Data operates at the center of the electronic commerce and payments industry, serving as the motherboard to power integrated, end-to-end payment solutions worldwide. Through its Western Union® division, businesses and individuals can transfer money around the globe using the company's proprietary money transfer network. First Data's STAR Network offers PIN-secured debit acceptance at 1.7 million ATM and retail locations. Financial institutions, as well as retailers, rely on First Data for complete debit services, from ATM and PIN-secured payments, to bill payment and risk management. First Data also provides merchants a full range of payment solutions, including credit, PIN-secured and signature-based debit, wireless, stored-value, and purchasing cards; electronic benefits transfer; as well as loyalty and check services. As the leading provider of electronic commerce payment solutions for businesses and consumers worldwide, First Data is leading the way in electronic payments. ■

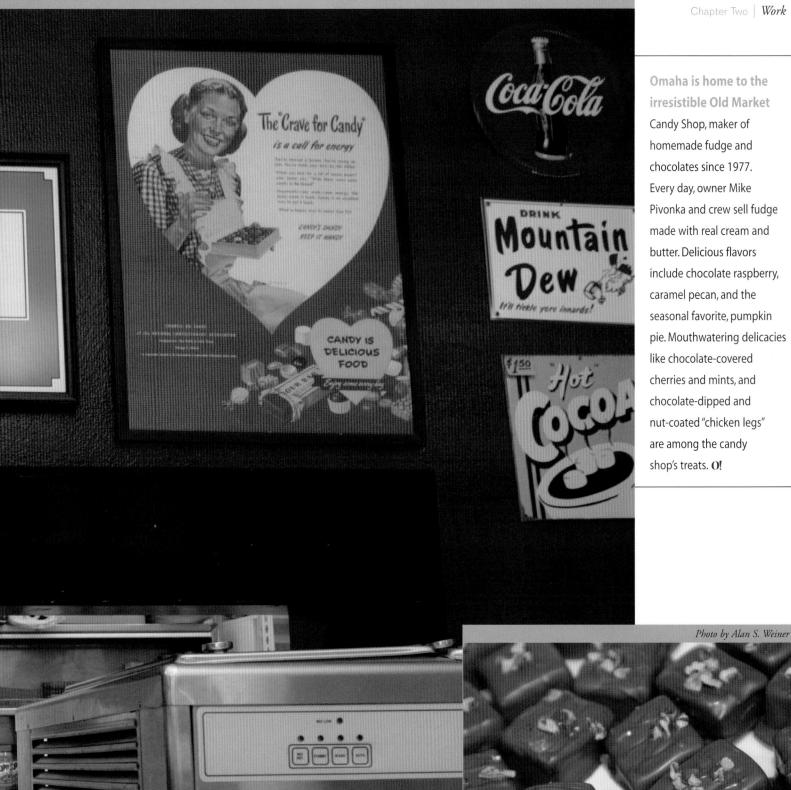

Omaha is home to the irresistible Old Market Candy Shop, maker of homemade fudge and chocolates since 1977. Every day, owner Mike Pivonka and crew sell fudge made with real cream and butter. Delicious flavors include chocolate raspberry, caramel pecan, and the seasonal favorite, pumpkin pie. Mouthwatering delicacies like chocolate-covered cherries and mints, and chocolate-dipped and nut-coated "chicken legs" are among the candy shop's treats. O!

Photo by Alan S. Weiner

Photo by Alan S. Weiner

Gallup associates Aaron Burklund and Jeremy Knuth work in Gallup's Global Network Operations Center. Fifty-two sites from around the world are monitored and managed from this Omaha location. ■

The Gallup
Organization

In a world where information is power, then the right information can turbocharge leadership. No company knows this better than The Gallup Organization. From the world-renowned Gallup Poll to measurement of employee and customer engagement, the company's expertise on human behavior has transformed Gallup into a worldwide consulting firm.

While the Gallup Poll is a household name, the respected peek inside America's mind is just one facet of this dynamic and composite organization. "Gallup's umbrella mission is to advise the 10 million people who manage, govern, and lead the world on what the 6 billion people of the world are thinking," says Jim Clifton, chairman and CEO. Gallup's unique consulting services are utilized by Fortune 1000 companies. Gallup understands the importance of human emotion, opinion, and behavior, and has been

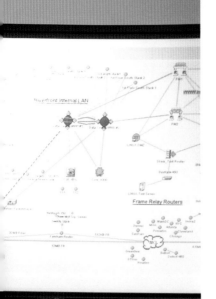

Omaha is home to Gallup University's Riverfront campus, where managers and executives from Gallup's clients come to Gallup University for training and consultation. The site also serves as Gallup's operational headquarters. ■

Photo by David Gibb

Photo by David Gibb

"Gallup's umbrella mission is to advise the 10 million people who manage, govern, and lead the world on what the 6 billion people of the world are thinking."

able to illustrate the link between those items and harder business measures of productivity and profitability. Clifton explains that by first understanding the human aspect of the business—the employees as well as the customers—Gallup can help rearrange, change, and transform its clients' companies for organic growth.

Through research examining the linkages between key elements of a healthy business, The Gallup Organization has developed a model that describes the path between the individual contribution of every employee and the ultimate business outcome of any company—an increase in overall company value. Aptly named The Gallup Path, the model's key tenets demonstrate that behind every successful business are engaged employees who, in turn, drive customer growth. This requires selecting professionals who are not only capable but also whose talents fit their role. When employees' talents fit with their role, they can develop them into real strengths, making them more productive and enthusiastic each day.

Having engaged employees and customers is not simply an emotional phenomena, but Gallup's proven road to helping businesses grow organically. Beyond the A-list clients they serve, Gallup firmly grounds its business practices in these principles. Rather than buying or acquiring resources, Gallup finds the value of selecting talented people, giving them great management, and keeping clients engaged. With stock earnings growth exceeding 20 percent each year for the last decade, and a strategy to increase its personnel by 5 percent every year, Gallup is reaping the rewards of sowing the seeds of organic growth with its clients. ■

Photo by Jackson Hill

It's all in the family at the Lithuanian Bakery, a delectable mainstay in Omaha since 1962. Founded by Lithuanian immigrants Vytautas Mackevicius and his wife Stefanija, the bakery is known for its old-country recipes for breads and tortes. The Napoleon Torte, a mouth-watering masterpiece of eight wafer layers laced with butter creams, takes three days to create, and usually only seconds to devour. Today the Lithuanian Bakery is managed by the Mackevicius sons: Algrid, Alfonsas, and Vytas. **O!**

Photo by Jackson Hill

" *In order to make my Maine wedding special, I chose Lithuanian Tortes as a reminder of my Omaha family traditions.*"

Lisa Ewert Poyer, former Omahan

Photo by Thomas S. England

Close your eyes and imagine. Is it Paris? Milan? No, it's Omaha, the Dundee neighborhood to be precise, but it could be any number of sidewalk cafes, beer gardens and outdoor dining options situated conveniently throughout the city. With Omaha's average summer temperature of 76.9 degrees, who needs Milan? O!

Managing shareholder Jerry Bland and senior manager Jason Tonjes visit with the management team of the Lund Company. The Lund Company, a longtime client of the firm, is one of Omaha's most successful commerical real estate companies.

Bland &
Associates

I t's given that most businesses rely on certified public accountants for tax and auditing expertise. However, smart businesses turn to CPA firms like Bland & Associates for broader guidance. More than a traditional accounting firm, the Bland & Associates team members serve as business consultants to their clients by providing proactive strategies for building wealth and business growth. "We're trying to see what we can do for our clients today that will help them tomorrow," says Jerry Bland, managing shareholder and founding partner.

With more than twenty-five accountants on staff, Bland & Associates serves clients with resources that mirror the national accounting firms, but with a personal, hometown approach. Through a strategic alliance with BKR International, a worldwide association of CPA firms, Bland & Associates provides high-level services for small and medium-sized businesses at more reasonable costs than that of national firms. In addition to traditional accounting services, the firm offers a variety of specialized projects including research and development tax credit studies, cost segregation studies, and multistate tax assistance, business valuations, litigation support services, forensic accounting, and QuickBooks consulting.

The core management team of Bland & Associates is Jason Tonjes, senior manager, David Riley, shareholder, and Jerry Bland, managing shareholder. ■

Photo by Doug Henderson

Photo by Doug Henderson

"Bland & Associates serves clients with resources that mirror the national accounting firms, but with a personal, hometown approach."

John Lund, of The Lund Company, says his company has benefited from Bland & Associates' expertise. "The quality of their work is extraordinary. They have been proactive in suggesting business improvement projects. Most recently, they completed cost segregation studies on several of our properties, which resulted in significant tax benefits," Lund explains. "They are always available to answer questions, and are extremely knowledgeable about our business and issues related to our industry."

The firm's innovative approach to customer service is rooted in an environment that allows the staff to be thoughtful and imaginative, and to work smoothly as a team. "It's not uncommon to have impromptu meetings with the partners and the staff to discuss a client's situation, or to develop a new approach to solving a client's problem," says manager Jason Tonjes. "We're always looking to improve clients' current business situations. Some may think these are ancillary services, but we think this proactive approach is the most important thing we do," he adds.

Jerry Bland founded the firm based on a shirtsleeve approach to client service. Today, the Bland & Associates team continues to work with clients in this fashion—always ready to get under the hood and identify opportunities for improvement.

In addition to their core entrepreneurial clients, Bland & Associates works with a variety of not-for-profit and governmental agencies, and Tribal governments. The firm's public sector experts take a similarly proactive approach in serving clients. "We aim to help improve clients' operations and make their organizations more efficient. We provide useful management advice as part of each of our engagements," says shareholder Dave Riley. In essence, Bland & Associates is committed to excellence in client service.

The Winnebago Tribe of Nebraska certainly appreciates the responsiveness of Bland & Associates. "They travel here for our council meetings, and always show initiative when handling our services," says Darwin Snyder of the Winnebago Tribe. "They do exactly what we ask of them, and they're always dedicated to getting things done the right way." ■

Photo by David Gibb

Like everyone at Children's Hospital, the facility's physical and occupational therapists make caring for children their sole focus. The hospital offers rehabilitative services for children through age twenty-one, using activity, play, and specialized equipment to help minimize the effects of disease, injury, and other health concerns that limit a child's abilities. O!

HELPING OTHERS

Photo by Thomas S. England

Omaha's corporations are visible in the community in many ways. Most, like Blue Cross and Blue Shield, are involved in sponsoring events for the greater good. Whether it is a mobile health screening van available to visit other businesses, or employees dedicating precious time and talent by volunteering for non-profit organizations, Omaha businesses are shining examples of what it means to be good corporate citizens. O!

Photo by Eric Francis

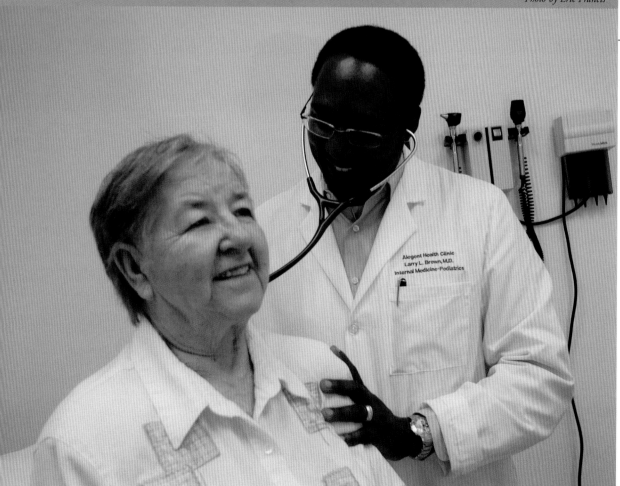

"Sometimes I see a child in the morning who says, 'You're gonna see my mom this afternoon,' and when I see the mother, she says, 'You're seeing my mother tomorrow.'" Dr. Larry Brown, who specializes in internal medicine and pediatrics at the Alegent Health Clinic, often treats all the members of the family, "from zero to whatever." As if that is not enough to keep him busy, Dr. Brown is also a minister of the Mount Carmel Baptist Church in Bellevue, Nebraska. His father, Herman Brown Sr., is both founder and senior pastor of the church. Asked how he manages two full-time professions, Dr. Brown smiled and said, "I have a very understanding wife." O!

SITEL
Corporation

People across the globe depend on the power of communications to keep their lives and livelihoods running smoothly. Whether they're reporting a lost credit card, configuring a complicated piece of electronics, or rushing an injured child to the emergency room, SITEL Corporation is there to help.

As a global leader of outsourced customer support services, SITEL specializes in the design, implementation, and operation of multichannel customer contact centers for over three hundred of the world's leading businesses. By providing the latest in customer acquisition, sales, and care; technical support; and risk management services, SITEL helps improve the lives of millions of individuals and businesses each day.

Founded in 1985 by James F. Lynch, SITEL has grown to include operations in twenty-five countries throughout North America, Europe, Asia Pacific, and Latin America. At SITEL, success is measured one

SITEL specializes in the design, implementation, and operation of multichannel customer contact centers for over three hundred of the world's leading businesses.

SITEL's headquarters in Omaha supports the company's worldwide operations, which includes ninety-one customer contact centers in twenty-six countries. Executive management and staff provide thirty-two business units with operational, financial, and marketing support. ■

Photo by Doug Henderson

phone call at a time, as thirty-one thousand of the industry's most skilled customer service personnel log over 1 billion minutes of customer contact per year, including 18 million follow-the-sun call routings, 15 million e-mail and Web chat contacts, 150 million sales contacts, and over 400 million inquiries. And they do it in more than twenty-five languages and dialects.

SITEL has developed into one of the few companies in the industry with the scale, expertise, and technological resources necessary to serve the worldwide needs of large corporations, while never losing sight of the fact that behind the numbers lie real people seeking real solutions. On behalf of clients such as major financial services companies, banks, brokerage firms, and credit card issuers, SITEL handles millions of credit card holder contacts regarding balances, transfers, available credit, and interest rates. The company's contact care centers utilize the latest in advanced technologies to immediately access the data needed to answer questions and solve issues, while safeguarding the security of customer information.

Customers such as major utilities also seek SITEL's expertise in helping them manage costs and sustain high levels of customer satisfaction, from connection and service to billing and risk management. When power goes out in a community, SITEL establishes an automated network and voicemail system that tells callers what they need to know, simultaneously routing calls to a live operator for service—24 hours a day, 365 days a year. With SITEL on the job, utilities are better able to concentrate on delivering vital services to their customers.

In response to emerging technologies and the growth of the Internet, SITEL provides expert, up-to-the-minute support to some of the world's most

Continued on page 266

Photo by Eric Francis

Continued from page 265

sophisticated technology clients. Whether speaking high tech or low tech, SITEL's customer care personnel are able to provide immediate assistance through a variety of channels—including telephone, interactive voice response, fax, traditional mail, and all Internet channels.

Additionally, SITEL specializes in troubleshooting, technical support, and service dispatch for cable companies, Internet service providers, and telecommunications companies, realizing that in today's high-speed world, the difference between good and bad support can make or break a service provider.

And when there's a personal emergency, SITEL is there to connect people to friends, family, and vital services. Communications companies such as domestic and international long-distance providers, local exchange carriers, and PCS providers worldwide have come to count on SITEL's customer service personnel to effectively handle, with cool heads and calm voices, all manner of emergency calls, directory assistance, and technical support.

SITEL has twenty years of experience serving clients across the key industry verticals of Automotive, Consumer, Financial Services, Insurance, Media Services, Technology, Telecom, and Utilities.

At SITEL, it all starts with a phone call. It ends with improvements in the way people across the globe live, work, and grow their businesses. ■

SITEL's customer support professionals assist clients' customers 2 million times a day in twenty-five languages and dialects. ■

The Durham Research Center on the campus of the University of Nebraska Medical Center (UNMC) is one of the many projects of HDR, a worldwide architectural, engineering, and consulting firm headquartered in Omaha. Noted for its expertise in health-care design, HDR created a world-class facility functionally and aesthetically. The facility can meet current and future needs, as the building is sited so that an additional research tower can be built. The center is the hub of the UNMC's research enterprise—where more than fifty scientists advance the latest breakthroughs in a number of medical fields, including cancer, cardiovascular disease, neurosciences, transplantation, and genetics. With 289,000 square feet for 116 research laboratories, twelve conference room, three classrooms, and an auditorium, the center offers an environment that fosters discovery and collaboration—prime ingredients for success.

Photo by Rod Reilly

Nature comes to life for students in the educational programs at Omaha's Henry Doorly Zoo. Whether "adopting" an animal, taking a tour, or participating in a special "edzoocational" program, the facility offers a host of nontraditional ways for generating interest in the animal world. Through internships, students shadow the zoo's various professionals working in every area of the property, where they learn all about animal care, nutrition, and environment. Dedicated to conservation, research, recreation, and education, Omaha's Henry Doorly Zoo is home to a world-class collection of mammals, fish, birds, and insects in their natural environments. **O!**

The Omaha Police Department's motto, "To Serve and Protect," includes policing the metropolitan area from the sky as well as on the streets. The department's Air Support Unit includes helicopters that perform a variety of services, from search and rescue to providing support to patrol officers and detectives on the ground investigating criminal acts. O!

The Mounted Patrol is one of the more visible units of the Omaha Police Department—chiefly because the officers on horseback tower above their surroundings. The mounted patrol hit Omaha's streets in 1989 with just two officers, two horses, and a temporary home at the old Ak-Sar-Ben racetrack. Today, the eight officers, their sergeant, and their horses occupy an impressive four-hundred-thousand-dollar training facility and barn built by ConAgra Foods on land it donated at Seventh and Leavenworth Streets. O!

Photo by Dennis Keim

There, In the Window, Isn't That . . .

One of the unofficial landmarks of the Old Market is a seven-foot-tall reproduction of the Statue of Liberty, painted in bright red, white, and blue, that looks down upon visitors from the window of a Howard Street condo. The statue, named Lucy by her owners, has been known to come down and take part in the occasional Fourth of July parade. Lucy is a fixture at nighttime as well, with a string of white holiday lights draped around her torch and shoulders. O!

Natural gas is delivered
safely and reliably to more
than one hundred communities
in the eastern third of Nebraska.
As new subdivisions are created,
Aquila employees install new gas
lines to serve the needs of the
residents. ■

Photo by David Gibb

Aquila

We help
encourage existing
companies to
stay and expand,
and to find and
bring new business
to communities.

For more than 75 seventy-five years, communities and organizations in the Metro Omaha area have turned to Aquila for safe, reliable natural gas services. Aquila delivers more than natural gas energy to communities, consumers, and businesses. The investor-owned utility (NYSE: ILA) provides economic development energy as well as direction and support through its strong community partnerships.

"We help encourage existing companies to stay and expand, find and bring new business to communities, and improve the area's assets and market them to the world," says Jon Empson, senior vice president, Regulated Operations. Through its economic development partnerships, Aquila has assisted hundreds of communities with a variety of project proposals, lead-generation activities, community infrastructure planning, organizational development, and innovative, cost-effective energy solutions.

The company's focus on helping communities grow and prosper through economic development partnerships is also mirrored in its community relations initiatives. Whether through charitable contributions, employee involvement, energy assistance funding for needy customers, or purchasing policies that embrace diversity, Aquila believes in the power of synergy.

Formerly known as Peoples Natural Gas, Aquila is regulated by the Nebraska Public Service Commission and delivers safe, reliable natural gas service to more than 190,000 customers in 110 communities in the eastern third of Nebraska. ■

What's better than purchasing fresh produce on a daily basis? Picking your own! And that's just what customers throughout the area love about Wenninghoff's. Family owned and operated, Wenninghoff's has been growing and selling fresh produce to individuals and local grocers since 1928. Today, it sells as many as thirty different varieties of fruits and vegetables daily from 10 a.m. to 7 p.m., April through the end of October. Customers are welcome to bring a bushel and pick from the fields—beans, strawberries, tomatoes, and onions are favorites. Wenninghoff's is also known for several varieties of sweet corn available from July 4 through Labor Day. Wenninghoff's delivers fresh produce to fifteen area senior centers each week. O!

Photo by Eric Francis

Photo by Eric Francis

Borrowing for a new car or a better education—and everything in between—is easy at OFCU. Just ask Bob Kokrda (pictured with his two kids, Lily and Russell). His OFCU home equity loan helped him purchase this beautiful backyard fountain. ■

Omaha Federal
Credit Union

Omaha Federal Credit Union (OFCU) employees have more than eight thousand bosses, and they would not want it any other way. In addition, there are no customers at the OFCU, only members. Because the nearly seventy-five-year-old credit union is a cooperative, each member truly owns and operates the financial institution. The result? Better service, a wide range of financial services and products, a fair return on savings, and a solid capital base. Simply put: an organization committed to members' best interests.

Just ask recently retired federal prosecutor Bob Kokrda. A member for more than thirty years, Kokrda has utilized nearly all of OFCU's services. From auto loans to online banking services, he says the credit union experience has always been more user-friendly than traditional banks. "There's just a feeling at Omaha Federal that they are here to serve you," he says.

Omaha FCU employees Cheryl Mathis (upper left) and Chris Byous (upper right) enjoy their role as Santa's "community elves" distributing toys to (from left to right) Richie, Renee, Samantha, James, and Danielle in conjunction with the Open Door Mission's Operation Santa Toy Drive. This event is one of the many community partnerships of Omaha FCU. ■

Photo by Alan S. Weiner

Photo by Doug Henderson

Because the nearly seventy-five-year-old credit union is a cooperative, each member truly owns and operates the financial institution.

Big enough to serve you. Small enough to know you. That's what OFCU strives for. With close to $50 million in assets, seven branches, and a commitment to leading-edge technology, OFCU works hard to make the members' money work for them, yet makes financial transactions as accessible and convenient as possible. A recent charter change now allows OFCU to serve all residents of Omaha and surrounding communities.

"We look very much like any other financial institution," says Alan Ruff, a civil engineer who is also OFCU's chairman of the board. "The difference is that the person using the services is a member of the credit union. It's a friendly, family-like institution."

Members put their money in a variety of savings accounts, and that money, in turn, is lent to members. After operating expenses and reserve requirements are met, loan income is returned to all members in the form of dividends and comprehensive financial services.

This structure also allows the credit union to keep service charges at a minimum and interest rates competitive. When Kokrda went shopping for a new car, he found a sign on the model in the dealership that indicated a four-thousand-dollar discount to buyers who were credit union members. On top of the discount, Kokrda received special financing with a low interest rate from OFCU. "It was as if the credit union had that car waiting for me," he says.

Serving its members isn't the only goal of OFCU. "We try to meet the needs of the community as well," says president Steve Johnson. Every year OFCU is the title sponsor for Operation Santa, collecting toys and cash for more than four thousand children. In addition, OFCU supports the Children's Miracle Network, proceeds of which are designated for the local children's hospital. "We give 100 percent effort toward those charities and organizations we support," explains Johnson. "That's what a credit union is all about: people helping people." ■

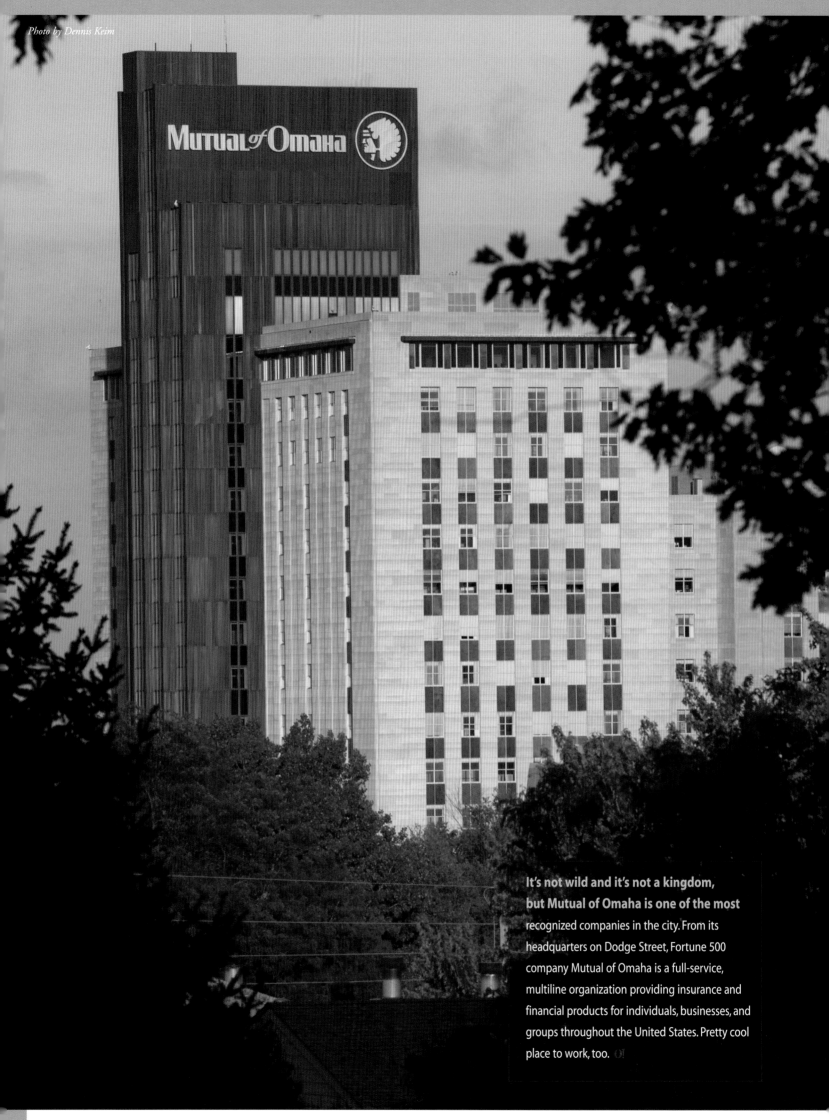

Photo by Dennis Keim

It's not wild and it's not a kingdom, but Mutual of Omaha is one of the most recognized companies in the city. From its headquarters on Dodge Street, Fortune 500 company Mutual of Omaha is a full-service, multiline organization providing insurance and financial products for individuals, businesses, and groups throughout the United States. Pretty cool place to work, too.

GROW Omaha!

Photo by Rod Reilly

Every Saturday at 8:00 a.m., Omaha residents are treated to an hour of the most enlightening economic development talk on the radio. That's when Coldwell Banker Commercial World Group founder and president Trenton Magid and vice president Jeff Beals present *Grow Omaha*, a News Talk 1290-AM KKAR show that discusses Omaha's thriving economy, urban growth, and commercial real estate development. The show's hosts bring special guests into the studio, such as Greater Omaha Chamber of Commerce president and CEO David Brown, and David Sokol, chairman of the Metropolitan Entertainment and Convention Authority; and call-in guests including Lou Dobbs of CNN. With their guests each week, Magid and Beals explore an array of themes that relate to Omaha's present—and future. **O!**

U.S. Bank
Nebraska

Omaha's U.S. Bank gives its customers a money-back service guarantee. Unusual? Not for this bank. If a customer waits more than five minutes in a teller line, they get paid five dollars. If a deposit fails to get credited on time, the bank refunds the service charge.

This dedication to customer service holds true in every department. The bank's Private Client Group provides trust and estate planning services as well as a personalized, individual approach to the financial needs of business professionals. The Commercial Banking area offers businesses an array of services including lending, depository, treasury management, international banking, and leasing. All of these products and services are delivered by banking professionals dedicated to building solid, long-term relationships of mutual trust.

This has been true since day one. For the first 120 years, U.S. Bank operated as Omaha National Bank. In 1986, it joined three other Nebraska banks to form FirsTier Financial, Inc. Ten years later FirsTier became part of First Bank System. In 1998, First Bank changed its name to U.S. Bank.

For more than twenty years, U.S. Bank has sponsored an exhibit featuring works from art classes at their Adopt A School partner, Omaha South High School. Parents and teachers join the bank in honoring the young artists at a reception. The art work, pottery, and jewelry are on public display in the Woodmen Tower bank lobby, and visitors can purchase pieces before these talented youngsters become famous. ■

Photo by Thomas S. England

Photo by Thomas S. England

"Our major goal is to provide customers with the best possible service and products to help them succeed."

Only the names have changed. "U.S. Bank still provides agricultural loans so ranchers can buy cattle and business loans so entrepreneurs can start new businesses," said Steve Erwin, Nebraska market president. "Our major goal is to provide customers with the best possible service and products to help them succeed."

Today with the backing of U.S. Bancorp's $195 billion in assets, Omaha's U.S. Bank provides a wide range of high-tech services locally, nationally, and internationally—each one handled with hometown friendliness.

When asked about the best part of his job, Wood Hull, vice president and manager of Private Client Group/Trust services, quickly answered, "The clients. Over the eighteen years I've been with the bank, I've worked with some of the most successful families in our community, and I learn from them every day. It isn't unusual for us to build relationships that span generations. That's both a privilege and a great responsibility."

Karen Nelsen, vice president and commercial banking relationship manager, agrees. "Like a lot of people here, I've been with the bank many years and developed both personal and professional friendships. Part of what makes my job interesting is being able to offer such a wide variety of products and services on a local level."

Many Omaha residents know U.S. Bank through its sponsorship of community events and volunteers who donate their time. U.S. Bank is a presenting sponsor for the Riverfront Jazz and Blues Festival. It also supports education through the Strategic Air and Space Museum, Creighton University, the University of Nebraska, Junior Achievement, and an Adopt A School partnership with South High School, among others.

In 1886, reputations rested on the cornerstones of integrity, honesty, courtesy, and reliability. At U.S. Bank they still do. ■

Musicians rehearse for a wedding in the Main Waiting Room of the Durham Western Heritage Museum, one of Omaha's favorite spots to exchange vows. Adjacent to the waiting room is the beautifully designed art deco–style Swanson Gallery, a favorite for receptions and other events. At just over forty-four hundred square feet and accommodating up to 250 people, the ballroom welcomes guests in grand fashion. The décor, consisting of simulated Travertine stone trimmed in painted silver leaf and imitation patent leather complemented by six transportation-themed murals, evokes the gallery's early railroad days, when it served as the Union Station Restaurant. It's a textbook blend of historic charm and contemporary elegance. O!

Photo by Joe Guerriero

The Lund Company was key in redeveloping Regency Court, providing a better level of service for existing tenants such as Borsheim's Fine Jewelry & Gifts while attracting prominent tenants such as Pottery Barn to Omaha. The Lund signs throughout the metro area remain a strong symbol of the company's growth, strength, and reach in the community. ∎

The Lund Company

The Lund Company is designed to meet every client's unique commercial real estate needs, completely and effectively.

"There's no greater feeling than looking around Omaha and seeing all the places in which we've helped others achieve a higher level of success," says John Lund, president and chief executive officer of The Lund Company. "By helping businesses succeed, we're helping Omaha thrive. . . . I'm proud to be a part of that."

In 1981, John Lund started this company focused on property management with just a few strong client relationships. The company has never lost sight of those beginnings, putting clients at the forefront of a successful business model. To meet its changing needs, The Lund Company expanded its commercial real estate portfolio to offer a full array of services including consulting and development.

Community involvement is fundamental to The Lund Company. John Lund is an active member of the Greater Omaha Chamber of Commerce's Board of Directors and participates in numerous sponsorship events. The Lund Company's property management department has been recognized locally and nationally for innovative and efficient energy use in several of its managed properties.

Any business owner knows that the right real estate choices directly correlate to success. The Lund Company values its reputation as one of Omaha's best commercial real estate companies, helping businesses

The Lund Company developed this **115,200-square-foot** Customer Contact Center for PayPal, an eBay company. The state-of-the-art Workstage building is the first of its kind in Nebraska and houses more than thirteen hundred employees. ■

"By helping businesses succeed, we're helping Omaha thrive. . . . I'm proud to be a part of that," says John Lund, president and chief executive officer of The Lund Company.

across the metro area make vital decisions. Lund Company signs blanket all corners of Omaha and represent Lund's growth, strength, and reach in the community.

One notable client success story is PayPal, an eBay company, that offers online payment solutions. In 2002, after reviewing the Omaha marketplace in search of a location for PayPal's newest call center facility, Lund determined that buildings were available, but none of the sites were versatile enough for PayPal's ever-changing industry. PayPal didn't want to be just another call center.

"We were in desperate need of a commercial real estate solution that met our space requirements, recruiting goals, and aggressive timeline," says Ryan Downs, PayPal's vice president of operations. "Lund helped us sort through all the options and select the perfect solution."

The Lund Company, with its partner Workstage, a design-build firm, was able to develop a high-tech, high-performance building within a six-month timeframe. The quality of the building has certainly helped PayPal recruit the staff it needs to support its explosive growth.

"PayPal's applicant pool has never been stronger," Downs says. "We have comfortable, efficient work spaces and outstanding amenities, such as the basketball court, fitness center, and café. Our employees love coming to work in this type of environment, and they encourage their friends and family to apply."

It all goes back to caring about the community and the companies that exist within it. Finding that perfect solution is what keeps clients coming back to The Lund Company.

"Helping a business find its way to Omaha makes us a success," Lund says. "We are focused on building a strong Omaha—a solid future for this city that we all call home. We take pride in being Omaha's local commercial real estate experts, and, like Omaha, we see a strong future ahead." ■

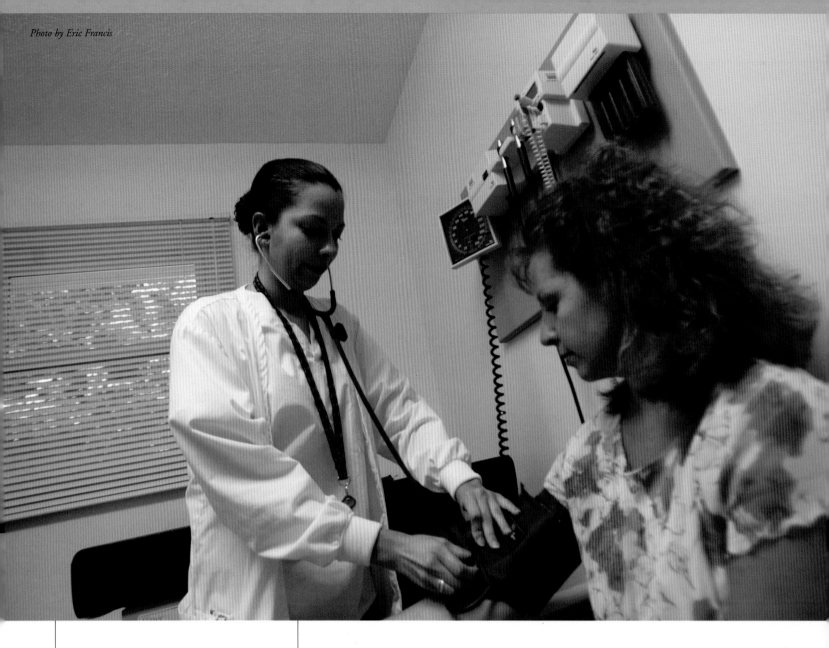

The Native American community in Omaha is a vital, living link to the city's history. At the Fred LeRoy–Ponca Health and Wellness Center, some eighteen hundred Native American patients receive care for everything from general medical conditions to dental treatment. Owned and operated by the Ponca Tribe of Nebraska, the center offers outpatient care, tribal traditional healing, a pharmacy, community outreach, public health nursing, and transportation for people representing over sixty tribes. O!

Dr. Kiran Gangahar, a native of New Delhi, India, works with a patient at the Westroads Office Park Clinic, one of four Heart Consultants' facilities located throughout the city. Dr. Gangahar, whose specialty is cardiology, graduated from University of Nebraska Medical Center in Omaha, where she also did her residency, and has been with Heart Consultants since 2003. O!

Photo by Eric Francis

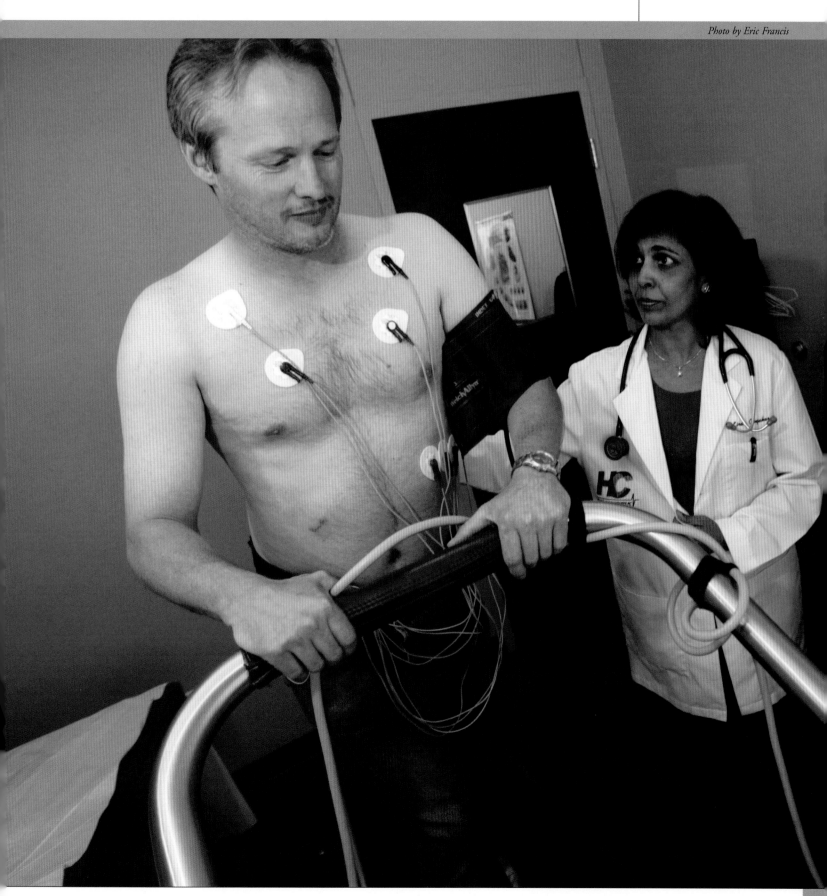

INVESTMENT
CENTER

SAVE
for Retirement

PLAN
for Your Child's Education

PROTECT
Your Assets

DEVELOP
a Financial Plan

SAVE
for a New Home

Commercial Federal investment and insurance products and services empower clients to take control of their financial futures. ■

Photo by Thomas S. England

Commercial Federal
Bank

One of Commercial Federal's newest branches in Omaha features a retail-style design with the latest in banking technology. ■

Photo by Thomas S. England

At Commercial Federal Bank, success isn't solely measured by dollars and cents, but by the number of lifetime partnerships established between the bank and its customers. Since its founding, Commercial Federal has remained committed to a set of principles that emphasizes financial strength and stability, excellence and innovation of service, and proactive identification of its clients' financial needs. By remaining true to this service-oriented philosophy, Commercial Federal has evolved into more than just a bank. To generations of its customers, it's become a trusted financial advisor.

With its roots firmly planted in Nebraska soil and a history of familial involvement since its founding, Commercial Federal Bank's commitment to regional growth remains unmatched. Yet its progressive spirit has led the bank to extend its reach beyond the region, resulting in continual growth and the ability to anticipate client needs with evolving products and services.

Commercial Federal Bank was established in 1887 as South Omaha Loan and Building Association with ten thousand dollars in assets. The first manager was James J. Fitzgerald. Young, ambitious, and talented, Fitzgerald would eventually be named to the Board of Directors in 1893 and as president in 1943.

Fitzgerald family members have held leadership roles ever since, helping to guide Commercial Federal through years of steady growth to its current position as one of the largest, most stable financial institutions in the central United States. Today, Commercial Federal supports two hundred branch offices located in high-growth markets throughout Nebraska, Iowa, Colorado, Kansas, Missouri, Oklahoma, and Arizona. Backed by the Commercial Federal family of financial services, which includes insurance, investment, and realty investment companies, Commercial Federal Bank continues to uphold its mission to provide better banking, every day, for every client.

Through its development and use of the latest technologies, Commercial Federal has greatly enhanced the scope of its products and services. In addition to consumer, commercial, and mortgage banking, consumer, commercial, and small business lending, and insurance and investment services, today's clients have access to a host of high-tech products and services tailored to their specific needs.

The bank's AccessOnline® service provides customers with free-of-charge Internet account management services that allow them to easily pay bills, view and print canceled checks, make credit card payments, maintain and reconcile their accounts via an online check register, and view their mortgage history. Similarly, AccessNow provides a convenient, twenty-four-hour bank-by-phone service, and the online EZ Change Kit allows customers to establish or transfer accounts from the convenience of their homes or offices.

Business customers also appreciate Commercial Federal Bank's attention to their specific needs, from basic checking and savings accounts to comprehensive cash management tools and investment advice. The bank's Business Banking area for small business is specially qualified to help clients select the accounts and services to

With its roots firmly planted in Nebraska soil and a history of familial involvement since its founding, Commercial Federal Bank's commitment to regional growth remains unmatched.

Continued on page 288

Photo by Mark Romesser

Continued from page 287

The bank has become
synonymous with its annual
concert at Memorial Park,
Commercial Federal Celebrates
America, which commemorates
July 4th. Chairman and CEO Bill
Fitzgerald addresses the crowd
of nearly sixty thousand people
enjoying the free concert and
spectacular fireworks finale. ■

reach their short- and long-term business goals, whether it be through a line of credit, a loan in conjunction with the Small Business Administration's guaranteed lending program, or advice through the bank's Small Business Advisor newsletter, which covers topics ranging from managing cash flow to improving collections.

Larger commercial clients receive the same personalized attention geared toward their specific needs, as do specialized businesses, such as car dealerships. Through its indirect lending program, Commercial Federal Bank offers new vehicle franchises in Iowa, Kansas, Missouri, Colorado, and Nebraska; a three-tiered program designed to give the new vehicle dealer maximum flexibility for customer financing needs, including quick contract funding and the most accessible underwriters in the industry.

Photo by Eric Francis

Residents throughout the
Omaha area benefit from the
various cultural and educational
sponsorships Commercial Federal
provides. These girls are viewing
the Smithsonian exhibit at the
Durham Western Heritage Museum
that the bank supported for the
community's enjoyment. ■

In addition to striving to be the bank of choice for dozens of communities across the region, Commercial Federal Bank also strives to be one of the most outstanding corporate citizens within those communities. Working year after year with a number of organizations and causes throughout the seven states it serves, Commercial Federal Bank donates both time and money to causes that promote education, social services, the arts, and community growth.

Whether at home in Nebraska or at any number of locations throughout the central United States, the people of Commercial Federal Bank strive to provide Better Banking. Every Day. It's not just a slogan; it's a guiding principle that results in outstanding and innovative financial services, trustworthy long-term business partnerships, and community enrichment and growth. ▪

Photo by Joe Guerriero

Helping families achieve the dream of home ownership, particularly in under-served communities, is one aspect of Commercial Federal's commitment to serving the community. This Omaha family is one of many who have benefited from the bank's community reinvestment initiatives. ▪

From the Omaha "war room" of Cornerstone Energy to many other area businesses, Commercial Federal meets clients' unique needs. ▪

"Sell cheap and tell the truth." That's the philosophy late Russian immigrant Rose Blumkin followed for her business, the Nebraska Furniture Mart. When "Mrs. B" opened shop in the basement of a small store in downtown Omaha, little did she know that her idea of the American Dream would become a Midwest retailing legend. The Omaha store includes a 450,000-square-foot showroom, a separate electronics and appliance store, a clearance center and factory, and a warehouse and distribution center. When billionaire investor Warren Buffett in 1983 paid $60 million for a 90 percent interest in "the Mart," he and Mrs. B sealed the deal with a handshake. O!

Photo by Mark Romesser

Photo by Mark Romesser

Photo by Mark Romesser

After years of admiring the beautiful, historic homes in the midtown Blackstone neighborhood, Jim and Barb Farho purchased one of their own. Today, the proud owners of a home built in 1892, have made considerable headway in their efforts to restore the structure to its once majestic stature. Called "the secret garden house" by the four Farho kids, the home once belonged to a banker whose fortune was lost in 1929 when the stock market crashed. The home's one-acre property, which houses a carriage house and garage, offers the Farhos plenty of opportunity for outdoor creativity as well. O!

Photo by Alan S. Weiner

Great Western
——Bank

"Great Western Bank takes pride in serving its communities through financial leadership, community participation, and hands-on support."

Great Western Bank knows how people view money. "It's a means to an end — not an end in itself," according to Harlan Falk, executive vice president of the bank. "We understand that it's not about money as much as it is about how your money helps you achieve the important goals you have in life."

For that reason, Great Western Bank takes banking to the people, staying at the forefront of technology and structuring its products and services for the greatest convenience. It was the first in the state to offer Internet banking, and its retail branches, located in metro-area Wal-Mart SuperCenters, operate twelve hours a day. "We go to where the people are instead of making them come to us," explains Falk.

The bank's ability to deliver to the individual customer stems in part from a strong reputation in commercial lines, a heritage forged since the doors opened in 1932. Business clients have always appreciated Great Western Bank's ability to respond quickly to decisions, a factor derived from the bank's independent ownership at the local level.

Today, Great Western Bank's nineteen Omaha locations make it one of the largest banks in the city. The bank also operates in Iowa, Missouri, and Kansas, and is part of a holding company with additional charters in South Dakota and Iowa that manages $2.6 billion in assets.

Wherever it is found, Great Western Bank takes pride in serving its communities through financial leadership, community participation, and hands-on support. Such assistance contributes to Great Western Bank's role as an essential resource for Omaha-area families. ∎

A little north of Lewis & Clark Landing sits the impressive *Monument to Labor* sculpture created by Matthew Placzek. Eight Omaha union locals, and twenty-six companies and individuals gave more than $1 million in funding and labor to make the monument a reality. One of the key facets of Omaha's vibrant and diverse economy is our well-educated and highly-skilled labor force. For the counties within a fifty-minute radius of Omaha, the labor force totals more than 650,000 persons. It is a productive force, as data from the Census Bureau indicate that compared to the national average, Nebraska workers produce 18 percent more goods for every dollar of wages paid. O!

The thirty-story Woodmen Tower has served as the Woodmen national headquarters, or Home Office, since 1969. Woodmen has called downtown Omaha home since the organization's founding in 1890.

Photo by Dennis Keim

Woodmen of the World
Life Insurance Society

In the heart of Omaha's central business district stands the Woodmen Tower, the thirty-story national headquarters, or Home Office, of Woodmen of the World Life Insurance Society. When completed in 1969, the Woodmen Tower—the tallest building at that time between Chicago and the Pacific Ocean—helped bring about a revitalization of the downtown area that ultimately strengthened the community and enhanced the lives of Omaha's citizens.

This is particularly fitting because these very same goals—enriching lives and strengthening communities—are the driving forces behind Woodmen, and have been since the organization's founding in 1890 in Omaha.

Today, Woodmen is one of the nation's leading fraternal benefit organizations, providing eight hundred thousand members with insurance protection, financial security, valued benefits, and community service opportunities. These members are served by six hundred employees, or associates, who work at the Woodmen Tower, and fifteen hundred sales associates who represent Woodmen in communities across America.

Members of an Omaha-area Woodmen lodge work with other volunteers to repair playground equipment at a local homeless shelter. Across the nation, Woodmen lodges conduct thousands of volunteer projects each year that benefit individuals, organizations, and communities. ■

Photo by Eric Francis

Woodmen is committed to helping members reach their financial goals at every stage of life through a wide range of life insurance options and annuities, as well as long-term care insurance, cancer insurance, and a daily hospital supplement plan. These products are complemented by home mortgage and refinancing options, investments, and other financial services.*

However, as Woodmen president and CEO James Mounce explains, "Woodmen is much more than simply an insurance provider. As a fraternal organization, we're committed to serving our members and their communities."

This is achieved through an array of member benefits, family-centered social activities, and volunteer opportunities.

Member benefits, which are available at little or no additional cost, include financial aid following the diagnosis of certain illnesses, monetary assistance for the orphaned children of members, a newborn insurance benefit, a prescription drug discount benefit, and recreational programs for youth and senior members. A highlight of the youth program is a unique summer camp experience for members between the ages of eight and fifteen.

Woodmen also helps members connect with their communities through the social, volunteer, charitable, and patriotic activities of its two thousand local lodges.

Throughout the year, Woodmen lodges bring members together for cookouts, group outings, holiday parties, and other social gatherings. Lodges also conduct numerous volunteer projects that benefit individuals and organizations and provide charitable support to nonprofit agencies. Woodmen's disaster relief partnership with the American Red Cross enables members to work on Disaster Action Teams (DAT) in their hometowns. In Omaha, for example, the Woodmen DAT has responded to more than two hundred house fires and other emergencies.

Through its Patriotic Program, Woodmen lodges present more than one hundred thousand U.S. flags annually to schools, churches, and nonprofit groups and provide American Patriot's Handbooks to libraries and newly naturalized citizens. Every September 11, lodges conduct ceremonies that salute the heroes and victims of 9/11 and recognize local heroes, like police officers and firefighters.

Across the nation, and here in Omaha, families are enriched by the financial security, valued benefits, and volunteer opportunities offered by Woodmen. They're all part of the organization's mission to benefit members through every stage of life. ■

Enriching lives and strengthening communities are the driving forces behind Woodmen, and have been since the organization's founding in 1890 in Omaha.

*Residential mortgage loans are offered through Woodmen Mortgage Services, Inc., a wholly owned subsidiary of Woodmen. Securities are offered and processed through Woodmen Financial Services, Inc., member NASD, SIPC, a wholly owned subsidiary of Woodmen.

After a year of careful rearing, it's time for J&C Simmentals of Blair to bring their cattle to market. At their auction in Fremont, the company's cattle, full-bred and crossbred black Simmentals, attracted registered buyers from sixteen states. Native to Europe, Simmentals are now well established in the U.S. cattle industry. O!

National Retailers Embrace Omaha

As one of a growing number of national retailers to join the
vibrant Omaha market, Whole Foods Market's landmark Midwest
store—which serves as a community gathering spot and a fresh approach to
grocery shopping—is a welcome addition to the city's robust economy. Other
national retailers and entertainment venues that have entered the Omaha
market include Dick's Clothing and Sporting Goods, Sharper Image, P.F.
Chang's China Bistro, Red Robin restaurants, Dave & Buster's, Scheels All
Sports, and Pottery Barn. Existing retailers such as Home Depot, Lowe's Home
Improvement, Target, and Wal-Mart are expanding. Omaha is a great place to
do business—on both sides of the counter. **O!**

Security National Bank depends on its senior management and officer staff to promote its "high-tech meets high-touch" approach every single day. Their collective ability to make each customer's banking experience both pleasant and personalized has allowed the organization to cultivate a loyal and satisfied patron base over the course of the bank's storied history. ∎

Security National Bank
of Omaha

Clarence L. Landen Jr. has always been known as an idea man. So when he decided to establish a national bank in Omaha, his friends and colleagues anticipated great things from his pioneering venture. They were not disappointed. In April 1964, Landen and a small group of banking executives secured a national charter and opened the doors to the city's first national bank in more than thirty years. Today, thanks to strategic planning and an unwavering community-minded outlook, Security National Bank is one of Omaha's most trusted financial institutions.

Twelve banking locations offer customers a complete suite of personal and business banking services, as well as a comprehensive portfolio of mortgage, home equity, and auto loans. Additionally, clients have access to an independent investment company, an Internet banking center, a trust division, and much more.

"We want to be a leader as a community bank in providing services to our clients," says president James

Security National Bank's corporate headquarters building, located at 101st and Pacific Streets, is a testament to the financial institution's impressive growth within the Omaha market over the years. Built in 2002, it houses the Bank's corporate offices, as well as Business and Private Banking, the trust division, a mortgage lending center, a retail branch, and an independent investment service. ■

Photo by Doug Henderson

Photo by Eric Francis

Today, thanks to strategic planning and an unwavering community-minded outlook, Security National Bank is one of Omaha's most trusted financial institutions.

E. Landen, who succeeded his father in the family business.

Therefore, the organization blends sophisticated technology with high-touch, personalized attention as its most distinctive characteristic. "We are an organization that's never left its origins of high touch," Landen continues. "We want to have a personal relationship with the client. But we also want to be high tech. So it's a combination of high tech and high touch that we believe delivers a suite of products and services that our clients expect and want from us."

Managing a solid organization that balances the unique needs of customers, employees, and shareholders is of the utmost importance to the Security National Bank family. That's the way it has always been, and that is the way it will continue to be as future generations of the Landen family join the company. Maintaining this vision and its reputation as a dedicated community bank, says Landen, is what sets the organization apart. "We're very focused on having a good strategic plan that goes well into the future," he explains. "We like being in the banking business, and we've tried to deal with all of the issues that cause banks to be sold. We have a long-term game plan in place to consistently serve the community."

The reason for this approach is simple. The community itself is as much a part of the bank as the tellers and ATMs. That's why Security National Bank also participates in numerous charitable activities through-out the city. "We're a company of people serving people, and we're serving the community we call home," Landen notes. "We live here and work here every day, and we want the best to happen for this community. Our actions can impact that, so we're focused on being a good corporate citizen and giving back to the community." ■

handful of business leaders, d hospital administrators he groundwork for what e Blue Cross and Blue braska.

In those days, our claim payments were carefully recorded in a handwritten ledger book; the single membership premium rate was 75 cents a month. The mission was simple: help people protect themselves against catastrophic medical bills.

Donald J. Burke
Second President of Blue Cross, 1941-1944

1948 – Nebraska Blue Cross and Nebraska Blue Shield companies move into new offices on the fifth floor of the Kilpatrick Building in downtown Omaha.

In 1949, Arthur L. Coud becomes the fourth president of Blue Cross. That same year, Inter-Plan Bank is created, which connects individual Plans and allows members to receive benefits for care when traveling in other states.

Arthur L. Coud

Photo by Alan S. Weiner

BlueCross and BlueShield of Nebraska's longevity in the community is depicted through a unique three-dimensional relief that serves as a focal point in the company's lobby.

The artwork, designed and installed by local vendors, makes it easy for employees and visitors to follow the milestones of the insurer's history. Originally separate companies, the Associated Hospital Service of Nebraska (Blue Cross, founded in 1939) and the Nebraska Surgical Plan (Blue Shield, founded in 1944) came together in 1974 to launch today's company, a not-for-profit mutual insurer that provides coverage or benefit administration to more than five hundred thousand people. **O!**

" It's our community, it's a giving community. It's a concerned community. It's a caring community. It's a community with people whose thoughts are dominated a lot more by 'our' than are dominated by 'me.'"

Stuart Chittenden,
business development director

Photo by Jackson Hill

Security National Bank employees volunteer to serve hot meals to the homeless and less fortunate through the Salvation Army's Winter Night Watch program. The van began making the rounds in the city in the early 1990s, and is now serving more than twenty-five thousand meals each winter season. "This keeps me connected to my community and reminds me that we are all vulnerable to hard times," says Angela Barry (front). "The individuals and families we make contact with are thankful, kind, and humble." Valeria Smedlund (back) adds, "What we were doing didn't feel like it was enough, but to some it seemed like we gave them the world." O!

Photo by Eric Francis

Family owned and operated, John A. Gentleman Mortuaries takes pride in its highly personalized approach. FRONT: Rosemary Flecky, Karl Rohling, Laura Engen, Thomas Belford. CENTER: Marty Bowman, Carla Cooper. BACK: Anthony Whelchel, Jim Ely, Brian Sunseri, Steve Halstead, Anthony Allmon, Matt Honz. ■

John A. Gentleman
Mortuaries

A few minutes spent talking to Thomas M. Belford, president of John A. Gentleman Mortuaries, makes it clear that this firm is extraordinary. First, in this day of national conglomerates, John A. Gentleman is a family company that has been locally owned since 1906. "We feel the most important thing we offer is consistency, so one funeral director takes charge of all the arrangements and is responsible for all the corresponding details," said Belford. "Rather than telling families how services should be conducted, we ask, 'What would you like us to do for you to create an event that celebrates a life?'"

To make decisions easier, John A. Gentleman has already thought through a number of details. Their facilities include community rooms with catering available for after-service lunches. Floral arrangements

A unique program, families can celebrate the life of a loved one through "living memorials" in the Lauritzen Gardens, Omaha's Botanical Center. FRONT: Lavonne Muller, Marty Bowman, Dusty Stark. BACK: Doug Schroeder, Thomas Belford. ■

Photo by Eric Francis

and sympathy cards are available on site. Even the selection process has been redefined. "We have a small area where the family can see corner sections of several types of caskets. We find this is far less overwhelming than walking into a large room filled with full-sized caskets," Belford explained.

One of the truly outstanding aspects of their service is aftercare. "Our service does not stop at the cemetery. Our motto, 'Service Beyond the Service,' means we provide whatever a family needs to help them during their healing process." They offer several free six-week sessions for adults; these groups provide support and education for rebuilding at a time of loss. There is a trained bereavement facilitator on staff who works with the support groups. In addition to the groups sponsored by John A. Gentleman, the firm also has a referral service for other local support groups which focus on different ages and different types of loss.

The Living History Class is yet another innovative service offered by John A. Gentleman. Everyone has their personal triumphs, big and little victories, and favorite memories of their relationships with other people. These life reviews, autobiographies, and family histories are treasures that future generations will cherish.

A unique program offered is the John A. Gentleman Botanical Memorial. For every family they serve, a planting is made in the deceased's name in the Lauritzen Gardens, Omaha's Botanical Center. This provides a living memorial. Families are invited to the annual dedication and the unveiling of the names of their loved ones on a memorial plaque. "We are very proud of this program because it not only honors those we serve, but it also supports one of the best programs to improve our city and provide a beautiful, peaceful, green space," Belford explained.

Thomas A. Belford founded his funeral home in Council Bluffs, Iowa. He passed the mantel to his son Thomas J., who relocated and expanded the business significantly. In turn he passed it to his son Thomas M., who continues the tradition of serving the Omaha area with old-fashioned, personalized service plus innovative new ideas. ■

"Our motto, 'Service Beyond the Service,' means we provide whatever a family needs to help them during their healing process."

Photo by Alan S. Weiner

FRESH

ON T

Blackstone Stou

Firehouse ESB

Root Beer

Dundee Scoto

American W

India Pale

The Upstream Brewing Co. here in the Old Market and at its west Omaha location hit the mother lode with its O! Gold Light Beer. One of a dozen beers the brewery and restaurant offers on tap, O! Gold has proved to be as popular as the city it promotes. It's had "absolutely phenomenal" results, says Upstream president and CEO Brian Magee. "It quickly became one of our top three beers."

As the focus of the $300 million First National Center, the First National Tower sits at the corner of 16th and Dodge Streets, in the heart of downtown Omaha. It is the tallest building from Chicago to Denver.

First National
Bank

Photo by Rod Reilly

Since 1857, First National Bank has been guided by one driving principle: to provide its customers with quality products and superior service. This unwavering commitment has earned First National more than 6.6 million customers across all fifty states.

With more than twenty branches and over seventy ATM locations in the Omaha metropolitan area, First National Bank is committed to quality products and superior service. ■

The dedication to quality is also evident in the First National Tower, the bank's corporate headquarters in the heart of downtown Omaha. Standing at 633 feet and more than forty stories high, it ranks as the tallest building from Chicago to Denver.

First National Bank's beginnings were slightly more modest. Founded in 1857 by two brothers, Herman and Augustus Kountze, the bank opened for business when Omaha was barely a village. It had been settled a short three years prior, and Nebraska had yet to become a state. The Kountze Brothers Bank's first office was a small wooden building, close to the banks of the Missouri, where they traded primarily in gold dust and buffalo hides.

After six arduous years, the Kounzte brothers applied for and received the first national bank charter awarded in Nebraska, a major distinction, which granted their enterprise some much-needed prestige. That same year, the bank reorganized with new partners, including the well-known telegraph entrepreneur Edward Creighton as president. This charter places them as one of the oldest banking companies west of the Mississippi River.

From its humble start, First National Bank has grown into one of the fifty largest banks in the United States. The bank prides itself on being a family-owned business. Bruce Lauritzen, chairman of First National Nebraska, is Herman Kountze's great-great-grandson, making First National Bank a sixth-generation family enterprise. Today the company employs more than seven thousand employees and has assets of more than $16 billion.

Just as it was the first chartered bank in Nebraska, success has been marked by staying ahead of the curve. First National was one of the first banks to issue credit cards, as early as 1953. This commitment to innovation has served them well, as First National is the fifth-largest in-house credit card processor, the sixth-largest merchant processor, a top-ten commercial card issuer, the twelfth-largest issuer of bank cards in the United States, a top-twenty electronic funds processor, the fifth-largest agricultural lender with customers in 49 states, as well as one of the leading providers of project finance to the ethanol industry.

While acknowledging the importance of technology, the bank has never lost sight of the fact that banking is still very much a human transaction. "When people want to talk about money, they want to talk to a person," says Dennis O'Neal, president of the Corporate Bank. "They may enjoy the convenience of online banking, but when it comes to loans or their account information, they want to see someone face to face."

Continued on page 308

While acknowledging the importance of technology, the bank has never lost sight of the fact that banking is still very much a human transaction.

First National is pleased to provide free jazz concerts two days a week on our outdoor plaza during the summer months for all downtown employees to enjoy over the lunch hour. ■

Photo by Dennis Keim

Continued from page 307

The focus on people and dedication to the customer are the driving forces behind First National Bank's community involvement. From their $300 million investment that breathed new life into downtown Omaha to the employees who volunteer so much of their time, you would be hard-pressed to find an organization that gives back more to its city. "We feel that Omaha is a special community," says O'Neal, "and we believe that if the community prospers, then we prosper. In short, we think you've got to give in order to make your community what it needs to be."

Taking care of customers is the first priority. A key ingredient to this strategy is having satisfied employees. That's why First National Bank invests in its employees as much as its customers, offering employees benefits like flexible scheduling and a Child Development

Photo by Jackson Hill

The First National Technology Center has state-of-the-art security access, as shown here with iris recognition technology. The iris of the eye is unique, therefore ensuring access only to those individuals with security clearance. ■

First National Bank built our very own Child Development Center, where more than two hundred employees' children receive exceptional child care. ■

Photo by Jackson Hill

Center, where more than two hundred employees' children receive exceptional child-care. First National Bank has also been recognized by *Working Mother* magazine year after year as one of the *"100 Best Companies for Working Mothers."*

"We look at people as an investment," says O'Neal, adding that the bank believes in building a qualified staff through education. "We feel that people who are better trained or qualified will be more loyal to the company."

These tenets of quality products, superior service, an investment in people, a commitment to technology, and community involvement have proven to be universal in their appeal. The success of its approach has spurred First National Bank's growth into several other states. "We see ourselves as a growth company, serving growth markets," says O'Neal. "In time, we will see our footprint covering markets throughout the Midwest." ■

Located in the old Nenemann's Bakery building on South 24th Street, the Latino Center for Financial Education opened in July 2005. First National Bank is committed to helping the Latino community reach their financial goals. ■

Photo by Eric Francis

Every Friday, community guests have the chance to sample delectable cuisine during gourmet lunches courtesy of the talented students from the Institute for the Culinary Arts at Metropolitan Community College. This local program, which allows students to choose career options that range from food service manager to culinary chef, ranks as one of the top three culinary schools in the country. It is jointly accredited by the American Culinary Federation Accrediting Commission and the Commission on Accreditation of Hospitality Management Programs and offers hands-on experience under the tutelage of award-winning faculty. And while most comparable culinary programs cost upwards of forty thousand dollars, tax-supported education allows Metro to provide the same level of superior instruction for thirty-five hundred dollars. Here, a few of these culinary wizards work their magic on a variety of appetizers in the Fort Omaha campus six-thousand-square-foot training facility. O!

Photo by Thomas S. England

Presenting art to suit each sense and mood. These colorful banners depict the various arts organizations' performances at the Orpheum Theater. From opera to Broadway in Omaha, the Orpheum is a popular and elegant venue that attracts audiences from well beyond Omaha's city limits. O!

Omaha's impressive role in the formation of the United States began in 1803, when Thomas Jefferson completed the Louisiana Purchase. It included an uncharted territory on the west bank of the Missouri River inhabited by the Omaha Indians, whose name means "upstream people" or "against the current." One year later, William Clark and Meriwether Lewis reached the territory and noted that it could be a good location for a trading outpost. In 1863, President Abraham Lincoln sealed the city's fate by selecting Omaha as the eastern terminus of a new transcontinental railroad, the Union Pacific. Four years later, Nebraska was admitted to the union. Just after the turn of the century, it was determined that Omaha needed a larger courthouse. Completed in 1912, the Douglas County Courthouse, shown here, is an outstanding example of the Renaissance Revival style of architecture. The rotunda has a stained-glass dome and murals depicting the history of Douglas County, while the rotunda floor is a beautiful mosaic. Decorative stonework adorns the building's exterior. The courthouse, which is still in use today, remains a landmark in downtown Omaha. **O!**

McGrath North
Mullin & Kratz, PC LLO

McGrath North Mullin & Kratz, PC LLO is an Omaha-based law firm that offers its clients a comprehensive, nationwide legal practice with the personal attention and reasonable cost of a mid-sized midwestern firm. The firm was founded in 1959 with two attorneys and has grown into the second-largest firm in Nebraska with over seventy-five attorneys. Our growth and success are a direct result of our focus on delivery of good results for clients. We innovate, expand, and adapt our services to meet our clients' changing needs.

McGrath North offers our clients a broad range of legal experience with expertise in virtually every area of the law, including corporate and business law, general and specialized litigation, tax and estate planning, legislative/governmental regulation, marketing and advertising, antitrust, white-collar criminal defense, employee benefits, environmental, health care, insurance, international, labor, intellectual property, and real estate. Our attorneys coordinate efforts across specialization groups so that McGrath North clients are assured of receiving the most efficient and effective legal services.

We are committed to providing our clients with the personal attention and resources necessary to deliver innovative and practical solutions, regardless of the size or complexity of our clients' projects. The firm employs a support staff of nearly one hundred paralegals, secretaries, information technology specialists,

Photo by Alan S. Weiner

Our attorneys coordinate efforts across specialization groups so that McGrath North clients are assured of receiving the most efficient and effective legal services.

administrative assistants, and other personnel to assist our lawyers in delivering legal services in a timely and cost-effective manner. The firm occupies five floors of the city's premier office space located in the First National Tower in the heart of downtown Omaha. Our offices are conveniently located across the street from the federal courthouse and a short walk to the Douglas County Courthouse.

Our clients include Fortune 500 companies, small and medium-sized businesses, and individuals and entrepreneurs from virtually every industry, including agriculture, food processing, information technology services, manufacturing, real estate, financial services, health care, aviation, and banking.

In addition to providing our clients with high-caliber legal services today, the firm is dedicated to developing the legal professionals and leaders of tomorrow. We have funded a scholarship program and a legal research center at the Creighton University School of Law. In 2004, the firm's foundation announced a $1 million pledge to establish the McGrath North Mullin & Kratz Endowed Chair in Business Law at the Creighton University School of Law. We have also endowed a scholarship fund at the University of Nebraska College of Law. The firm maintains a comprehensive summer associate program, providing law students from multiple law schools the opportunity to work closely with our attorneys and to experience the day-to-day challenges of the legal profession. McGrath North lawyers are active in our community, volunteering their time on many civic, charitable, and bar association activities. ∎

Photo by Eric Francis

“We live where the work ethic of the Midwestern farm meets with the intellect and sophistication of the urban environment. It's something that cities around the country just can't replicate. It makes us unique.”

Jason Lauritsen, director of corporate talent acquisition

Photo by Eric Francis

Photo by Eric Francis

Fontenelle Nature Association bird-banding volunteer Betty Grenon carefully removes a small songbird caught in a netting. Since 1996, the Fontenelle bird-banding project at the Neale Woods Nature Center nets, bands, and records data on native and migrating songbirds in Nebraska. A federally trained and permitted bander, Grenon enlists the help of close to a dozen volunteers to erect a series of mist nets at feeders throughout a ten-acre area. Once a bird is caught, other hands help fit it with a band containing a unique nine-digit number, which is entered into a nationwide database, along with such vital information as the bird's species, overall health, and day and location of the catch. O!

MAX, the mascot for SAC
Federal Credit Union's
Money Bunny Club, visits the
children at Anderson Grove
Elementary School in Bellevue,
Nebraska. MAX makes saving
fun! ■

SAC Federal
Credit Union

From its beginnings as a twelve-member financial cooperative to its current position as a leading provider of financial products and services in four counties, SAC Federal Credit Union has consistently promoted financial health among its members and their communities.

This tradition began in November 1946 when SAC Federal Credit Union was organized at Andrews Field, Maryland. In August 1949, it moved to Offutt Air Force Base, Nebraska, where it developed financial products to serve the needs of its military members. In 1993, the Board of Directors approved the Credit Union's request to change its field of membership from occupational to geographical. Today, with ten branches and $290 million in assets, SACFCU proudly serves a diverse membership of more than fifty-four-thousand people with the majority of its members residing in Nebraska's Douglas, Sarpy, and Cass counties, and Pottawattamie County, Iowa.

Loyal and progressive leadership has contributed greatly to SACFCU's growth and success. Under James A. Guretzky's leadership as President since 1984, the institution has grown into a full-service financial cooperative providing a host of benefits to members and the community alike. In addition, Chairman of the Board Paul E. Norton, with SACFCU since 1967 and set to retire in 2006, provided invaluable

SAC Federal Credit Union takes pride in a long history of distinguished leadership. From left to right: Chairman of the Board Paul E. Norton and President James A. Guretzky. ■

Photo by Doug Henderson

guidance in maintaining the credit union's longtime commitment to its military members while working toward integrating its new membership.

As a result, all owner/members now benefit from competitively priced products such as low-cost checking and savings, insurance, credit cards, and a variety of low-interest loan options. Members also have access to the latest in financial services technologies, including conveniently placed ATMs, audio response, electronic tax filing, e-statements, and online account access and bill paying.

Although technologically savvy, SACFCU has never sacrificed its commitment to personalized service. Accessible and hands-on, Guretzky sets the example with an open-door policy he extends both to members and employees. And when problems arise, he personally works towards a solution.

SACFCU's value system and service-driven culture from top to bottom differentiate the institution and give it a distinctive strategy for competing in its marketplace.

In keeping with its purpose to promote savings as well as provide credit, SACFCU offers members several innovative and free-of-charge money management services. BudgetSmart, a downloadable program available from SACFCU's Web site, helps members track their spending and create an effective budget. Those interested in establishing additional financial goals can take advantage of the professional, in-depth services provided by Accel Financial Education and Counsel, and SAC Financial Services.

Since it's never too early to start learning about money, SACFCU's Max the Money Bunny Club teaches children age twelve and under how to develop good savings and spending habits that will last a lifetime.

Continued on page 320

SACFCU offers members several innovative and free-of-charge money management services.

Photo by Joe Guerriero

Continued from page 319

As part of its extensive community involvement, SAC Federal Credit Union participates in the Douglas, Sarpy, and Cass Counties Relay for Life Fundraisers. Here the SAC Employee team prepares for the Sarpy County Relay for Life at Bellevue East High School. ■

Volunteerism also starts at the top, and again, Guretzky sets the example. Not only is he personally involved in numerous community events and initiatives, he also inspires his Board of Directors, employees, and community business leaders to give unselfishly of their time, talent, and guidance in countless organizations and charitable causes, including local Chambers of Commerce and the American Cancer Society's Relay for Life.

While honoring its past and continuing to make great strides in the present, SAC Federal Credit Union works to ensure the organization's prosperity well into the future. With ten branches and a strong presence in Omaha and western Iowa, SACFCU will continue to use leading technology to respond to member needs; offer progressive, competitive, and convenient products; and prove that caring, personal service is not just a trend. It's a tradition. ■

Each summer, SACFCU participates in at least twelve community parades throughout the various counties it serves. One of the largest events is Ralston's Independence Day Parade, which is the highlight of the town's two-day celebration. ■

Photo by Eric Francis

Photo by David Gibb

From Lisa's Radial Café in midtown Omaha to family-owned cafés throughout the city, the bread is always fresh and the coffee cups never go dry. Whether it's a breakfast meeting over golden hash browns and crispy bacon, a leisurely mid-morning visit to read the newspaper, or dropping in to check out the lunch special, Omaha's hometown restaurants are a treat worth experiencing. And don't forget to try the pie! O!

Photo by David Gibb

Photo by Dennis Keim

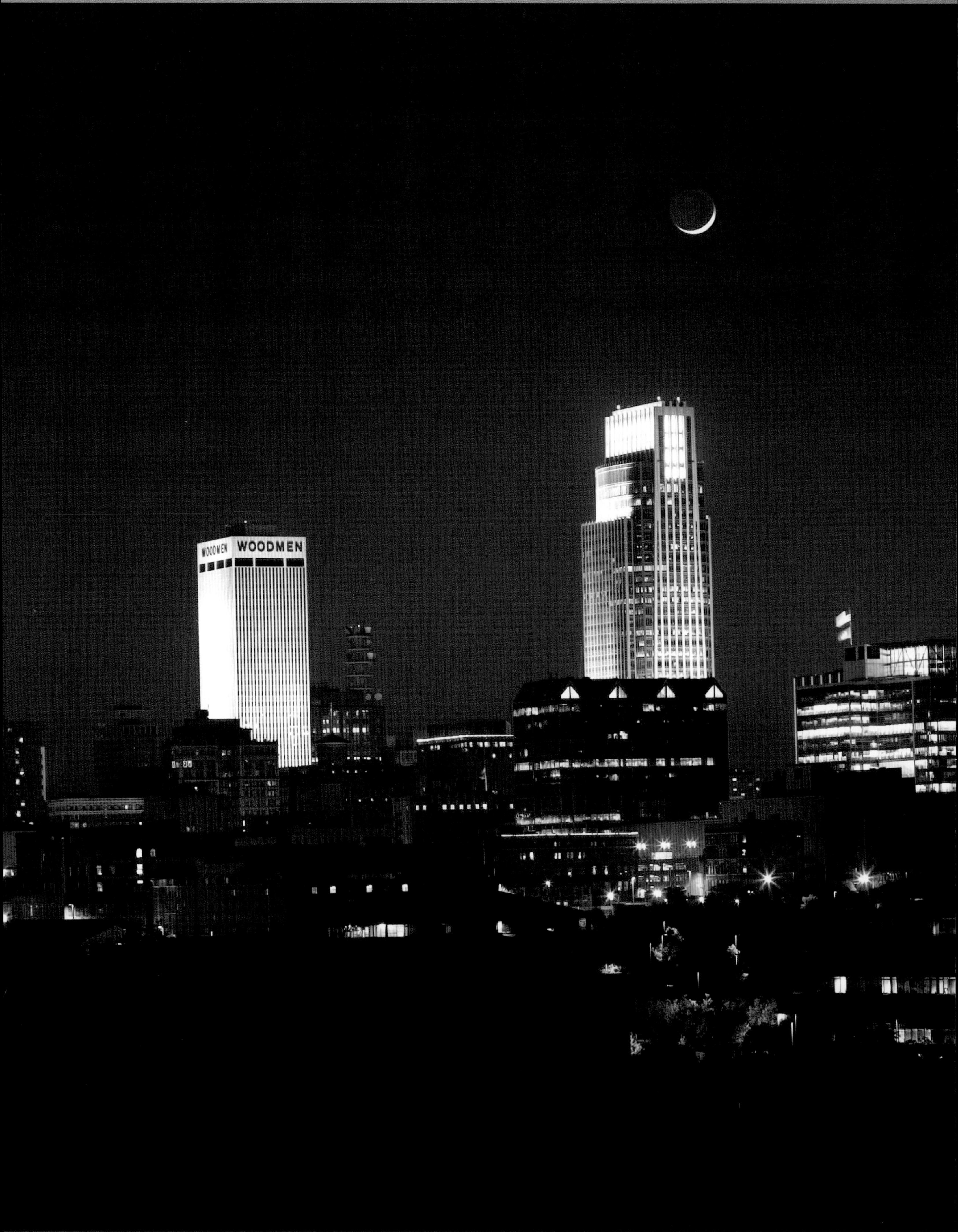

As the sun sets over the Omaha skyline and the city's twinkling lights dance in a rippling reflection on the Missouri River, it's almost hard to imagine what this now-progressive metropolis was like when a ferry company laid its foundation in 1854. At that time, a collection of log buildings constituted the whole of the city. Today, Omaha is a flourishing commercial hub, home to major industries, corporate headquarters, and burgeoning small businesses. It also is a tight-knit community that caters to residents of all ages and interests, offering every individual the chance to pursue—and realize—his or her dreams in the true heartland of America.

O! LIVE

Photo by Eric Francis

The March of Dimes walk-a-thon and 5K run is one of many fund-raising events held in Greater Omaha. Nearly every weekend, runners, joggers, and walkers can lace up their shoes and take a few steps to benefit national charities and their local chapters. **O!**

Throughout Greater Omaha, old and new come together to form a natural harmony and balance.

Stately historic neighborhoods boast mansions listed on the National Register of Historic Places. Destination Midtown's innovative mixed-use redevelopment affords a vibrant urban experience. Suburban neighborhoods incorporate convenience and comfort with the latest in styles and materials. Picturesque rural communities in Sarpy, Washington, and western Douglas counties offer acreages complete with stables, ponds, and natural woods—still within minutes of the city.

No matter their age, all these neighborhoods share the same amenities that make Omaha so attractive. Marvelous educational opportunities, from day care and prekindergarten to more than a dozen universities, colleges, and medical schools. Convenient retail centers, places of worship, hospitals, and medical facilities. Parks, playgrounds, bike paths, jogging trails, and swimming pools. Plenty of features. Plenty of options.

Our people are as unique as the homes in which they live. Omaha is the forty-third largest city in the nation. More than a million people live within a fifty-minute radius. For them, the city is the center of attention. For jobs. For recreation. For excitement.

Greater Omaha is affordable. Median home prices, along with the cost of consumer goods and services, rank below the national averages.

It is accessible. You can commute anywhere from here—across town or across the country—and spend less time doing it.

It is beautiful. Our healthy climate brings forth the charm of each season, from the first snowfall in winter to the first blossoms in spring.

Big enough to offer a bit of everything. Suit every taste. Satisfy every lifestyle. Small enough to offer room to grow. A family. A business. A future.

Omaha is a wonderful place to live. And more. **O!**

As the resident dance company of El Museo Latino, "CHOMARI" Ballet Folklorico Mexicano shares with its audiences the vibrant traditions of Latino dance. "CHOMARI" means "deer" in the indigenous language of the arahumara people and also refers to the popular folklorico Dance of the Deer. Comprising around thirty college and high school students, some of whom have been studying with the Ballet since 1993, "CHOMARI" performs at the museum, at schools, and at special events throughout the region. Opened in May 1993 by Magdalena Garcia, founder and executive director, El Museo Latino is the first Latino art and history museum in Nebraska. Throughout the year, El Museo Latino features exhibits by local, national, and international artists, as well as educational programs that include art, music, dance; and theater classes; lectures; workshops, and a visiting artist series. **O!**

Photo by Rod Reilly

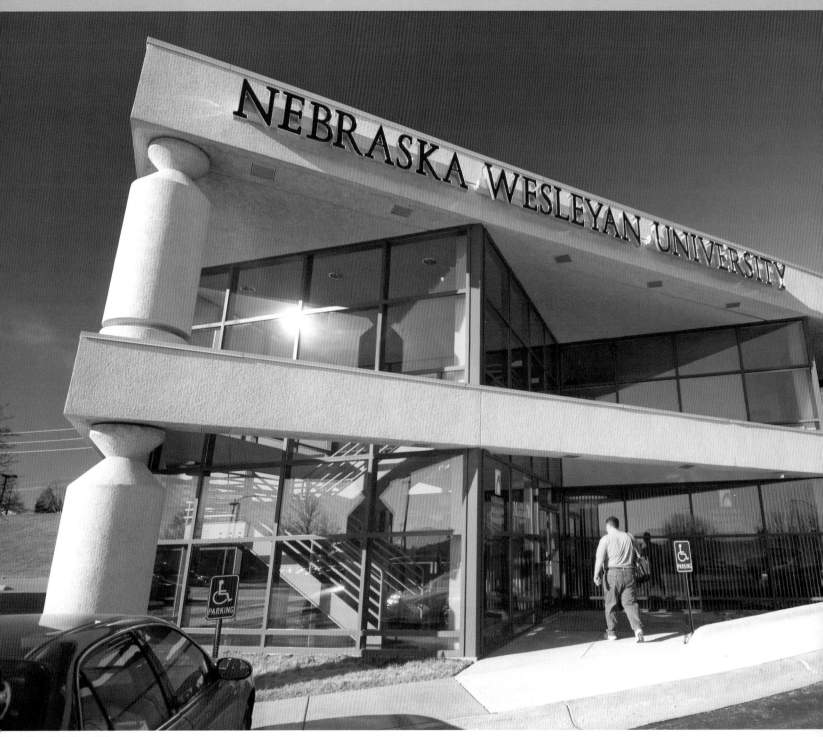

Photo by Jackson Hill

Nebraska Wesleyan
——University

J eff Genoways could be called nontraditional. Still, he is much like many other Nebraskans and Americans. Genoways is part of a growing trend of working adults going back to college to gain a career advantage. In the academic world, these returning students are referred to as "nontraditional," and research shows that adult students are the fastest-growing educational demographic in North America.

In Omaha, people looking for that same edge are choosing Nebraska Wesleyan University's Wesleyan Advantage program for its affordable, quality education, its flexible schedule, and its adult format—all requisite features for adult students balancing many responsibilities. "The students enrolled in Wesleyan Advantage are focused. They are willing to work hard to attain a degree that replicates the high standards and academic intensity of our traditional undergraduate program," says Stacey Ocander, Associate Dean, University College, and Director of Wesleyan Advantage.

Wesleyan Advantage's flexible five- and eight-week course format, faculty-to-student ratio, and engaged faculty and staff are ideal for the nontraditional, adult student. "We gear toward everything an adult faces—from job changes, promotions, marriage, and family—so adjustments can be made easily," says Stacey Ocander, associate dean, University College, and director of Weselyan Advantage. ▪

Through close relationships with key health-care organizations, Wesleyan Advantage can focus on giving nursing students like Tracey Ozello hands-on learning. And, for nurses pursuing career development, the program offers a seamless transition from bachelor's to master's degree. ▪

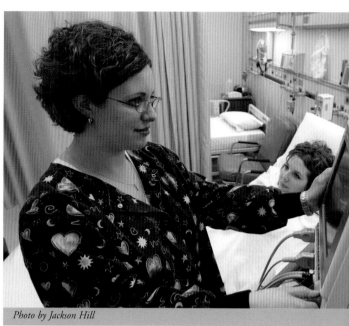

Photo by Jackson Hill

The students enrolled in Wesleyan Advantage are focused. They are willing to work hard to attain a degree.

Genoways, a project manager at Werner Enterprises, agrees. "This was a program that seemed tailor-made for me," he says. "The coursework was rigorous, but the adult format of five- and eight-week sessions fit my schedule. I also knew that I would earn a degree from a high-caliber institution."

Additionally, students appreciate the fact that the Wesleyan Advantage faculty is composed of business professionals like Brian Ridder, a Wesleyan alumnus and senior vice president of an area bank. "We have an intimate classroom experience where the faculty-to-student ratio is very appealing," explains Ridder. "I personalize the experience from the textbook by bringing in real-world examples, as do the students." This collaborative exchange results in strategies that students can apply immediately in the workplace.

The program's streamlined bachelor of science in business administration, for example, is designed to give students a broad understanding of business concepts and practices, which ultimately complements a variety of careers and work environments. Nontraditional students can also pursue either a bachelor's or master's degree in nursing —both of which continue to be in great demand. "We work in tandem with the key healthcare organizations in Nebraska to provide the quality education at the BSN and MSN levels that these employers require," explains Ocander. "In doing so, we prepare them for lifelong learning in their field, whether that is professional development or an advanced degree."

Nebraska Wesleyan University, founded in 1887, is the leading liberal arts college in Nebraska. Its traditional students are some of the state's most advanced, with more than 25 percent of freshmen having graduated in the top 20 percent of their high school class. The nontraditional Wesleyan Advantage students, equally motivated, excel in the program's rigorous adult format. By encouraging the most advanced students to attend the University, and by providing each of them with an honors-quality education, Nebraska Wesleyan has developed a reputation for producing successful graduates. ▪

Photo by Tom Kessler

The serenity of nature and spirit brings visitors to the Holy Family Shrine on the bluffs overlooking the Platte River Valley southwest of Omaha. Created to give people the opportunity to discover and develop the Catholic faith, the Holy Family Shrine is an interactive journey beginning at an entry spire into a beautiful chapel, and wandering along natural trails that lead to a labyrinth sculpted into the prairie grasses. **O!**

Photo by Tom Kessler

Photo by Kirsten Case

Photo by Kirsten Case

Photo by Ann Kraft

Through Youth Leadership Omaha (YLO), a program of the Greater Omaha Chamber of Commerce, high school sophomores from throughout the metropolitan area receive the opportunity to demonstrate and strengthen their abilities to become community leaders. The philosophy behind YLO is that leaders are made, not born. The goal is to instill an appreciation for the diverse people, places, and opportunities available in Omaha and to encourage young people to bring about positive changes and make meaningful connections in the community. YLO graduates participate in the Ambassadors program in their junior and senior years. Ambassadors meet monthly and use their YLO skills to organize quarterly service projects and a large citywide youth forum as well as participate in a grant-making project with the Omaha Community Foundation. **O!**

Photo by Kirsten Case

Youth Leadership OMAHA

" *Youth Leadership Omaha has added color and excitement to a faded picture. I can't pinpoint one event that made me feel this way, but the care and love and drive for excellence I have seen here astonish me.*"

Ben Amdor, YLO graduate

STORE

US POST OFFICE

Students in Lower School make frequent visits to the James Lower School Library to check out books and read independently. ∎

Photo by Alan S. Weiner

Brownell-Talbot
School

B rownell-Talbot School is truly a community of learning, where lessons reach beyond the rigorous curriculum. Honoring the individual student, Brownell-Talbot School initiates an excitement for lifelong learning, cultivates character, embraces diversity, offers a variety of extracurricular activities for all age levels, and develops good citizens. A Brownell-Talbot education is an investment in your child's success in college and in life.

"We have focus and direction, and we have had them since our beginning in 1863," says Dianne Desler, headmaster of Nebraska's only independent, coeducational private college prep school. "As the premier college preparatory school in the region, our expectations are high. With an emphasis on a traditional liberal arts curriculum delivered in a nurturing environment, our students receive the best educational opportunities with the appropriate level of challenge to develop their potential fully."

Comprehensive education at the coeducational Brownell-Talbot School begins in preschool and culminates with the graduation of high school seniors. Technology is used across the curriculum. In the Lower

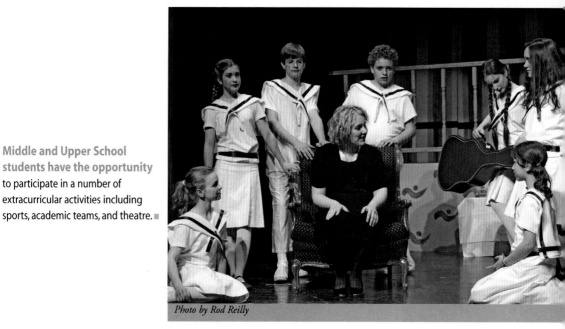

Middle and Upper School students have the opportunity to participate in a number of extracurricular activities including sports, academic teams, and theatre. ▪

Photo by Rod Reilly

We have focus and direction, and we have had them since our beginning in 1863.

School (preschool through fourth grade), students study many thematic units, resulting in a cross-disciplinary educational experience that provides a solid foundation for continued success. "Small class size allows us time for enrichment," explains first-grade teacher Twyla Baker. "We're able to challenge each child beyond his or her perceived ability."

In the Middle School (fifth through eighth grade), individual attention is critical. Not quite young adults but no longer children, middle school students have unique needs. "I go to great lengths to find success in the product that each student creates," says English and speech teacher Chris Hamel. His approach includes individual conferences with the students where he helps them compare their work, not to that of their peers as many tweens are apt to do, but rather to their own previous work. Consequently, the students recognize their progress and, subsequently, gain confidence.

The Upper School builds on the foundation of independence by offering students choices in academic courses and extracurricular activities. When young adults in grades nine through twelve are free to explore and make decisions, they often develop interests for life, as well as a better understanding of the decision-making process. "At Brownell we excel at educating the total child, helping them build on their strengths and strengthen their weaknesses, so that when they go out in the world, they have options," explains Upper School faculty member Jackie Byers. Upper School students also use wireless laptop computers in all classes.

By the time of graduation, Brownell-Talbot students are poised to embrace the many opportunities available at the nation's finest colleges by virtue of the strength of the school's academic program, coupled with college counseling that begins formally in the eighth grade. Even with the highest graduation requirements in Nebraska, 100 percent of Brownell-Talbot seniors traditionally gain admittance to the college or university of their choice. In addition, more than two-thirds receive college scholarships. Clearly, a Brownell-Talbot education pays dividends for a lifetime. ▪

Spotlight on O!

For the coaches, the players and their parents, cheerleaders, fans, and the band, there is something magical about Friday nights in the fall that takes high school football to a level all its own.

Local TV cameras capture the perfect pass and the winning touchdown for the 10 o'clock sports report. Writers from the high school paper to the *Omaha World-Herald* record the highlights and miscues. Any single play can be the one that takes your team up or down in the rankings. Every yard gained and point scored is important, because from one of these fields a team will emerge to be crowned state champion.

All that took a back seat one Friday night in the fall of 2004 as Tom Jaworski coached the Creighton Prep Junior Jays against the No. 1–ranked Millard West Wildcats.

Photo by Eric Francis

Rallying from a 6-0 deficit, the Junior Jays put thirteen points on the board in the second half. With the game on the line, less than one minute to play, and the Wildcats' offense inside the Prep one-yard line, the Junior Jays' defense put forth a goal-line stand that would make the pros proud. The crowd of forty-five hundred people roared its approval, for there was more on the line that night than a No. 1 ranking.

For Jaworski, Prep's 13-6 win was his 294th victory in 33 years of coaching. That gave the proud Prep graduate the state record for most

Every

Photo by Eric Francis

Photo by Eric Francis

victories for a high school coach. He received a plaque from school administrators, and the Prep team presented him with a football, signed by every player.

There were a couple dozen games played that night in Greater Omaha. Each one meant something to the players, coaches, and fans. Because, in a season of Friday nights, every game, every play, every tick of the clock can be the one that makes a dream come true.

Just ask Tom Jaworski. **O!**

Photo by Eric Francis

Second Counts

Children from one of several downtown-area day-care centers cool their feet in the water at the Gene Leahy Mall. Whether it's in-home day care, a day-care center, or care provided in-house by a growing number of businesses and corporations, a vast array of child-care options exist throughout Greater Omaha. Nebraska law requires that anyone providing child-care services to four or more children at any one time be licensed. Regulations and inspections, as well as a community-wide commitment to protecting the safety and well-being of all children, ensures the availability of quality day care. And the treats are tasty, too! O!

Kickin' Back

Darren and Susan Harsin, and family dog Cooper, take a walk to survey their property. The Harsins grew up in town, but chose to move out to the country to raise their three boys: Zach, Josh, and Drew. While their forty-eight-acre homestead is only twenty minutes from metro Omaha, and less than five minutes from the town of Blair, the Harsins feel they are in the perfect place away from it all. "We enjoy the outdoors and wanted to live where our boys could have the freedom to explore and play. It's a lot of work to maintain the place, but we've seen how the boys have been able to grow up, and we're happy we made that decision," says Darren, a teacher at Blair High School. O!

Photo by Doug Henderson

Photo by Doug Henderson

Creighton University
Medical Center

Since before the turn of the twentieth century, physicians, teachers, and researchers have joined together at Creighton University Medical Center (CUMC) to provide some of the best possible medical care to patients throughout the region. Through the academic medical center's affiliation with Creighton University, one of the nation's twenty-eight Jesuit Catholic educational institutions, these highly skilled specialists have based their comprehensive efforts on a long-standing philosophy and enduring healing mission.

"Nationally, we're one of the few hospitals that is associated with a Jesuit medical school," explains Philip Gustafson, CUMC hospital president and CEO. "What that implies is that it's not just the teaching mission, but it's teaching healthcare that's grounded in the principles of Jesuit education and service to others."

At CUMC, offering quality patient care involves treating the whole person by staying on the cutting edge of some of the most sophisticated medical treatments and advancements, while having access to a large

---

Creighton University Medical Center is an academic medical institution, teaching tomorrow's healthcare professionals while striving for excellence in diagnosis and treatment today. ■

By associating research and teaching with advanced medical care, CUMC has built a national reputation in multiple fields.

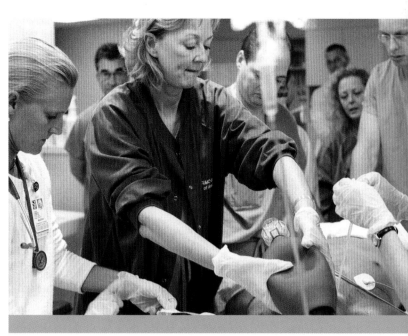

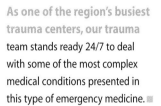

As one of the region's busiest trauma centers, our trauma team stands ready 24/7 to deal with some of the most complex medical conditions presented in this type of emergency medicine. ■

network of resources. The organization includes Saint Joseph Hospital, a 334-bed acute care facility; Creighton University Schools of Medicine, Nursing, Dentistry, Pharmacy, and Health Professions; Creighton University Medical Laboratories; Center for Health Policy and Ethics; and Creighton University Medical Associates, a network of nearly three hundred physicians who practice in clinics and outreach sites throughout Nebraska and southwest Iowa.

"In addition to providing exceptional care to patients," Gustafson notes, "we're conducting research, and we're also training future doctors, pharmacists, nurses, physical therapists, and occupational therapists."

By associating research and teaching with patient-focused medical care, CUMC has built a national reputation in multiple fields. Today, the organization boasts of quality cardiac care, cancer services, high-risk obstetrics, trauma services, blood conservation surgery, and much more. In fact, Solucient, a leading source of healthcare information, recognized CUMC as one of the top one hundred U.S. teaching hospitals, and HealthGrades™, ranked it number one in Omaha for overall cardiac services. The facility also is internationally recognized for advancements in cancer, genetics, osteoporosis, and minimally invasive surgery.

This type of acknowledgment is a result of CUMC's pledge not only to provide advanced care, but also to be forward-thinking and generate new therapies, paving the way for others in the medical field. "As a teaching hospital, our physicians and staff strive to develop new technology and serve as early implementers for new treatments," states Dr. Stephen Lanspa, senior vice president for medical affairs.

Charles Filipi, MD, FACS, who focuses on minimally invasive surgery and its development, concurs, asserting, "There's some very important work being done here. Part of our mission is research, and the underlying core value

Continued on page 342

Continued from page 341

is to advance medical science. The local community and society-at-large are going to benefit if we can successfully do that."

Fortunately, in areas like general surgery, CUMC's physicians have been able to apply a wide range of sophisticated procedures, from gallbladder and esophageal laparoscopic surgeries using the da Vinci® Robotic Surgery System to the Breast Clinic's minimally invasive breast cancer treatments and same-day tissue diagnosis. In fact, the ability to study and implement these techniques has attracted not only some of the foremost experts to CUMC, but also other qualified physicians who want to learn from those specialists.

CUMC is one of the few hospitals in Nebraska to operate the amazing da Vinci™ robot. Using the da Vinci surgical robot, tiny instruments are inserted into the body through two small incisions. Each incision is less than a half inch. The endoscope, inserted through one incision, becomes the surgeon's eyes. The endowrists, inserted through the second incision, are his hands. Smaller incisions mean less scarring and reduced recovery time. ■

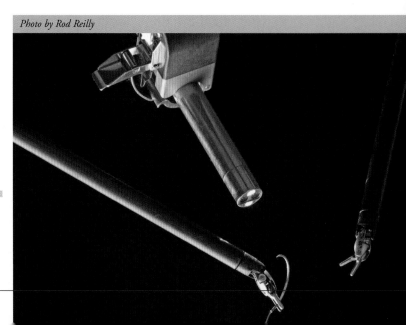

Photo by Rod Reilly

Dr. Henry Lynch is a pioneer in hereditary cancer research. In 1967, when cancer was thought to be triggered almost solely by environmental causes, Dr. Lynch pursued the genetic link to certain cancer risks. He manages a database of thousands of family pedigrees tracing various hereditary cancers. His detailed histories and tissue collections have provided substantial evidence leading to the discovery of gene mutations such as BRCA1 and BRCA2 mutations that contribute to hereditary breast cancers, rare strains of colorectal cancers in Native Americans, and the strain of hereditary nonpolyposis colon cancer dubbed the *Lynch Syndrome* in his honor. ■

Photo by Rod Reilly

Photo by Dennis Keim

A medical technologist in the Clinical Virology Laboratory loads patient specimens onto the Roche LightCycler®, an instrument which performs a polymerase chain reaction (PCR) to rapidly detect minute quantities of Herpes simplex and other viruses. ■

One such magnate is Robert Fitzgibbons, Jr., MD, FACS, globally known as an authority on hernia repair. As a member of the CUMC team, he sees firsthand how the facility works to benefit patients both locally and from around the world, particularly in regards to laparoscopy. "What's important is the fact that we're doing research—not only the surgeries," he observes. Furthermore, he remarks, "I hope local area residents know what a great resource they have. We're more than a hospital," pointing to the clinical research projects that have come to fruition and undoubtedly will garner CUMC even more consideration.

Clearly, the work being performed at CUMC has made the medical center a valuable regional, national, and international resource, with about one-third of the organization's patients coming from outside of the Omaha area. Nevertheless, CUMC's commitment to the local community has never waned. The center sponsors major community events and supports nonprofit organizations' activities year-round. It also coordinates communication between the hospital and neighborhood clinics to provide continuity of care while serving as a regional trauma center four days a week.

Creighton University Medical Center is a major part of people's lives, as they know they can count on the Center's high-level care 24 hours a day, 365 days a year. "We care for some of the region's most critically ill patients, smallest infants and the most complex injuries and illnesses," Gustafson continues. "We are an academic medical center that brings together some of the most innovative patient care, teaching, and healthcare research in the region." ■

Photo by David Gibb

Whether they are in the Ak-Sar-Ben Aquarium standing face-to-face with the largest catfish on display in the country, viewing any one of the other fifty species of native Nebraska fish, or wandering through the fish hatchery museum, visitors to Schramm Park State Recreation Area will find something to keep them entertained. The park is situated along the Platte River south of metropolitan Omaha. **O!**

Photo by David Gibb

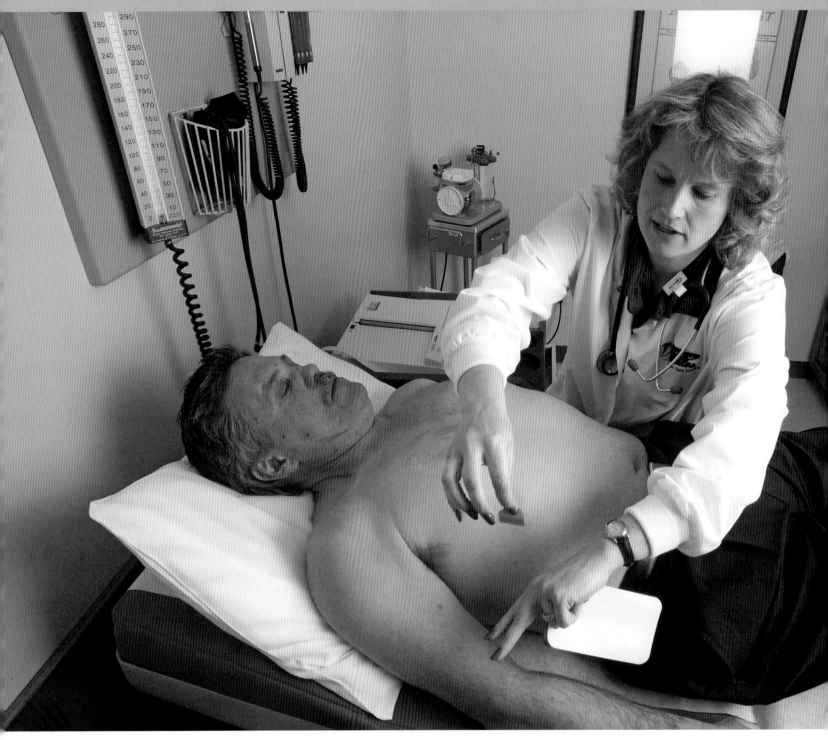

Midwest Minor Medical
Urgent Care Centers

It is early Sunday morning, and your child has a sore throat and high fever. Where do you go? The touch football game got a little rough, and you think you strained a muscle. Where do you go? You are working late and get a cut that might require stitches. Where do you go?

For Omaha residents the answer is simple. You go to one of the three clinics of Midwest Minor Medical, which has been providing quality care and convenience seven days a week since 1982. Midwest Minor Medical was the first urgent-care center in Omaha.

Today, Midwest Minor Medical is an independent medical group owned by five doctors: Dr. Robert Byrnes, Dr. Sylwia Jedruska-Witt, Dr. Yvonne Stephenson, Dr. Louise Winter, and Dr. John Otto. These doctors and the other physicians on staff have up to thirty years of experience. The company employs seventy-five medical and administrative workers.

Dr. Otto, the founder of Midwest Minor Medical, was an emergency room physician in 1982. He read

As a convenience to their residents, nursing homes in the Omaha area occasionally request the services offered by Midwest Minor Medical Centers. Physicians, such as Dr. Robert Byrnes, travel to the facilities to do routine exams such as checking heart rate and blood pressure, as well as administering flu shots. ■

Photo by Rod Reilly

Photo by Rod Reilly

Midwest Minor Medical was set up to take care of people's minor injuries and illnesses, and to save them time and money over a trip to the emergency room.

about a new type of clinic that opened in New York the previous year, and thought it would work in Omaha.

"That urgent-care idea sounded like a great alternative way of providing care for people," Dr. Otto remembered. "Often times the emergency room would be inundated with people who really had only minor conditions, but who had nowhere else to go. Midwest Minor Medical was set up to take care of people's minor injuries and illnesses, and to save them time and money over a trip to the emergency room."

Midwest Minor Medical has a twofold mission: to provide families with prompt treatment for minor injuries and illnesses, and to offer businesses a variety of occupational health services.

Everyone should have a primary care doctor, but not all injuries or illnesses happen during regular business hours. It can also be difficult to get a last-minute appointment with your regular doctor. At Midwest Minor Medical, patients never need an appointment. Just walk, run, or limp in. Usually within thirty minutes, one of their experienced doctors will be available.

Families have come to rely on Midwest Minor Medical to take care of many nonemergency medical conditions. They can treat allergic reactions, sports injuries, nausea, infections, lacerations, and other aches and pains that come up. Each clinic also has complete X-ray services.

As a partner with business, Midwest Minor Medical offers health services such as preemployment and DOT physicals, tetanus shots, hepatitis shots, drugs of abuse screening, and so on. They also provide workers' compensation care for minor on-the-job injuries.

Never forgetting its mission to provide convenient, quality care, Midwest Minor Medical participates with most insurance companies, HMOs, PPOs, and workers' compensation carriers. They can set up multiple corporate accounts for businesses and they also accept most major credit cards. ■

Photo by Mark Romesser

Whether running a relay, clearing a hurdle, or vaulting clear of the bar, the young men and women at the 2005 Great Plains Athletic Conference Outdoor Track and Field Championships in Blair were giving it their all. Thousands of athletes from colleges and universities around the state participated in nearly two dozen events, including one-hundred- to ten-thousand-meter races, high and long jumps, and the discus, hammer, and javelin throws. O!

Photo by Mark Romesser

Photo by Mark Romesser

Photo by Dennis Keim

Photo by Dennis Keim

For two days each May, over eighteen hundred area fifth-graders learn all about the aquatic environment through a unique environmental education field day known as Water Works. Sponsored in part by the Papio–Missouri River Natural Resources District and held at Schramm Park State Recreation Area and the Eastern Nebraska 4-H Center, Water Works is conducted by various water-related experts who not only teach their young participants to canoe and fish, but also provide instruction in water quality, erosion, and resource management. **O!**

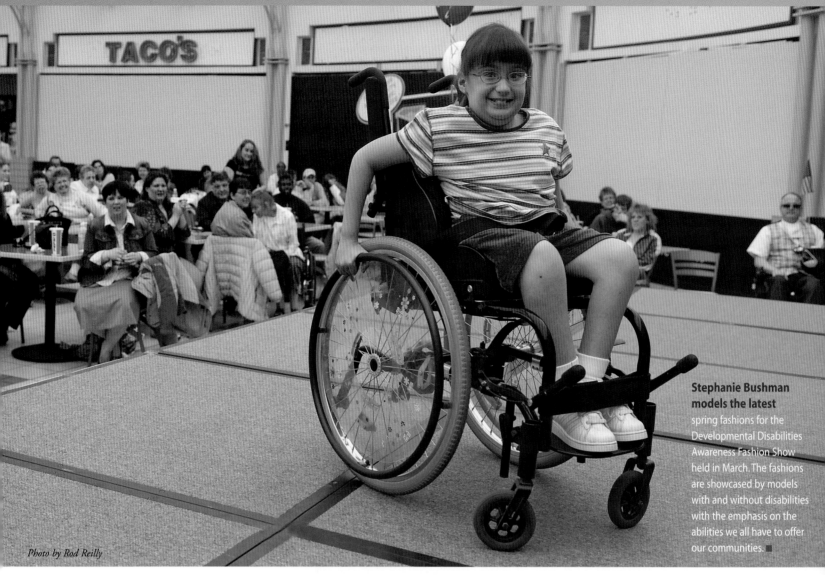

Stephanie Bushman models the latest spring fashions for the Developmental Disabilities Awareness Fashion Show held in March. The fashions are showcased by models with and without disabilities with the emphasis on the abilities we all have to offer our communities. ■

Photo by Rod Reilly

The Arc of Omaha at the
Ollie Webb Center, Inc.

Pilot Parents matches experienced parents who can offer information and support with other parents of children with disabilities.

Since the 1950s, the Ollie Webb Center has been discovering untapped abilities, improving the quality of life, changing perceptions, and influencing the legislature for families and people with developmental disabilities. Previously known as GOARC (the Greater Omaha Association for Retarded Citizens), the center was renamed for Ollie Webb in 1998. A former resident of the Beatrice State Home, Webb became a national spokesperson for self-advocacy.

She was a founding member of Project II, a social, educational, and self-advocacy program for adults with developmental disabilities. Project II is just one of five innovative programs sponsored by the center.

Pilot Parents matches experienced parents who can offer information and support with other parents of children with disabilities. Teenagers have their own support group in Just Friends. In this mentoring-friendship program, teens without disabilities share typical activities with teens with disabilities. "I never heard my daughter giggle with a friend until she got involved in this program," said one grateful parent.

The PRISM project (Parent Resource Information and Support Meetings) has monthly evening gatherings during the school year, offering information, education, and support. The Quality of Life Trust allows parents to provide, through their estates, for personalized advocacy, as well as emotional and social support for their children.

"We are starting a sibling group, and we're always expanding our other services," said Laurie Ackermann, executive director. "We've found it amazing what individuals can accomplish with a little help from their friends, family, and the community." ■

Photo by Eric Francis

A little nose squeeze and face painting are all part of the team spirit of the "Get Blue" National Game Viewing Day for the Creighton University men's basketball team. Before the Bluejays take the court at Qwest Center Omaha, hundreds of alumni and friends gather for the annual big pregame pep rally, complete with music, games, and of course, Billy Bluejay. With six NCAA tournament appearances in seven years, the Bluejays are a hot ticket, ranking among the national leaders in attendance with an average home crowd of more than eleven thousand.

"Get Blue"

The Joslyn Castle was the private home of George and Sarah Joslyn, who came to Omaha looking for opportunity and found it in the printing business. Built in 1903, the Castle now serves as the site of events and regular tours and is one of the many unique treasures of Destination Midtown. ■

Destination
Midtown

Midtown Omaha is more than a geographic label. It is a unique combination of ages and lifestyles, historic architecture, places of higher learning, large and small businesses, and active neighborhood associations.

It is also home to a unique partnership known as Destination Midtown, a cooperative effort of public and private interests working together to return the midtown area to prominence and make it a destination of choice in Omaha.

The initiative focuses on a 3.6-square-mile area from 24th Street on the east to Saddle Creek Road on the west, Cuming Street on the north to Center Street on the south. It encompasses twenty-eight thousand residents, eleven neighborhood associations, forty-three thousand employees, twenty-two churches, sixteen schools, seven parks, and thirty designated historic landmarks, including the Joslyn Castle, St. Cecilia Cathedral, and the Blackstone building.

Representatives of each aspect of the area have come together with city government and the Greater Omaha Chamber of Commerce to develop a plan of action that promotes economic development opportunities and advances neighborhood goals.

As part of its effort to beautify midtown Omaha and improve the quality of life, Destination Midtown has established "identity gardens" throughout the area's eleven neighborhoods, as in the historic Field Club neighborhood near the birthplace of former President Gerald R. Ford. ■

Photo by David Gibb

"Individually, people realized the need to preserve and enhance the area's assets. Destination Midtown is the cooperative response to that need."

"The public-private partnership is what really sets Destination Midtown apart," says Tawanna Black, Destination Midtown executive director. "Individually, people realized the need to preserve and enhance the area's assets. Destination Midtown is the cooperative response to that need."

The partnership links the people and entities that share a stake in the area's success and a vision for its future, says Bob Bartee, chair of the Destination Midtown board. "It made sense for them to form an organization to work collaboratively for implementation. That partnership is the foundation of Destination Midtown."

The initiative recognizes the need to promote home ownership as well as the renovation and revitalization of the historic mixed-use neighborhood business districts.

Jim Champion, business owner and executive director of the Midtown Business Association, says the area holds great opportunity for new businesses. "We're looking for small business districts blossoming from the project to enhance all of our businesses in the long run."

Bartee says Destination Midtown is cooperation at its best. "We are proactively addressing priorities in a way that ensures the interests of one facet of the project do not harm the success of another facet."

The work has led to the formation of the Midtown Neighborhood Alliance. The alliance links the eleven neighborhood associations within the Destination Midtown boundaries to provide input to decision makers, developers, and potential funders of development initiatives.

"We saw a need for us to come together as one voice to work with the Destination Midtown effort to make it a success," says Jim Farho, Midtown Neighborhood Alliance president and Destination Midtown board member. "Although we are still independent organizations, we have one larger organization that can speak for us."

By working together, those involved in Destination Midtown are affecting progress, preservation, and great pride in the city's midtown. Their efforts will enhance the vibrancy of the heart of the city and intensify midtown's attraction to families, young professionals, interested visitors, and all Omahans. ■

Photo by Eric Francis

Photo by Alan S. Weiner

OMAHA–Where Imagination Meets Opportunity | 357

On weekends and snow days when school is cancelled, kids of all ages rush to Memorial Park, where the hills around the World War II monument are perfect for sledding and snow boarding. Omaha's annual average snowfall is about thirty inches, enough to delight cross-country skiers and sledders who find the parks throughout the city perfect for wintertime fun. O!

As part of VNA's commitment to community health, nurses care for children living in local homeless shelters through the Shelter Nursing program. Nurses assess each child's immediate physical needs as well as long-term health issues, administer immunizations, and conduct health screenings. While in the shelter, each child also receives weekly follow-ups. ■

Visiting Nurse Association

L ike a guardian angel of health care, the Visiting Nurse Association has provided over one hundred years of healthcare services and education to individuals and families throughout Omaha and its surrounding communities with a mission to serve the most vulnerable and high-risk populations.

Established in 1896, VNA remains a mission-driven, freestanding, nonprofit healthcare organization that focuses its services in three major areas: homecare, hospice, and community health programs.

Over 75 percent of VNA's 250 employees are direct-care providers, representing the most competent, experienced, and credentialed clinicians in the field. As a result, on any given day, up to 2,000 individuals in the Omaha area receive care from a VNA healthcare provider. Whether these patients reside at home or in a nursing facility, community setting, shelter, or transitional living situation, they can count on VNA to deliver a variety of healthcare services throughout one's life, from birth to hospice.

With its century-long mission to foster dignity while promoting independence and self-care, VNA is

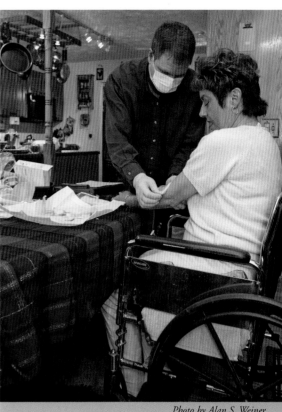

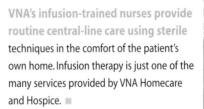

VNA's infusion-trained nurses provide routine central-line care using sterile techniques in the comfort of the patient's own home. Infusion therapy is just one of the many services provided by VNA Homecare and Hospice. ■

Photo by Alan S. Weiner

Photo by Alan S. Weiner

On any given day, up to two thousand individuals in the Omaha area receive care from a VNA health-care provider.

also a tireless advocate for healthcare education and illness prevention. Since the cornerstone of the agency's services has always been its work with women and children, VNA's comprehensive pre- and postnatal care programs also include proactive health and education services. Additionally, VNA works in collaboration with other community groups to strengthen services for those less fortunate. The group's public health nursing team, for instance, provides nursing services to the homeless and those in transitional housing, as well as connecting them to other community resources.

Making all this possible is VNA's close ties to the community. In addition to revenue received from insured clients, funding sources include United Way, individual, corporate, and foundation donations and grants. These relationships allow VNA to subsidize its care by more than $1 million a year and to invest in community health outreach programs and services.

Community support also allows VNA to offer the most up-to-date home healthcare technologies. Because of its legacy of excellence, VNA was chosen by HomMed as its Partner Agency for telehealth in the Omaha area. The agency is now the area's exclusive provider of HomMed's daily home monitoring system. This system allows VNA clients to monitor their vital signs at home and transmit this information directly to an RN at VNA. With such advanced home monitoring technology at its disposal, VNA is able to reduce crisis situations such as emergency visits and rehospitalizations.

By providing affordable access to the latest medical technologies, caring for patients regardless of their ability to pay, and advocating for the disadvantaged, VNA makes a positive difference in the lives of thousands of patients in the Omaha area. ■

Photo by Alan S. Weiner

Team

Photo by Alan S. Weiner

Photo by Alan S. Weiner

Current students and boosters alike can't get enough of the Creighton University Bluejays. An afternoon or evening spent at Qwest Center Omaha watching this talented NCAA basketball team meet the competition is a surefire slam-dunk. In recent years, the Jays have captured seven straight postseason bids and six twenty-win seasons, giving their fans plenty to cheer about. Over the years, the team has supplied the NBA with such players as Benoit Benjamin, Paul Silas, and Kyle Korver. Here, the team controls the court as they face off against the Southern Illinois Salukis. In typical Jays fashion, the skilled players exhibit dynamic action on the floor, keeping the energized spectators in the stands revved up. O!

Spirit

Home Instead Senior Care has provided affordable care to nearly 1 million clients, many of whom tell us their caregiver made the difference for them between counting the years and living them. ■

Home Instead Senior Care

Home Instead Senior Care's services include companionship, meal preparation, medication reminders, light housekeeping, errands, and shopping.

Independence is a concept dear to all Americans, but it is especially important to seniors who want to remain in their homes and function on their own. Home Instead Senior Care allows them to do just that. The company, which is the world's largest provider of non-medical companionship and home care services, was founded in 1994 by Omaha natives Paul and Lori Hogan. Today, more than twenty-seven thousand CAREGivers℠ provide one-on-one assistance through more than six hundred locally owned franchise offices in this country, Canada, Japan, Portugal, Australia and Ireland. Local offices are located in Omaha, Bellevue and Fremont.

Home Instead Senior Care's services include companionship, meal preparation, medication reminders, light housekeeping, errands and shopping. Their services are also available to families seeking help with Alzheimer's care. For those who purchase franchises, Home Instead Senior Care provides extensive training programs for both their owners and the CAREGivers they hire. "I've learned to step inside the world of the person with Alzheimer's. The training prepared me to give my clients all the respect, compassion, and patience they deserve," said a Home Instead CAREGiver.

Home Instead Senior Care has been recognized by *Inc.* magazine as one of the country's fastest growing private companies. *Entrepreneur* magazine ranks it as the number one non-medical senior care company in the nation, and Home Instead Senior Care is regularly honored as one of Omaha's top twenty-five fastest-growing companies.

For older adults, Home Instead Senior Care can be the difference between counting the years and living them. ■

During the warm months, a visit to the Heartland of America Park is a popular way to cool off, enjoy scenic views, and relax in the great outdoors. The thirty-one-acre park and fifteen-acre lake represent the last step initiated by the city to develop a park extending from downtown east to the Missouri River. Heartland of America Park also connects via walkways, trails, and a footbridge to Lewis & Clark Landing. The park has picnic areas, arbors, a concert lawn and concession pavilion, memorial statues, public restrooms, benches, a concessionaire who provides boat rides on the lake, and two fountains. The Heartland of America Fountain, in the middle of the lake, has colored lights and jets that shoot water three hundred feet into the air.

Photo by Dennis Keim

The lobby at Children's Hospital serves as a comforting refuge for patients, families, and visitors. Features include a flowing stream, live trees, and playful cranes. The entire hospital was designed to put children at ease. ■

Children's Hospital

Photo by David Gibb

There is a jewel in the center of Omaha. Though its windows glitter in the sunlight, not until you learn of its amazing programs do you realize that the real splendor is what's happening on the inside.

With its curving walls and glittering windows it is easy to see that even from the outside Children's Hospital at 8200 Dodge Street puts its young patients and their families at ease. ■

Omaha is one of the nation's smallest communities with a freestanding hospital dedicated solely to the care of children, yet Children's Hospital is home to several pediatric subspecialty programs that are found in only a dozen or fewer communities across the United States. Its physicians in such pediatric specialties as neurosurgery, craniofacial surgery, osteogenesis imperfecta (brittle bone disease), cardiology, cardiac surgery, and critical care are widely recognized as some of the country's best.

To attract these quality physicians, the hospital caters exclusively to the distinctive needs of pediatric patients. "Everything we do, day in and day out, is focused upon the needs of children," explains Gary A. Perkins, president and chief executive officer of Children's Hospital. "Children are not small adults. They react very differently to illnesses; they react differently to treatment. That's why caring for children isn't just a part of what we do. It is uniquely what we do."

That singularly focused care is delivered by a multidisciplinary team tending to the physical, psychological, and even spiritual well-being of every child. The caring extends to family members as well. "We view the family as a very important part of the care team," says Perkins. "Because this is a very emotional, sometimes traumatic time, our staff is also attuned to the family's needs. We empower family members to be part of the support for their child."

One piece of helping families through a child's health crisis is providing them with a healing environment. Children's Hospital's state-of-the-art facility was designed to promote healing, with comforting features like child-friendly décor, single-occupancy rooms, on-demand meal service, and open visitation for families.

As a vital member of the Omaha community, Children's takes an active role in the welfare of its neighbors, donating millions of dollars in care and serving as a teaching site for tomorrow's healthcare professionals.

In 1948, Children's Hospital was formed by a community that supported the idea of providing its young people with quality care. "The financial contributions of the community have been instrumental in our ability to accomplish our goals and objectives," says Perkins.

Over time, that backing has remained a strong part of the hospital's heritage, enhancing its ability to tailor programs and services. Today, those comprehensive offerings include inpatient and outpatient services, critical and emergency care, home health, psychological counseling, and over twenty specialty clinics.

The dedication of everyone working at Children's Hospital, aided by the ongoing support of the community, ensures that the children of Nebraska and the region will continue to receive the quality care they need and deserve. ■

"Everything we do, day in and day out, is focused upon the needs of children," explains Gary A. Perkins, president and chief executive officer of Children's Hospital.

Photo by Eric Francis

Downtown living and magnificent views make the Riverfront Place condominiums and townhomes the city's signature for downtown residential development. Adjacent to the Gallup University campus and minutes from Eppley Airfield, Riverfront Place is within walking distance of the Old Market, Qwest Center Omaha, and Holland Performing Arts Center. "We think Riverfront Place captures the exciting momentum this city is building for downtown life," says developer Ross L. Robb. "It is truly progressive for cities like Omaha to send a message that downtown is more than just a place to work—it's a place to live." From left to right, homeowners Bob and Mary Gerken, Riverfront Place partner Kim McGuire, and project manager Greg Peterson view an architectural model. O!

Photo by Thomas S, England

Perhaps no other building in Omaha had as many close calls as the distinctive Flat Iron Building, whose triangular shape resembles an old-fashioned clothing iron. Saved from the wrecking ball three times, the former 1911 hotel was permanently preserved in 1978 when it was added to the National Register of Historic Places. In 1995, Steve and Kathleen Jamrozy renovated its main floor and opened the very popular Flat Iron Café. Says Kathleen of the community support: "We've been so lucky. People were behind us the whole way, and they still are. We're part of the glorious rebirth of downtown Omaha." O!

Photo by Dennis Keim

Every day, the Jewish population of Omaha, sixty-five hundred strong, celebrates its rich culture and heritage. And on no day is this more apparent than Yom Ha'atzmaut—Israeli Independence Day. Hosted by the Jewish Federation of Omaha and held at the thirty-seven-acre Jewish Community Center of Omaha, the event, shown here, is as entertaining as it is educational. It also is a testament to how unified the city's Jewish community is and how dedicated its people are to observing important milestones and traditions. Throughout the year, this commitment to faith and custom can be found at any of Omaha's three synagogues—Temple Israel, Beth El, and Beth Israel. The spirit also is demonstrated at the Jewish Community Center, known locally as "the J" and home to a number of agencies, such as the Anti-Defamation League/Community Relations Committee, the Jewish Press, and the Jewish Family Service. The center's campus offers a range of activities for young and old, a state-of-the-art fitness center, child care, a health spa, swimming pools, and much more—all part of its mission to create "a positive Jewish environment in which to build, strengthen, and preserve Jewish identity and traditions." O!

Photo by Dennis Keim

Hundreds of pairs of little feet take to the street on the ConAgra Foods campus for the annual ConAgra Foods Race for the Kids. The noncompetitive one-mile run/walk for kids and adults is designed to promote physical activity and benefits All Our Kids, Inc., an organization that helps at-risk young people through one-on-one mentoring. During the event, participants take part in the race and are treated to games, food, prizes, and a T-shirt. This child-centered effort is an integral part of ConAgra's commitment to enhancing children's lives—an endeavor that has also included the opening of numerous ConAgra Foods Kids Cafés throughout the nation. Every year, the ConAgra Foods "Feeding Children Better" Foundation partners with America's Second Harvest and local communities to establish the cafés, which provide evening meals five nights a week for children in need. O!

Photo by Dennis Keim

There's nothing quite as exciting as hearing a baby's first words, and this is especially true with parents of hard-of-hearing or deaf children. Teaching a child to listen and talk begins in infancy, and the Omaha Hearing School offers parents help and encouragement along the way. ■

Photo by Thomas S. England

The Omaha Hearing School
for Children, Inc.

The Omaha Hearing School is child-centered, family-focused, and community-based.

"I love you."

These are words parents wait to hear when their child begins to talk. Families of children who are deaf or hard-of-hearing have unique challenges, including teaching their children to talk. The Omaha Hearing School helps these families understand those challenges and become part of a team to help children learn to listen and talk.

The school works with families of children from birth through third grade. Today's digital hearing aids and cochlear implants offer even profoundly deaf children access to sound, helping them speak for themselves. This was the vision of the four doctors and their wives who started the school in 1952.

The Omaha Hearing School is child-centered, family-focused, and community-based. To reinforce the integration of its students, the school also has a neighborhood preschool for hearing children where deaf and hard-of-hearing children play alongside their hearing peers. In addition, the school developed a graduate program with the University of Nebraska at Omaha to prepare classroom teachers to use auditory/oral techniques.

The Omaha Hearing School helps the child and the family so that they can share the joy of hearing their child's first words and the satisfaction of giving their child the optimum opportunity to be successful in a hearing world. ■

Photo by Joe Guerriero

Eclectic is definitely the word for Frankie's Garden and Nature Trail at the Omaha Hearing School. Donated by and named after one of the first students to attend the school in 1952, the garden is designed with a wide variety of colors, shapes, smells, textures, and sizes. "The goal is to give our students lots of things to talk about," said Karen Rossi, executive director. Apparently it's working for Savannah and her young friends Megan and Maureen. The garden, which is the size of a residential lot, also has play equipment and a nature trail that promises other intriguing topics of conversation about lots of interesting creepy, crawly, squiggly, wiggly things. O!

A good read. The perfect cup of coffee. Classic Christmas decorations. Vintage clothing. Unique antiques. A delicious meal. Beautiful art. Eclectic gifts. A frosty microbrew. These are among the treasures and treats found in the historic Old Market in downtown Omaha. Whether it's a visit to buy, try, or just please the eye, the shops, galleries, coffeehouses, pubs, and restaurants between Farnam and Jones, and 10th and 13th Streets are sure to offer something for everyone. Once the heart of commercial enterprise in the Omaha of the 1800s, the area thrived in that capacity until well into the twentieth century. The Old Market's rebirth as an entertainment and shopping district is popular with visitors, like this woman from Canada, and local residents. O!

Photo by Joe Guerriero

Strawberry fields

When the weather warms, it's time to head over to the Bellevue Berry Farm and Pumpkin Ranch, where many Omahans go for scrumptious fresh-picked strawberries and raspberries. In fall, a trip to the pumpkin patch might include a spooky ride along the way. Starting in October, ranch attractions also include a frontier town, a lost gold mine, the animal corral, and much more. A barn is available for parties, and when Halloween rolls around, the Ranch of Terror is a fright to behold. **O!**

Photo by Thomas S. England

Professor David Volkman guides students in analyzing market movements during a class in the Investment Sciences Laboratory at the University of Nebraska at Omaha. Thanks to private support, the lab is equipped with twenty work-stations featuring high-end computer equipment and software used in the financial industry today. ■

University of Nebraska
Foundation

E very time someone gives to the University of Nebraska Foundation, that person increases quality at each of the University of Nebraska campuses.

"The core of the university is funded by state appropriations and tuition revenues, but to create real excellence in programs requires private dollars," explains Terry Fairfield, CEO of the Foundation. "Those gifts add the extra components, such as outstanding faculty and modern structures, that create a very positive academic environment and attract a diverse student body."

The University of Nebraska Foundation is a private, nonprofit corporation that has secured financial support for each of the university's four campuses since 1936. Through the Foundation, donors interested in advancing quality education are able to support their area of preference.

"What we try to do is create a giving method that will enable donors to see, during their lifetimes, the benefits of what they have funded," says Fairfield, adding that those gifts come in many forms and provide for the full scope of needs. "Donors are really quite sophisticated in their giving. They see it as an investment, one from which they will not receive economic gain but that they are very willing to make for the benefit of others."

Whether providing for a scholarship, funding a program with societal value, or supporting researchers in the discovery of new concepts, gifts to the University of Nebraska Foundation are a vital part of enhancing the programs of the university. ■

The last work created by world-renowned sculptor Victor Salmones, *Cancer…There's Hope,* **is the focal point of** Omaha's Cancer Survivors Park. Featuring cancer patients moving through various stages of emotions and treatment, the sculpture echoes the park's positive message. Established by Richard and Annette Bloch after Richard's successful treatment and recovery from cancer, the park encourages cancer patients to fight their disease and not accept death as the inevitable outcome. The park also features the Positive Mental Attitude Walk and a Road to Recovery, both of which include spaces for reflection, meditation, and inspirational and informational plaques on fighting cancer.

University of Nebraska
Medical Center

Ask chancellor Harold M. Maurer, M.D., to define the University of Nebraska Medical Center's (UNMC) role and he's quite clear: to research the best ideas, to educate the best students, and to provide the best care for patients in Nebraska and beyond. "We're developing into a world-class academic health sciences center," explains Maurer. "That means that we're excellent in all the work we do, and truly exceptional in specific key areas."

Under Maurer's leadership, UNMC's advances in research, education, and patient care not only put UNMC on the international map, but also contribute greatly to Nebraska's economic health. With a current research enterprise that exceeds $72 million, UNMC is truly an economic engine. For every $1 million generated in federal and state research grants, thirty-four jobs are created. Physicians, dentists, nurses, and allied-health professionals trained in Omaha at UNMC support smaller communities in the state. And when

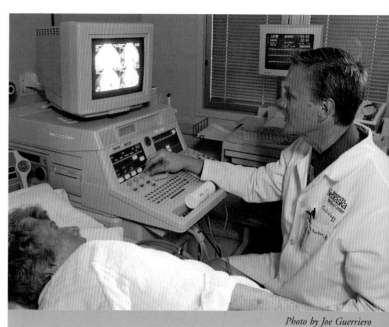

UNMC cardiologist Thomas Porter, M.D., right, has pioneered research of patented "microbubbles." The microbubbles can be used to study blood flow into the heart, as well as to target delivery of medications to specific blood-vessel locations within the heart or other organs. ■

Photo by Joe Guerriero

Photo by Joe Guerriero

Omaha's businesses recruit senior executives, the benefit of having a world-class academic medical center and its hospital partner, the Nebraska Medical Center, is key.

UNMC also is recognized for its innovations in educating students. From its leadership position in 1964 as the first academic health center in the country to use a telecommunications system for teaching, to current applications of learning-centered education, UNMC continues to develop innovative ways to train the best students in the most conducive manner possible. The use of information technology and interactive teaching techniques are essential to helping next-generation scientists and clinicians master the core competencies required for outstanding research and patient care.

From humble beginnings as the Nebraska School of Medicine in 1881, to today's academic health sciences center with a ninety-acre campus and an annual budget of more than $300 million, UNMC's contribution to advancing medical science and health has never been more important. "The citizens of Nebraska and beyond deserve the best in health care, the best in research, and the best in education," says Maurer. "We will deliver." ■

UNMC's advances in research, education, and patient care not only put UNMC on the international map, but also contribute greatly to Nebraska's economic health.

Photo by Doug Henderson

Laura Donigan, right, is one of many UNMC students who provide care for almost no cost at three student-run clinics in Omaha. Donigan is studying to become a physician. UNMC's community service also stretches across the state, including training opportunities for medical residents in rural areas. ■

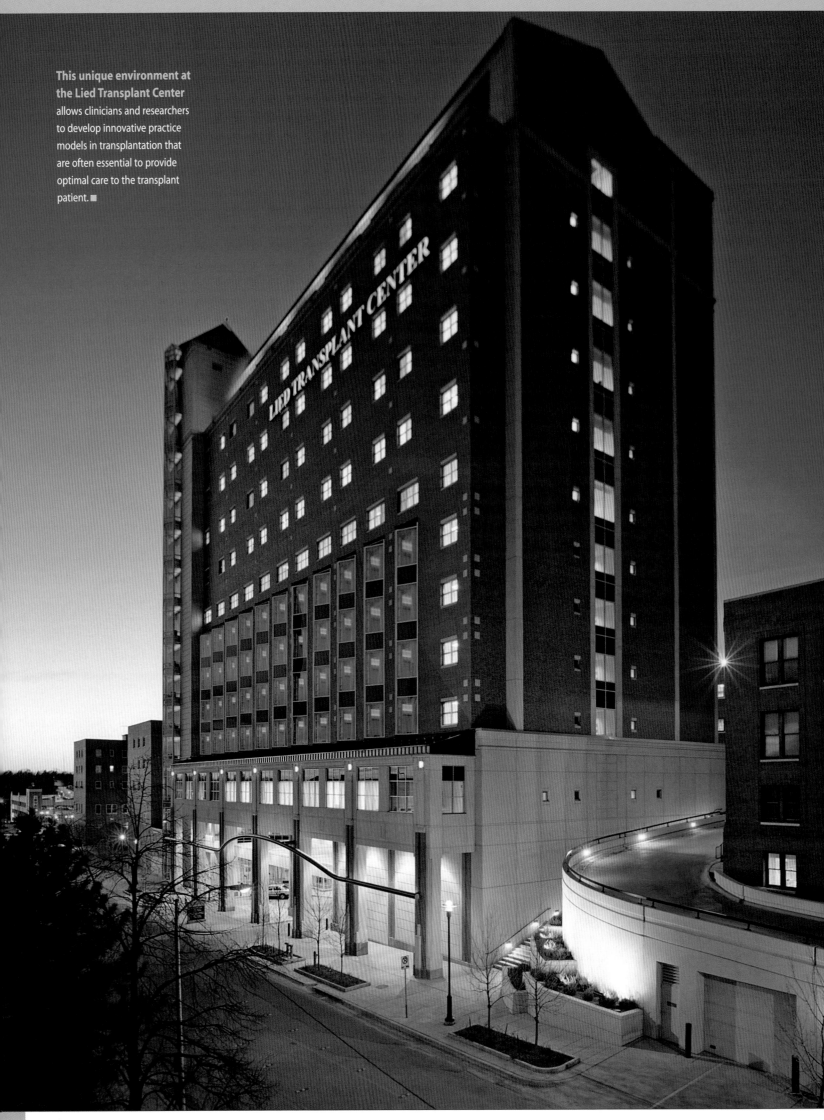

This unique environment at the Lied Transplant Center allows clinicians and researchers to develop innovative practice models in transplantation that are often essential to provide optimal care to the transplant patient. ■

The Partnership:
The University of Nebraska Medical Center and The Nebraska Medical Center

When advanced medical science meets patient care, the result is a level of health care found only in a few premier academic health sciences centers in the world. Fortunately for the people of Nebraska, that's found right here at home, through the collaboration of two nationally ranked organizations: the University of Nebraska Medical Center (UNMC) and its teaching hospital, the Nebraska Medical Center.

"Research is the underpinning of an outstanding educational program and outstanding medical care," explains Harold M. Maurer, M.D., UNMC chancellor. Since 1998, UNMC's research funding has risen from $30 million to more than $72 million, as top medical scientists from various disciplines explore ways to detect, treat, and in some cases prevent diseases in key areas: cancer, cardiovascular health, neurosciences, and transplantation among them. For example, UNMC's scientists are developing tailor-made vaccines to prevent recurrence of some slow-growing cancers that do not respond to standard treatment.

Glenn Fosdick, president and chief executive officer of the Nebraska Medical Center, reiterates the symbiotic relationship between the two institutions, and ultimately, the vital impact of research on patient care. "The integration of clinical care, education, and research across our partnership sets us apart," he says. "More importantly, it enables us to make breakthrough discoveries, deliver extraordinary care, train the best health professionals and scientists, and lead health outreach and prevention initiatives in our community." ■

College of Nursing professor Martha Foxall, Ph.D., left, instructs Michael Leach, middle, and Lesley Leach, using a patient simulator. Similar to real life, the "patient" blinks, responds to medication, and can be given an IV or tracheotomy. ■

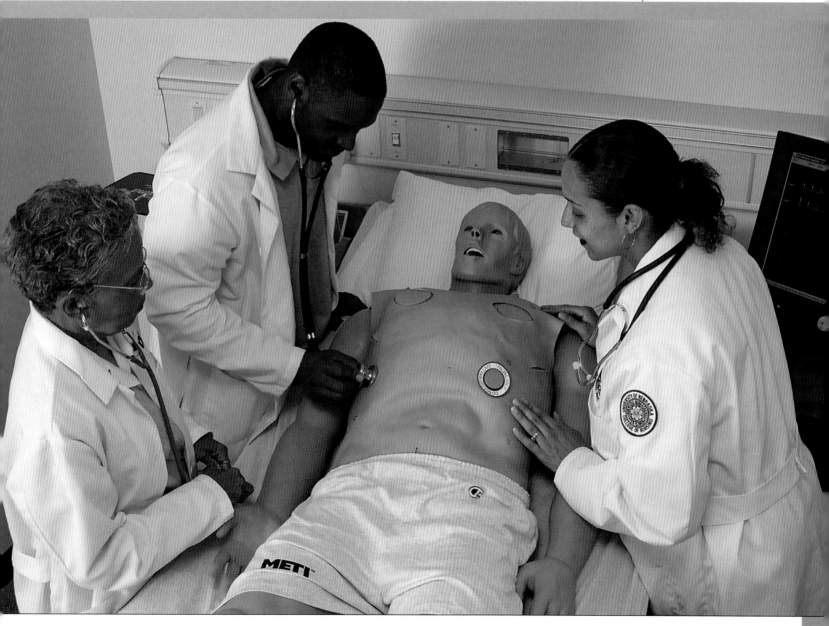

The Nebraska Medical Center

Every day, patients with serious, debilitating illnesses like cancer, Parkinson's disease, epilepsy, and heart disease come to the Nebraska Medical Center for treatment. Because of the complexity of these serious illnesses, the diagnosis and treatment is anything but "every day." As the teaching hospital for the University of Nebraska Medical Center, the Nebraska Medical Center and its nationally known physicians in academic and private practice provide extraordinary care for people who come here from Nebraska, as well as all over the world.

"The complicated case is our niche," explains president and chief executive officer Glenn Fosdick. "What we have is a unique collaboration of two nationally ranked organizations—the hospital and the University of Nebraska Medical Center—combined with physicians in private practice. That power of academic and private medicine gives us strength, credibility, and innovation."

The Nebraska Medical Center is nationally recognized for a number of clinical programs. The hospital's transplant program is one of only a few in the country that provides comprehensive treatment for diseases of the liver, small intestine, kidney, pancreas, heart, and lungs. The hospital is nationally ranked for cancer care by *US News and World Report*, and is particularly well known for its treatment of non-Hodgkin's lymphoma. In the field of neuroscience, the Nebraska Medical Center is a pioneer in the diagnosis and treatment of Parkinson's disease, epilepsy, stroke, and Alzheimer's disease. The hospital is also home to the only nationally certified stroke center in the region, and the largest biocontainment unit in the country.

"While physicians, nurses, and other health professionals can practice anywhere, they choose to come to the Nebraska Medical Center," says Fosdick. "We believe that's because we've honored the legacies of our founding institutions, while establishing our own identity—one that has earned the reputation for serious medicine and extraordinary care."

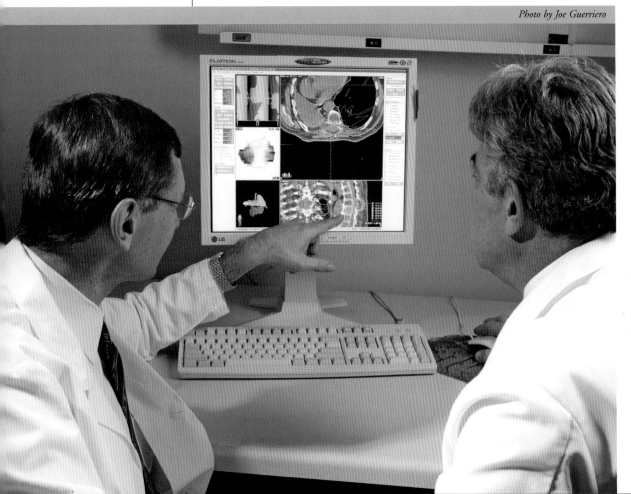

Photo by Joe Guerriero

IMRT enables the treatment team, which consists of a radiation oncologist, radiation physicists, and radiation technologists, to improve radiation targeting of tumors. This allows the radiation to attack the cancer with higher doses of radiation, without damaging healthy tissue and organs.

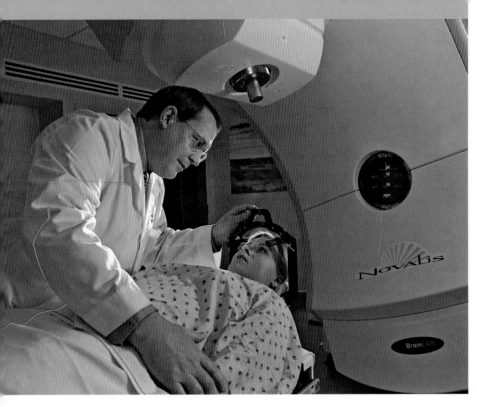

Novalis is the most innovative and advanced option available to treat tumors of the brain, head, neck, spine, liver, lung, and prostate without harming surrounding healthy tissue. ■

Due to advances in technology and techniques, cardiac catheterization is often performed on an outpatient basis, meaning that the patient may go home the same day. ■

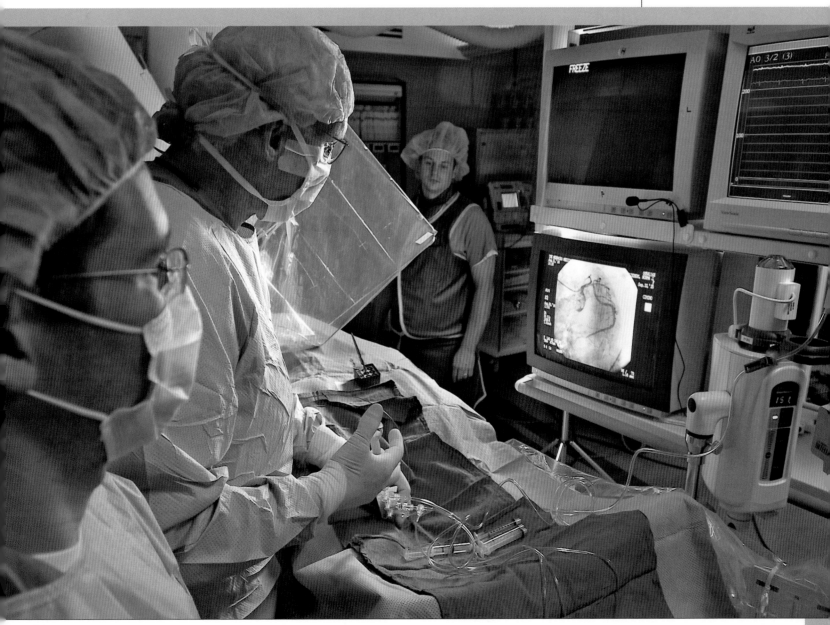

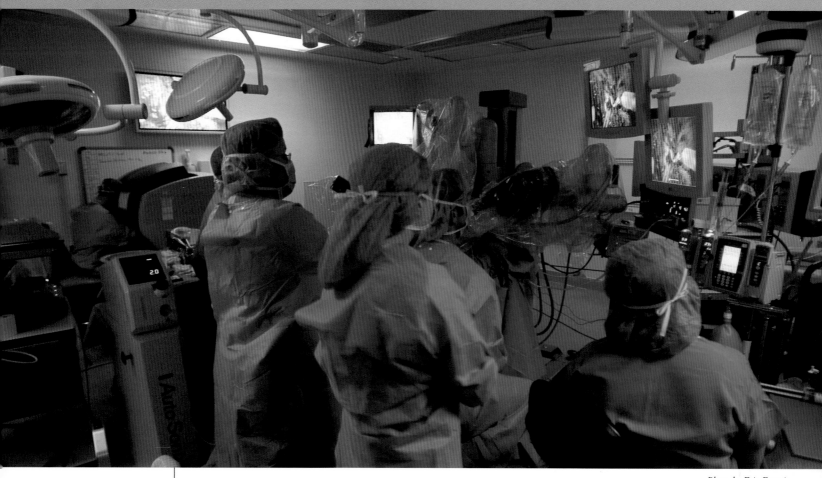

Photo by Eric Francis

Charitable Giving Augments UNMC Programs

As a medical center dedicated to improving the health of Nebraskans through health-care education, research, clinical care, and community outreach, the University of Nebraska Medical Center (UNMC) plays a vital role in the Omaha community and state of Nebraska.

Supporting UNMC's extensive effort is the University of Nebraska Foundation, a private, nonprofit corporation that has secured financial support for the medical center and three other University of Nebraska campuses since 1936.

In fact, over time, gifts to the Foundation have touched nearly every aspect of the medical center. From supporting the work of leading scientists, educators, and physicians to funding the construction of state-of-the-art buildings, private donations have helped advance excellence in medical research, patient care, and health-care education.

Among the more recent developments made possible by private funding is the Durham Research Center, a $77 million, ten-story structure housing over one hundred laboratories. In this center, private funding continues to support researchers in their pioneering efforts to reveal new and better discoveries.

Photo by Doug Henderson

A UNMC student and patient at the university's SHARING Clinic in South Omaha. The clinic provides health profession students of many disciplines the unmatched educational opportunity to participate in an actual patient setting. Charitable gifts to the University of Nebraska Foundation help offset costs associated with maintaining the high standards of care. ■

The achievements made at UNMC that benefit from private funding represent the power of the partnerships the Foundation continues to forge. These relationships also serve to strengthen the community by helping attract federal funding and by educating well over half of the health-care professionals in the state.

Gifts come in many forms to the University of Nebraska Foundation but each is made with the same intent: to create a healthier, better quality of life for the people of Nebraska and beyond. ■

Photo by Eric Francis

Dr. Robert Binhammer works with a group of medical students in the gross anatomy lab located at the University of Nebraska Medical Center's College of Medicine. Dr. Binhammer, who has been with the university since 1979, is currently professor, vice chairman, and head of gross anatomy at the college. In recognition of his years of distinguished service, he was a 2002 recipient of the Hirschmann Prize for Teaching, an award established in 2001 by two UNMC alums, Jerome Hirschmann and his son Richard. The Hirschmann Prize is awarded yearly by senior students at the College of Medicine to two faculty members who best exemplify excellence and innovation in their teaching methods. **O!**

Photo by Alan S. Weiner

Ice means heat for hockey fans, courtesy of the University of Nebraska at Omaha Mavericks. An NCAA Division I team since 1996, the Mavericks never fail to provide fans with heart-stopping action as they face off against challengers from the Central Collegiate Hockey Association. The Mavericks compete under head coach Mike Kemp, recipient of the CCHA Coach of the Year Award for the 2004–2005 season. O!

Photo by Alan S. Weiner

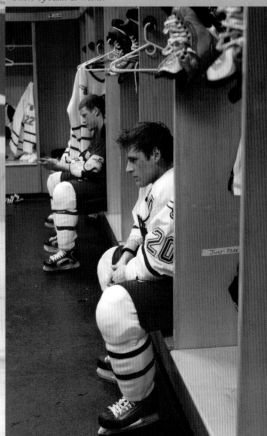

Photo by Joe Guerriero

University of Nebraska
at Omaha

F amed anthropologist Margaret Mead once said, "A city is a center where, any day in any year, there
may be a fresh encounter with a new talent, a keen mind, or a gifted specialist . . . but to play this
role in our lives, the city must have a soul—a university."

Nancy Belck, chancellor of the University of Nebraska at Omaha (UNO), often uses this quote
when talking about the sprawling midtown campus that has become part of the fabric of the state's
largest city. In fact, since its founding in 1908, UNO has worked hard to build a distinctive reputation
as Nebraska's metropolitan university. Students from all disciplines and backgrounds are offered a truly
unique educational experience where they are the center of the enterprise. Students are provided with
exceptional academic programs, as well as the chance to engage with the community around them.
UNO maximizes its "metropolitan advantage" by partnering with public and private organizations, not
only to enrich students' lives, but also to enhance the city.

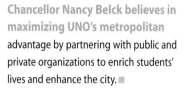

The Henningson Memorial Plaza, located in the heart of UNO's north campus at 60th and Dodge Streets, is a popular thoroughfare for students going to class, walkers out for a stroll, and the occasional cyclist. ■

Chancellor Nancy Belck believes in maximizing UNO's metropolitan advantage by partnering with public and private organizations to enrich students' lives and enhance the city. ■

Photo by Joe Guerriero

Students from all disciplines and backgrounds are offered a truly unique educational experience where they are the center of the enterprise.

"UNO is the soul of Omaha. As stewards of place, we believe UNO gives to the community as significantly as it gives to us," explains Belck. "We want to graduate students who understand they also need to give back to their community. We want to give them a sense of civic pride."

Of course, this starts in classrooms, serving fifteen thousand students with a comprehensive array of undergraduate degree programs, covering everything from the arts and business administration to information science and public affairs. "Surveys conducted of graduates showed that they chose UNO because of the quality of our academic programs," Belck states. Thanks to its solid reputation for scholastic merit, the university can boast that 94 percent of entering freshmen list UNO as their first or second choice of universities, and more than 92 percent would recommend the university to other college-bound students. "I think those are powerful numbers," she adds.

Additionally, the school offers four doctoral, two educational specialist's, and sixty-one master's degrees, along with nine graduate certificate programs to twenty-eight hundred graduate-level students. "We are very proud of our graduate programs. They are excellent, well-known, and attract students from a broad base," Belck continues, noting that nine graduate programs are recognized by U.S. News and World Report. The school's doctoral programs in information technology, public administration, and criminal justice are immensely popular and greatly praised.

Much of this acclaim can be credited to UNO's faculty and staff. Not only are many faculty the recipients of major honors and awards, but they show a great deal of care and concern for those in their classes. "I think most students would say that faculty really give of themselves," Belck notes. "So, you not only

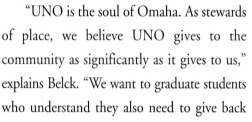

Continued on page 388

Photo by Alan S. Weiner

Home ice for the UNO Mavericks is the Qwest Arena in downtown Omaha, Nebraska's premier entertainment and sports venue. UNO is a member of the Central Collegiate Hockey Association, along with Notre Dame, Michigan, and Ohio State. ∎

Continued from page 387

have highly qualified faculty and staff, but they never forget that teaching is their most important role."

This kind of attention gives students the foundation needed to succeed as they take advantage of UNO's many service learning and internship opportunities. Students can really see the benefits of the relationships that UNO has built with the Omaha community over the years. Partnerships with private and public, profit and nonprofit organizations offer a host of choices and the chance to acquire invaluable hands-on experience. And, as Belck reports, students who have successful

Photo by Dennis Keim

Commencement is a time of celebration and reflection. Pictured at right, new University of Nebraska at Omaha graduate Jessica Barsell pauses to absorb the moment before beginning her future. ∎

internships have a 90 percent chance of staying in Omaha, most likely working with the companies where they apprenticed.

Furthermore, UNO's impressive partnerships have allowed the school to boost its on-campus resources. For instance, in a partnership among UNO's College of Information Science and Technology, the University of Nebraska–Lincoln's College of Engineering and Technology, and private businesses throughout the city, the University of Nebraska Peter Kiewit Institute operates on UNO's south campus. This state-of-the-art facility provides a stimulating environment for students—and faculty—to explore and generate some of today's most innovative technological advances.

Sustained growth at UNO shows that students appreciate the university's efforts on their behalf. Over the last decade, enrollments have held steady at around fifteen thousand students, three new residence complexes have been added, and the school's Division II Mavericks, which also compete in Division I hockey, are ushering in a new era of accomplishment. During the past season, UNO women's teams took home conference titles in soccer, softball, swimming and diving, and tennis. On the men's side, the Mavericks finished first in football, basketball, and baseball in the North Central Conference, and the wrestling team captured the national Division II NCAA title for the second consecutive year. It's all due to a metropolitan model that lets UNO fully realize its potential.

"Omaha has just provided a super environment," says Belck. "We are lucky to be in a city and a state that value education." ■

Photo by David Gibb

The UNO Art Gallery, located in the Weber Fine Arts
Building on the west end of campus, is a vital cultural resource committed to serving the campus, the residents of Omaha, and surrounding communities. The gallery serves as an educational forum for the study, contemplation, and critical analysis of works of art. Pictured above, UNO students Seth Thompson and Frances Y. Osugi view a student exhibition. ■

Photo by Joe Guerriero

Matt Riley knows the score. The UNO computer science major, pictured at the University of Nebraska Peter Kiewit Institute, earned a perfect 36 on his ACT. The sophomore is considering a career in electronic entertainment. ■

Photo by Rod Reilly

Private Support Enhances the Quality of Students' Educational Experiences

Making quality education affordable and accessible is a primary emphasis of the University of Nebraska at Omaha (UNO). Enhancing the quality of that education is the main focus of the University of Nebraska Foundation.

"Whether funding a scholarship, a program with societal value, or researchers discovering new concepts, private funding is vital to the university's advancement," says Terry Fairfield, Foundation CEO.

A private, nonprofit corporation, the Foundation has secured financial support for each of the university's four campuses since 1936. Over the years, that funding has benefited every aspect of the university. "It's a circular effect," says Fairfield. "For example, funding that goes toward building research space will, in turn, attract good faculty who draw outstanding students that want to study with those on the cutting edge of their discipline."

Rounding out the cycle, UNO graduates often become benefactors themselves, helping to open doors for others. "Education is the key ingredient for how people can improve their lives," says Fairfield, "and private giving provides that opportunity for many who otherwise could not achieve it."

The results of private support designated to UNO can be seen in entities like the Investment Sciences Lab, connecting students with real-world financial issues, and the Sapp Fieldhouse, transformed in recent years into a state-of-the-art facility.

These are just two examples of the strength of a public-private partnership between the university and the community that will continue to foster a level of excellence in the University of Nebraska system. ■

Photo by Joe Guerriero

exigence
what your situation requires

When University of Nebraska at Omaha (UNO) graduates Jonathan Vonk (left) and Stephen Haberman decided to start a software development company in June 2004, they found the perfect home within the Omaha business community. The two young entrepreneurs launched Exigence Corporation, a firm that collaborates closely with clients to meet their ever-changing development needs. According to Vonk, the business has shown steady growth, thanks in part to its membership in the Greater Omaha Chamber of Commerce and the valuable relationships he and his cofounder cultivated with members of the UNO faculty and staff during their academic careers. The city's central location has also been a great advantage. "We enjoy Nebraska, and we feel comfortable here," Vonk says. "We've worked with several long-distance clients in New York and elsewhere from right here in Omaha." O!

Boys and girls, grab your baskets and start your search!
Approximately one thousand kids eagerly scrambled to find the
treasures provided by NRG Media and Verizon Wireless in an annual Easter
Egg Hunt, one of dozens held in parks and neighborhoods across the city.
The Elmwood Park public event featured plenty of plastic eggs filled with
candy and passes for free rides on the *River City Star*, a riverboat that cruises
the Missouri. O!

The most popular name for babies in Omaha is Methodist Hospital, the first hospital in Nebraska, and just the twenty-ninth hospital nationally, to earn the Baby-Friendly USA certification. Methodist annually delivers more babies than any other hospital in the region. ■

Photo by Thomas S. England

Methodist Health System

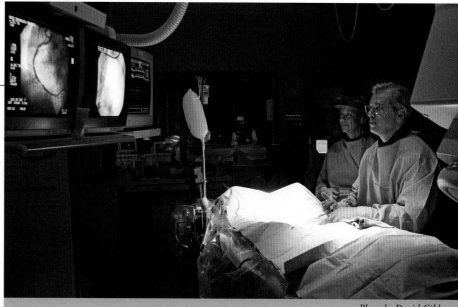

Photo by David Gibb

In 1982, patients throughout Omaha were introduced to Methodist Health System, a regional network of health-care providers, educators, and support services that were dedicated to delivering excellence in health care and health-care education. This integrated delivery system,

Jennie Edmundson Hospital in Council Bluffs, an affiliate of Methodist Health System, is the only hospital in southwest Iowa capable of performing emergency angioplasty procedures. Jennie Edmundson Hospital has been serving the community since 1886. ▪

composed of six affiliates anchored by two hospitals—each with more than 110 years of service to their communities—and five thousand employees, became the bedrock of a vast group of community-based medical programs designed to improve the quality of life for local residents.

"Our mission is simple: we are committed to caring for people," says CEO Stephen D. Long. "Therefore, we are steadfast in our effort to bring the latest health-care technology and treatments to this market, providing innovative, high-value solutions that meet the ever-changing needs of the consumer."

Today, Methodist Health System is a regionally recognized leader in the delivery of first-rate health-care services. It is the nonprofit parent of a family of organizations that provide treatment options to anyone who requires care, regardless of race, creed, lifestyle, or socioeconomic status. With the exception of Shared Service Systems, the affiliates are nonprofit entities and include Nebraska Methodist Hospital, a 430-bed acute-care facility that serves Omaha and its neighboring regions; Physicians Clinic, Inc., Nebraska's largest private, multispecialty group practice; Jennie Edmundson Memorial Hospital, a 230-bed regional health-care center that serves southwest Iowa; Jennie Edmundson Foundation, which supports its namesake hospital with a range of community programs and services; Nebraska Methodist College, a fully accredited health professions college; and the Methodist Hospital Foundation, which contributes charitable care to patients in need and promotes health-related programs. Shared Service Systems operates as a wholesale medical/surgical distributor and full-service centralized laundry.

From cardiology, neurosurgery, and women's services to cancer care, gastroenterology, orthopedics, and comprehensive diagnostic services, these organizations offer to patients with a wide variety of medical concerns unparalleled care and some of the most technologically advanced therapies and services in the nation. For instance, Methodist Health System can boast of Omaha's only Leksell Gamma Knife® surgery, a minimally invasive treatment for certain brain tumors. It also features computer-aided detection (CAD) mammography, two linear accelerators for radiation therapy, the daVinci® Robotic Surgery System, and more. In addition, the entire system is converting to an electronic health records system that provides medical professionals with better and quicker access to patient records and helps reduce errors.

"Public response has been very positive," Long notes. "Patient satisfaction has been evidenced by Methodist Hospital being the only Nebraska hospital to be awarded the Consumer's Choice Award by National Research Consultants every year that it has been bestowed." And the accolades do not stop there. Consumer surveys

Continued on page 396

"Our mission is simple: we are committed to caring for people," says CEO Stephen D. Long.

Patients at Methodist HealthWest, Methodist Health System's state-of-the-art ambulatory care center, were among the first in the region to benefit from a high-tech networking system that immediately transfers filmless digital "X-ray" images between medical facilities for faster diagnosis and treatment. ■

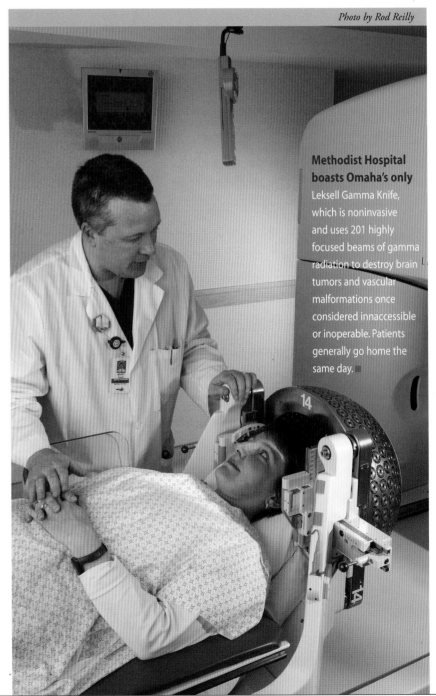

Photo by Rod Reilly

Methodist Hospital boasts Omaha's only Leksell Gamma Knife, which is noninvasive and uses 201 highly focused beams of gamma radiation to destroy brain tumors and vascular malformations once considered inaccessible or inoperable. Patients generally go home the same day. ■

Continued from page 395

recognize Methodist Hospital, Physicians Clinic, and Jennie Edmundson Hospital as leaders in providing quality care.

Methodist Hospital was the first facility in Nebraska to earn the coveted Magnet designation from the American Nurses Credentialing Center. This is a great honor for everyone within Methodist Health System, including its board of directors, which consists of some of Omaha's most respected business and civic leaders. More satisfying, however, is the ability of Methodist Health System's affiliates to assist the under-served community through facilities like the Renaissance Clinic, programs like the Methodist Hospital Foundation's "Works of the Heart" charitable programs, 55PLUS®, and services like free and reduced-price health screenings, educational programming, and medication assistance.

Long says the future holds exciting opportunities for Methodist Health System. "We will maximize our resources to provide care in the most efficient, cost-effective, and appropriate setting," he states. "We want to be as responsive as possible to the needs of the surrounding population by delivering, measuring, and publicizing results that show we meet the highest standards." ■

Photo by Dennis Keim

This colorful mural celebrating the dynamic Hispanic heritage of south Omaha is one of many that adorn buildings, walls, and public spaces around the city. The mural, titled *Discoveries*, was a Bemis Youth in Public Art project of the Bemis Center for Contemporary Arts program.

Photo by Timothy Keen

Photo by Timothy Keen

Coming

Photo by Timothy Keen

Photo by Timothy Keen

Native Omaha Days, which every two years celebrates African American heritage by bringing native Omahans and former residents back to the city for a week of festivities in August, is like "a family reunion where the common name is Omaha." The 2005 gathering, the fifteenth of its kind, attracted between eight thousand and ten thousand people. Presented by the Native Omahans Club Inc. and several corporate and civic sponsors, the week included a Gospel celebration at Salem Baptist Church, a tour of Omaha, a drill team competition at Creighton University, a boat ride on the *River City Star*, a golf outing, a music and cultural expo, a Welcome Home Dance at Qwest Center Omaha, and a Sunday afternoon picnic at Carter Lake Park. "I love it," said Donetta Allen, vice president of the Native Omahans Club Inc., pointing to the enthusiastic crowd at the drill team competition. "I'm in heaven." The events drew to a close with tearful goodbyes on "Blue Monday." O!

Photo by Timothy Keen

HOME

Photo by Thomas S. England

Students at the Elkhorn Valley Campus take classes that can transfer to many area postsecondary institutions. This high level of flexibility, as well as the numerous academic program options offered by the school, is what makes Metro so appealing to its student population. ■

Metropolitan
Community College

Photo by Thomas S. England

The students who attend Metropolitan Community College (Metro) mirror the diversity of the community. They hail from different backgrounds. They represent an array of ethnicities and age groups. They are urban, rural, and suburban men and women. Some are just starting out, while others are starting a new adventure. Yet, in the long run, they all have something in common: they recognize the power of choice, and that's why they've decided to pursue their postsecondary education at this highly regarded institution.

A comprehensive, full-service public community college, Metro prides itself on providing every one of its twenty-seven thousand credit students with options. From academics and student services to business and community opportunities, students are given the chance to craft an educational experience that meets their unique needs.

The commons area in the Sarpy Center lets Metro students mingle with patrons of the adjacent LaVista Public Library. This type of unique facility is part of the school's series of capital improvement efforts, which have benefited not only Metro's students, but also local area residents. ∎

A recent economic impact study showed that a Metro student recovers all costs of education (including wages forgone while attending college) in five years. Those who receive a two-year associate degree earn 112 percent more than someone without a high school diploma and 35 percent more than a high school graduate. Over a lifetime, the associate degree graduate will earn $286,810 more than the average high school graduate.

Metro's foundation is built upon a repertoire of more than one hundred associate degree, certificate, and specialist diploma programs in everything from business administration and computer technologies to culinary arts and nursing. In recent years, new programs in subjects such as elementary and secondary education, emergency management, and civil engineering have been added. The associate degree programs frequently serve as a stepping-stone for students who can continue their education by transferring their credits and pursuing a four-year degree at one of the area's universities. Conversely, certificates and specialist diplomas, often one-year programs, provide "quick skill acquisition for entry-level positions in some fields and highly specialized advanced programs of study in other areas," according to Randy Van Wagoner, vice president of Educational Services.

The college's Workforce Development Institute offers customized training for local businesses. Additionally, Metro boasts numerous noncredit continuing education courses, which attract more than twenty thousand lifelong learners annually.

The key to helping students take advantage of Metro's many offerings is convenient access. Classes are not only held days, evenings, and weekends at three main campuses and three educational centers throughout the Omaha area, but they also are presented through a series of innovative e-learning programs. From online classes to interactive television and DVD/video courses, students can tailor their academic schedules to fit their daily lives. This level of access is unparalleled, especially since Metro's faculty members teach the same content in both the virtual and on-campus courses. Furthermore, these

continued on page 402

A comprehensive, full-service public community college, Metro prides itself on providing every one of its twenty-seven thousand credit students with options.

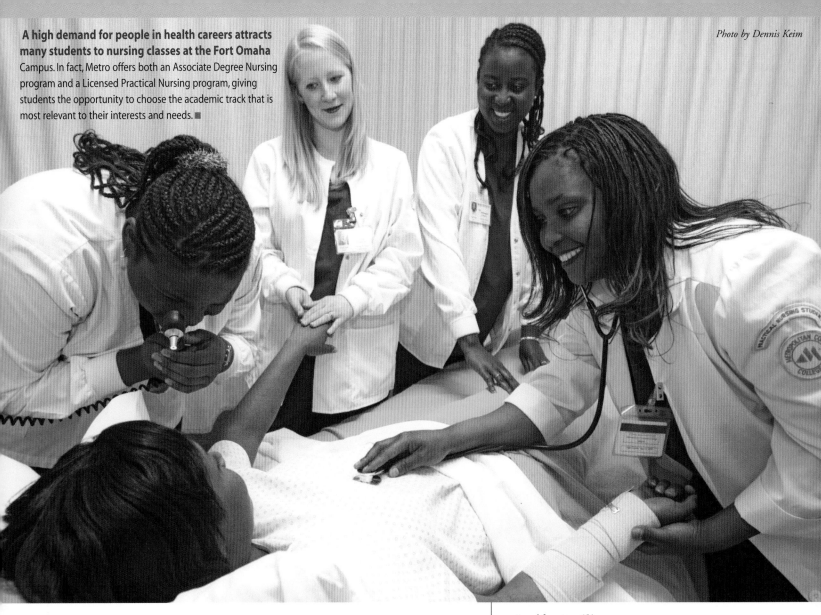

Photo by Dennis Keim

A high demand for people in health careers attracts many students to nursing classes at the Fort Omaha Campus. In fact, Metro offers both an Associate Degree Nursing program and a Licensed Practical Nursing program, giving students the opportunity to choose the academic track that is most relevant to their interests and needs. ■

Photo by Dennis Keim

With precision and skill, an automotive technology student runs a diagnostic test with state-of-the-art equipment at the South Omaha Campus. This type of exclusive hands-on training is what gives Metro students a truly competitive edge when they embark on their careers after completing their education. ■

continued from page 401

various learning options, reveals Van Wagoner, "allow the college to be more efficient in utilizing on-campus space and adds additional capacity to offer more classes."

It's no wonder that Metro has managed to maintain the largest enrollment of the state's six community colleges, while greatly impacting Omaha's social and economic growth. In fact, the school's continued development has sparked capital improvement projects across all three campuses, including a much-anticipated City of Omaha/ Metro Library on the South Omaha Campus. Each new project ultimately is designed to benefit residents of Dodge, Washington, Sarpy, and Douglas counties—Metro's service area.

"Metro has gained respect as a strong educational institution that provides outstanding value to students and serves as a great partner with business and industry as well as education at all levels," says Van Wagoner. "The college will seek to build on this legacy of success and serve the community in even more significant ways in the future." ■

Red Hat Society

Photo by Thomas S. England

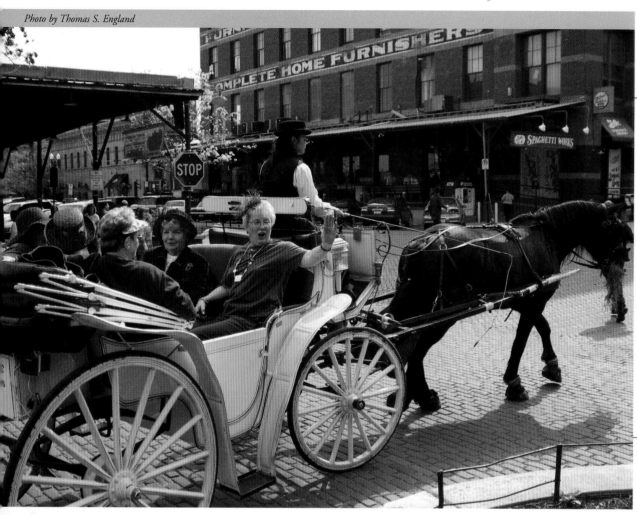

If fun under a red hat is your thing, the O!maha Hatters is one of more than 100 local chapters of the Red Hat Society, which formed in California in 1998 when a group of women went to tea dressed in purple clothing and red hats. Today, the Red Hat Society has an estimated 850,000 members and more than thirty-four thousand chapters across the United States These not-so-mad "Hatters" enjoy a carriage ride through the Old Market. O!

Gardening Fun

Photo by John Yochum

Three friends enjoy working in the garden at the Richmont Village retirement living community in Bellevue. The metropolitan area has a wealth of options for older adults to reside at independent, assisted living, and full-care retirement centers, and still live close to their family and longtime friends. O!

Photo by Mark Romesser

The Peter Kiewit Institute
Scott Technology Center

There are no diamond mines in Nebraska, but there is a rare jewel clearly visible just a short drive from downtown Omaha. The Peter Kiewit Institute (PKI), like the diamond, was created by bringing ordinary elements together in an extraordinary way—with one important difference. PKI went from concept to creation in less than three years. The PKI charter was approved by the University of Nebraska Board of Regents in December 1996. The first scholar recruits began in the fall of 1997, and its new facility opened in 1999. The first phase of the Scott Technology Center, an adjunct of PKI, opened in 2001, and four phases were operative by 2006.

The idea is brilliant in its simplicity and logic. PKI connects students directly to business and industry. The partners include the University of Nebraska–Lincoln's (UNL) College of Engineering and Technology, the University of Nebraska at Omaha's (UNO) College of Information Science and Technology, and

The Peter Kiewit Institute is a 192,000-square-foot facility with an exposed infrastructure and is located on the former Aksarben property. The colleges of Engineering and Information Science and Technology work together in a collaborative partnership with business and industry. ■

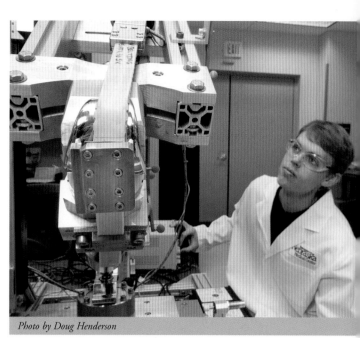

This machine simulates total knee replacement implant capability measuring kinetic and kinematic motion. It's the first in the world capable of using novel pneumatically acutated fluidic muscles. Engineering graduate Ben O'Brien works in this University of Nebraska Medical Center laboratory. ■

Photo by Doug Henderson

The idea is brilliant in its simplicity and logic. PKI connects students directly to business and industry.

business leaders working with real-world applications. These elements give PKI its competitive edge.

In this collaboration, traditional boundaries do not exist. The Colleges remain separate but work closely together, inviting students to explore courses through both entities. The end result, for example, can be a student who not only understands the issues of data collection, data mining, and systems architecture, but also has a working knowledge of the hardware requirements involved. "About one-fifth of our students take full advantage of this partnership by double majoring," said Winnie Callahan, PKI executive director.

Faculty and experts-in-residence from major companies introduce high-tech problems and share their expertise with students and faculty. Together they seek workable solutions that industry can tap immediately.

Students also take advantage of internships and summer jobs in their fields of study and establish connections with business leaders eager to turn bright students into tomorrow's expert employees—a win-win-win situation for business/industry, students, and faculty.

The Scott Technology Center mentioned above is a direct outgrowth of PKI. It was developed by the Suzanne and Walter Scott Foundation (a public, nonprofit organization). The Center capitalizes on the partnerships presented by the Kiewit Institute. In other words, the Center identifies and supports opportunities for the creation and development of emerging and disruptive technologies. It provides the tools and advantages critical to take concepts to market.

The Institute complex, located on the South Campus of UNO, includes PKI, Scott Technology Center, Scott Residence Hall, the Conference Center, and Scott Village.

Continued on page 406

Engineering students work in Institute structures lab on a prestressed highway bridge girder (Nebraska Department of Roads). The lab is robust, boasting of a twenty-five-ton overhead movable crane and reaction wall which sustains up to 1 million pounds of force. ■

Photo by Doug Henderson

Continued from page 405

The policies of the Institute are guided by a governing board of eleven CEOs who set direction and help facilitate partnerships. PKI has nearly two hundred business partners including local firms such as Mutual of Omaha, HDR, Union Pacific, and ConAgra; major national firms including IBM, Cox Communications, Gallup, Raytheon, and US Strategic Command; and international institutions such as Fraunhofer and KUKA Robotics of Germany.

The labs and work environments support new technology creation, developmental opportunities, and ongoing operations. In this multitenant space, corporate giants such as SAIC commingle with emerging companies such as Spiral Solutions Inc. This diverse population, which also includes professors and students from PKI, fosters cross-pollination of talent and stimulates innovation. Classroom ideas are transformed into marketable products.

PKI and the Scott Technology Center have been touted by the *Chicago Tribune*, *The New York Times*, the *Los Angeles Times*, *PC Week*, *Information Weekly*, and the *Omaha World-Herald*, to mention a few.

The Scott Technology Center, an outgrowth of the Peter Kiewit Institute, provides incubator, office, and lab spaces for companies partnered with the Institute. From corporate giants to startups, students and professors experience hands-on opportunities with the best in the industry. ■

Photo by Doug Henderson

Photo by Doug Henderson

This Scott Technology Center Board Room along with three other conference rooms provide excellent meeting spaces for tenants and businesses engaged in technology transfer and project collaboration. The Center serves as a hub for economic development strategies and planning. ■

University of Nebraska president James B. Milliken said, "There's probably no better example of public/private partnerships in the country than those found at the Peter Kiewit Institute."

Jimmie Haines, a senior engineer from Boeing, agreed. "I know of no other educational institution that is taking such a dramatic step in working with business and industry to reshape and build curriculum."

Forbes echoed those sentiments. "PKI operates one of the most respected and innovative information technology and engineering education programs in the United States."

The word is definitely spreading. PKI has students from more than thirty states and ten foreign countries. The core group of scholars rank among the nation's top 3 percent academically "Institutions like Carnegie Mellon, Stanford, Harvard, Penn State, Colorado State, and the George C. Marshall Institute, as well as others, have visited to learn more about what we're doing," said David Hinton, dean of UNO's College of IS&T. And no wonder: there is nothing like the brilliance of a rare and precious jewel to attract worldwide attention. ■

Photo by Doug Henderson

This Security Technology Evaluation and Analysis Lab (STEAL) is one of two labs providing students and professionals alike a premiere learning environment for the study of information assurance and cyber security. This is a National Security Agency Center of Excellence. ■

4-H youth from a nine-state region including Nebraska compete for prizes in the annual Knights of Ak-Sar-Ben 4-H Livestock Exposition, an event that goes back seventy-eight years in Omaha. But it was in 1982 that the 4-H show became a core event of the River City Roundup, conceived by Omaha's Knights of Ak-Sar-Ben philanthropic organization as a way to celebrate western heritage, educate youth and families in agricultural issues, and award more than $250,000 in youth scholarships. Held over four days each September at Qwest Center Omaha, River City Roundup festivities also include the popular Pace Picante ProRodeo Summer Tour Finale, televised on CBS, and the Douglas County Fair. A Heritage Parade, trail rides, the Ak-Sar-Ben Invitational Art Show, and the Nebraska Beef Council's "What's for Dinner" cooking stage provide additional fun for the whole family. OI

Photo by Eric Francis

Photo by Rod Reilly

Through the "Creatures Great and Small" summer day-camp
program, more than one thousand Girl Scouts from the
Omaha-based Great Plains Council learn how to care for animals. During
the weeklong program, the girls also learn how to help prevent animal
abuse and overpopulation, practice first aid on stuffed animals, make a
trip to Fontenelle Forest to study insects, and tour a local farm to learn
about agriculture and animal husbandry. Here, they spend the day at the
Nebraska Humane Society bathing and grooming dogs. Founded in
1875, the Nebraska Humane Society (NHS) is the fifth-oldest Humane
Society in the United States From its impressive facility near 90th and
Fort Streets, the nonprofit NHS provides education and animal control
services, gives sanctuary to animals, encourages adoptions, and promotes responsible pet ownership. **O!**

Photo by Eric Francis

Liberty Elementary public school opened in 2002 to accommodate the growing residential population in downtown Omaha. Liberty Elementary students reflect the diversity of the area. Because many of the students are learning to speak English, in addition to learning their ABCs and one-two-threes, providing a rich language environment is a key to success. To do so, teachers utilize poems, chants, and catchy words with the younger students. Older students expand their vocabulary by looking up the word, then writing and acting out their own definitions. "The strength of any school is good teachers, and our teachers are truly dedicated to the kids and concerned about building relationships with them," says principal Nancy Oberst. Liberty's teachers are able to strengthen their skills through the Gallup Organization's Clifton StrengthsFinders assessment, a management tool used by Fortune 500 companies. As one of the elementary's Adopt-A-School partners, Gallup employees volunteer in the classroom. **O!**

Liberty Elementary

Photo by Eric Francis

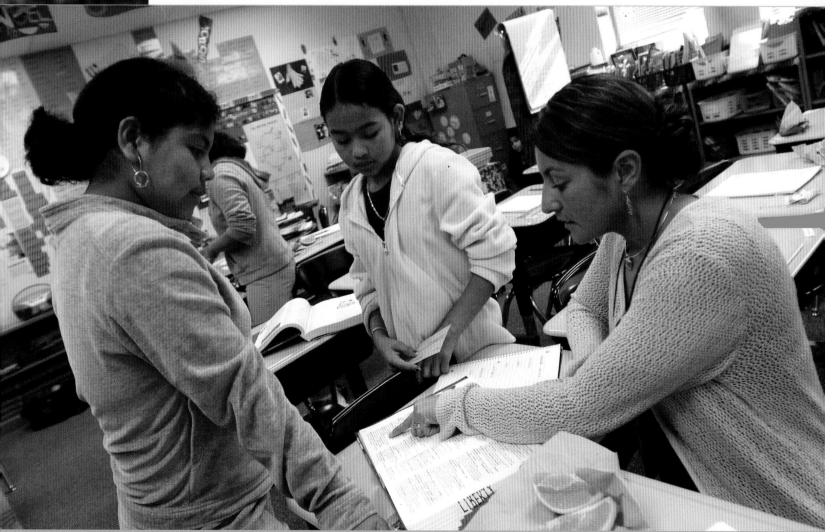

Photo by Eric Francis

Photo by Thomas S. England

Alegent
Health

Patients in the Joint Replacement Center at Alegent Health Bergan Mercy Medical Center—also referred to as "joint campers"—do their physical therapy as a group led by a physical therapist. The Joint Replacement Center is an award-winning, nationally recognized program that offers a unique approach to joint replacement where patients undergo recovery as a group in an environment that emphasizes teamwork and camaraderie. ■

Caring for the mind, body, and spirit—this is the Alegent Health way and the faith-based mission that inspires Alegent Health's higher standard of quality, compassionate care. "The people of Alegent Health know that faith makes a difference," says Wayne A. Sensor, CEO. "It empowers us to care for each patient as we would our own family." It also enables the nonprofit organization to focus on providing clinical care of the highest order in a healing environment, melding empathetic values of dignity, respect, and hope with the science of medicine and the support of innovative technology.

Born of the union between two premier health organizations with common core values—Bergen Mercy Health Systems and Immanuel Medical Center—Alegent Health's roots are deep, its branches wide. Providing medical services at more than one hundred sites across the area through nine acute-care hospitals and numerous ambulatory-care facilities, Alegent Health is the largest healthcare system in the Nebraska-Iowa region.

The comforts of home and top-notch medical care are combined in the Best Beginnings Maternity Center at Alegent Health Lakeside Hospital. The Best Beginnings Maternity Center offers a safe, secure, and private birthing environment. ■

Photo by David Gibb

"Alegent Health is fully aware of our greater responsibilities to seek out innovations that improve patient care and to extend our healing mission beyond our walls and into the communities we serve," said Larry Beckman, chair, Alegent Health Board of Directors.

In the increasingly complex world of health care, Alegent Health is committed to being a partner and a leader in innovation—working hard to understand and employ the best advances in technology, as well as innovations that improve the diagnosis, treatment, and efficiency of quality patient care. With a significant capital investment and a strategic alliance with Siemens Medical Systems, a leader in diagnostic and clinical solutions, Alegent Health effectively merges medical technology with information technology. The outcome is everything from efficient electronic medical records to digital imaging that allows for nearly instantaneous interpretation by clinicians.

"Technology is a tool to help us provide quality care," says Ken Lawonn, senior vice president and chief information officer. "It helps the physician to harness the vast information available and bring it to bear, real-time, to improve patient care."

In addition to a faith-based healing mission and a focus on exceptional quality care, Alegent Health has made a commitment to positively impact the health of the community as a whole. "Our mission calls for us to address the health status of the communities we serve," Sensor emphasizes. "This is not just limited to inpatient and outpatient services. It means that we reach into our community and find out what the needs are for all we serve."

"Our mission calls for us to address the health status of the communities we serve," Sensor emphasizes.

Continued on page 414

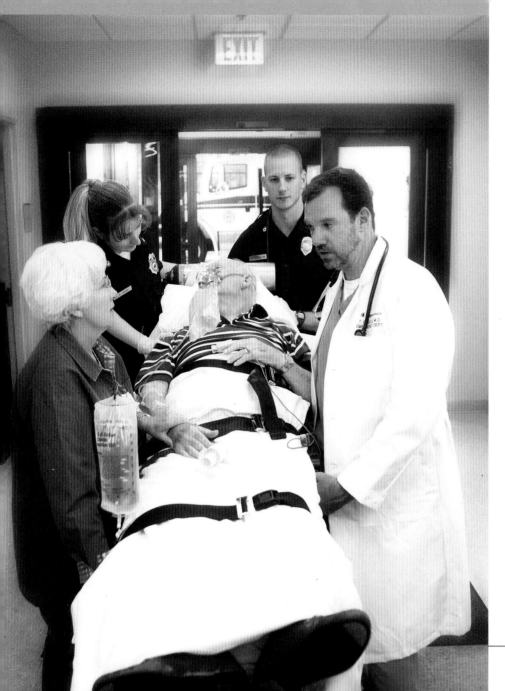

Continued from page 413

Sister Norita Cooney, senior vice president of Mission Services, explains how Alegent Health broadens its purpose. "We work collaboratively with other organizations in the community to provide support to them so that they can provide free clinics and free care to those individuals who have tremendous need," she says. Between $5 million and $7 million are allocated from net patient service revenues annually to support community programs through the Alegent Health Community Benefit Trust. Special emphasis is placed on assisting agencies that serve vulnerable populations.

As Sister Cooney says, "When you think about it, this is how we initially got started—trying to meet the unmet needs of the community." Sensor agrees. "Think about how many lives will be touched by this, how many organizations will be able to use that money to leverage their existing resources and their existing programs to truly improve the fabric of our community," he says. And that's the essence of Alegent Health's faith-based mission. It's the Alegent Health way. ■

Photo by Geoff Johnson

The physicians, nurses, and emergency medical professionals at the Alegent Health Midlands Community Hospital are specialists in emergency care. The Emergency Department at Midlands provides the latest technology with personalized care that centers on each individual person. ■

The Heart Center at Alegent Health Immanuel Medical Center is a state-of-the-art cardiac unit where levels of care step down as a patient improves. In addition to an experienced team of cardiologists and surgeons, patients also receive care from the region's first adult Intensivist program, which places critical-care physician specialists in the hospital around the clock. ■

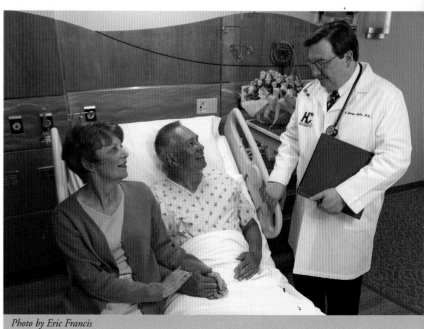

Photo by Eric Francis

Omaha Public Schools offer the region's most comprehensive complement of magnet schools. The King Science & Technology Magnet is one of the "stars." Offering fifth- through eighth-grade students the opportunity to study biology, chemistry, earth science, physics, and astronomy, the King Magnet ensures those students a minimum of four hours per week working with specialized science teachers in a laboratory setting. A favorite is the school's planetarium, where students meet out-of-this world astronomy and earth science learning goals as they explore the solar system and beyond. O!

Photo by Jackson Hill

From the dynamic African American community in north Omaha to the thriving Hispanic population in south Omaha and throughout the metropolitan area, efforts are under way to encourage the successful development of new and longtime minority-owned businesses. One of the programs is the Minority Economic Development Council of the Greater Omaha Chamber of Commerce, which assists various organizations' and agencies' community projects with an emphasis on economic development and employment opportunities. "Hard work, innovation, and the entrepreneurial spirit are the hallmark of these business owners," says Rodrigo Lopez, chairman of the development council, pictured below. "Our vital minority business community and its committed leaders add to the quality of life for the entire community. People here understand that diversity of businesses, like diversity of the population, adds strength and promise to Omaha's economic outlook. And Omaha is a great place for everyone to do business." O!

Photo by Timothy Keen

Photo by Eric Francis

Photo by Timothy Keen

Photo by Timothy Keen

Photo by Timothy Keen

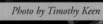

Photo by Timothy Keen

Photo by Alan S. Weiner

United Way
of the Midlands

O maha's businesses and human service agencies have a rich history of working together for the common good. United Way of the Midlands embodies this cooperative spirit by bringing people and resources together to make the communities of Douglas, Sarpy, and Pottawattamie counties strong.

Far more than a funding source, United Way is a catalyst in strategic planning, ensuring social service programs that meet the community's most urgent needs and that truly improve people's lives. "United Way is at the crossroads of our community," says Michael J. McLarney, president and CEO of United Way of the Midlands. "It starts with a thoughtful and thorough examination of local human issues. We work with a variety of partners to develop shared community strategies to address those issues, and then we measure the results. The ultimate goal is to make human services make sense."

United Way helps people find meaningful volunteer projects all year long. Employees of HDR and their families, for instance, give up a Saturday morning to help sort items in a homeless shelter's warehouse. If you'd like to start volunteering, call 342-LINK. ■

"United Way is a catalyst in strategic planning, ensuring social service programs that meet the community's most urgent needs and that truly improve people's lives."

One of the most entertaining exhibits at Omaha's Henry Doorly Zoo is the Hubbard Gorilla Valley, where the gorillas roam free and the visitors are captive. As people traverse this summer habitat through a window-lined tunnel, they can stop at enrichment stations where they interact with the gorillas in games such as pat-a-cake, tug-of-war, and wheel-spinning. The gorilla exhibit, as well as the breeding and research program, distinguishes the zoo as a leader in gorilla conservation!

"I love taking my grandchildren and our out-of-town guests to our zoo. No matter whether we sit and watch the penguins, an orangutan being bottle fed in the nursery, or sharks swimming overhead, the kids go home with good stories to pass along."

Kathy Menke, assistant university dean

Photo by Dennis Keim

Ensuring Qwest quality—
one customer at a time. ■

Photo by Dennis Keim

Creating a Cutting Edge
In the Middle of America

With a presence in Omaha that goes back 125 years, Qwest® has played an integral role in keeping the state of Nebraska on the cutting edge of telecommunications technology, while actively supporting numerous community service activities and organizations across the state.

As the largest telephone company in Nebraska, Qwest engages a statewide workforce of over seventeen hundred people. These professionals ensure service to more than eighty communities in Nebraska, and to various Qwest company-wide operations as well.

While Qwest is a leading provider of high-speed Internet, local and long-distance phone service, and wireless and broadband voice services, the company never forgets that behind the latest technologies are real people with real needs. They deliver the latest technology to millions of people at work, at home, and on the move in Nebraska—and in thirteen other states across the West and Midwest— as well as nationwide.

Qwest solutions keep business and businesspeople on the move. ■

Photo by Dennis Keim

Nebraska's telecommunications infrastructure utilizes Qwest's backbone network to provide very high-speed connectivity throughout the state. Additionally, Nebraska became the first state to receive nationwide and long-haul facilities, to establish WATS-line services and to deregulate telecommunications.

Through the years, Qwest technology has helped the state become a world leader in telemarketing, telehealth, and distance learning services. Qwest technology is also integral to the complex communications system at USSTRATCOM at Offutt Air Force Base.

Qwest is as committed to serving the people and community as it is to delivering the latest technology. Through the Qwest Foundation, the company promotes its core principle: to invest in people and communities today for a better world tomorrow. The primary function of the Foundation is to award grants to community-based programs that generate high-impact and measurable results, focusing on K-12 educational programs and economic development initiatives.

Likewise, the Qwest Pioneers work on projects that directly support their local communities. In Nebraska, Chapter 19 of the Pioneers comprises thirty-five hundred employees and retirees divided among six councils, including two in Omaha. These dedicated men and women lend their time and talents to such efforts as the Special Olympics, Habitat for Humanity, Ronald McDonald House, and Hug-A-Bears. They also have participated in the annual paint-a-thon that helps needy families renew their homes, and initiated cleanup and development projects at many of the state's parks and outdoor areas, including Fontenelle Forest and Ponca State Park.

No matter what may change in the industry, Qwest will always keep these principles at the forefront. So, too, do its employees pledge to create value through enterprising action; to maintain discipline and focus; to work with

Qwest is as committed to serving the people and community as it is to delivering the latest technology.

Continued on page 424

Photo by Dennis Keim

Continued from page 423

Qwest is real people serving real people's communications needs. ■

integrity and honesty; to seek out and encourage a diversity of contributions; to anticipate and meet the needs of customers and shareholders; and to work to always improve the future. Together, these corporate values make up Qwest's distinctive Spirit of Service in Action™.

When it comes to serving the needs of customers throughout Nebraska, Qwest has distinguished itself as more than just a telecommunications company. It has become a partner that can be relied on to provide exemplary products and services as well as invaluable community service, and to support the kind of entrepreneurship that has kept Nebraska at the cutting edge of the communications industry. ■

Photo by Dennis Keim

Communications solutions that work—for your life. ■

Photo by Mark Romesser

Harry Potter fans arrived in full regalia when the Bookworm bookstore held a big party to celebrate the release of *"Harry Potter and the Half-Blood Prince."* The festivities began at 10 p.m. with all sorts of fun activities and ended at midnight as fans lined up to purchase their copies. The Bookworm children's department manager, Ellen Scott, was wowed by the reception. "We expected three hundred people; close to four hundred showed up," she reports. Locally owned and operated by Beth and Phil Black, the Bookworm hosts promotions, readings, discussions, or book signings on a monthly basis. O!

Photo by Mark Romesser

Photo by Eric Francis

Photo by Eric Francis

From the Arapaho to the Ponca to the Winnebago, Nebraska has been home to many Native American tribes. The Omaha Indians, whose name means "upstream people" or "those going against the current," inhabited the area when Lewis & Clark first visited. So it's fitting that each year the Fontenelle Nature Association celebrates the culture and heritage during the Native American Music Festival. Pictured here, the distinguished, award-winning band Brulé performs contemporary Native American music, accompanied by dancers in splendid native dress. Brulé is one of the top-selling Native American recording groups, boasting more than 1 million CDs sold worldwide. Brulé has a tremendous fan base in Omaha and performs at events in the city several times a year, including the Summer Arts Festival downtown. O!

Westside High School students use laptop computers to review their French language lessons. In 2005, Westside Community Schools provided all high school students with this technology to enhance the learning that takes place in the classroom. ■

Westside Community Schools

E ducation at Westside Community Schools is an experience rooted in both community and innovation. "When you think of Westside, the first word that comes to mind is 'family,'" says superintendent Kenneth M. Bird, Ed.D. "New families joining our district become part of a bigger family, one that is dedicated to the nurturing of its children and that is willing to invest in the betterment of educational opportunities."

In fact, the desire to provide for an excellent education was the basis for merging existing districts in 1947 to form School District 66, later known as Westside Community Schools.

Since then, Westside has held true to its mission to ensure academic excellence and to serve the unique needs of all learners. As a result, the district now serves a preK-12 population of some six thousand students attending ten elementary schools, one middle school, and one high school.

Westside's innovations begin even before elementary school, with early childhood centers that offer comprehensive, nationally accredited programs for toddlers and preschoolers. At the elementary level,

Westside Community Schools superintendent Ken Bird spends time with kindergartners at Rockbrook Elementary. The school district's family-centered environment and commitment to quality, innovative education promote learning even before children reach this age of development. ■

Photo by Jackson Hill

Photo by Jackson Hill

"When you think of Westside, the first word that comes to mind is 'family,'" says superintendent Kenneth M. Bird, Ed.D.

Westside offers a well-rounded education that incorporates hands-on classroom activities. Spanish language instruction begins in kindergarten and is integral to the district's multicultural educational experience.

Westside Middle School, a National Blue Ribbon school, provides a nurturing transition to high school through programs like goal-setting in daily homeroom, club activities for every student, two-year language courses, exploratory laboratory work in the sciences, and PowerSchool that links classroom to home.

Technology is also a key component to Westside High School learning, where a performance-based focus instills a sense of personal responsibility. In addition to the school's student information system and a fully wireless building, students use laptop computers as a tool for learning. This school is especially noted for quality initiatives like modular scheduling, which tailors classroom scheduling to student needs.

Such visionary direction is made possible by the support of the Westside community. "Fundamentally, it starts with our board of education, whose desire is to offer the highest-quality, most innovative programs possible," says Bird, adding that empowering some of the state's most highly educated teachers also enhances the district's capabilities. "In addition, we believe in giving our teachers the freedom to develop new and exciting ways to engage students in learning."

Furthermore, says Bird, community interest is a key component to the district's success, and indeed the future of the district relies on the future of the community. "Our size allows us to give parents a voice, and in return, parents show their tremendous pride in their kids' education through active involvement in our schools. We know their support strengthens our schools and, in turn, makes our community a preferred neighborhood in which to live." ■

FALL means FOOTBALL!

Whether it's the University of Nebraska at Omaha Mavericks or the UNL Cornhuskers a bit farther south in our capital city of Lincoln, Omahans love football. Saturdays start with tailgate parties in the morning and last until the scoreboard lights have gone cold that night. Nebraskans adore the football experience, from the heart-stopping action on the field, to the bands, to the cheerleaders. Once we're all hoarse from yelling "Go Mavs!" or "Go Big Red!" all day, it's time to rest up—until next Saturday. **O!**

Omaha Public
Power District

D ay-to-day, it's easy for consumers and businesses to take for granted the electricity that powers their lives and their operations. That's because Omaha Public Power District does not. The utility takes its role as the energy partner for this community seriously, and in so doing it has earned a steadfast reputation for dependability and value.

"At OPPD, we're committed to helping our customers succeed by providing affordable and reliable power and professional energy services," says W. Gary Gates, president and chief executive officer. "We serve more customers at retail than any other electric utility in Nebraska, and in these changing times we know that customers expect more from their energy provider." OPPD focuses on understanding customer needs today and anticipates them for the future, and then works hard to meet those needs through strong strategic planning, solid financial management, and aggressive maintenance programs. As a result, even when

OPPD's Arboretum attracts many visitors, such as this local Girl Scout troop, and teaches the public about trees and power lines. ■

Photo by Thomas S. England

"At OPPD, we're committed to helping our customers succeed by providing affordable and reliable power and professional energy services."

customers utilize record amounts of power, OPPD power supply and delivery systems keep pace. Perhaps more importantly, customer satisfaction remains high, as evidenced by successive years of awards by J. D. Power and Associates.

Established in 1946 as a business-managed utility, OPPD's publicly elected board of directors establishes policies and rates guided by an approach to business that emphasizes exceeding customer expectations. OPPD serves fifty-three communities and surrounding rural areas in thirteen southeast Nebraska counties. OPPD operates two coal-fired baseload generating facilities and one nuclear generating plant—a mix that results in both economy and a system reliability of more than 99 percent, even during Nebraska's adverse weather conditions. "While other energy costs are rising, OPPD has maintained rates that are well below the national average, and we will continue to focus on maintaining that cost advantage for our customers," adds Gates.

In addition to being one of the nation's best electric utility systems, OPPD provides a number of innovative energy-related services to help customers become more energy efficient. Residential customers can obtain energy advice, payment protection insurance, and whole-house surge protection from OPPD, as well as streamline their bill-paying through automatic bill payment, or e-bills. Larger commercial customers can choose from a myriad of products and services all designed to help save energy, money, and time.

In addition, the utility continually looks for ways to help the area's economy prosper. Recently, OPPD played a vital supporting role in the development and revitalization of the city of Omaha's riverfront and downtown, with its personnel working behind the scenes in a complex job to orchestrate the coordination of all electrical services. For the Qwest Center Omaha, the area's high-tech arena and convention center, OPPD professionals logged approximately ten thousand hours of labor, installing hundreds of thousands

Continued on page 434

Photo by Eric Francis

Continued on page 433

of dollars of materials provided by the utility. OPPD also partners with rural communities, school districts, medical facilities, and individual businesses to help them evaluate and implement energy-efficient applications. By saving money on energy, these customers can focus on business.

Electricity is a vital component of modern life. It gives people the power to live, the power to grow, the power to heal, and the power to learn. OPPD fully understands its vital role in keeping Omaha and southeast Nebraska powered up safely, reliably, and affordably. "We value our customers and work hard to help them grow and add economic strength to our region. We enjoy the energy partnerships we've built in our communities and look forward to the opportunity to develop more," adds Gates. ▪

Through OPPD's Power Drive Program, Nebraska students design and construct safe, energy-efficient vehicles that they showcase during a series of rallies. This program provides an invaluable way for OPPD to invest in Nebraska's youth and our energy future. ▪

Even as one of the nation's largest publicly owned electric utilities, OPPD still keeps its promises: reliable energy delivered at the lowest reasonable cost, with customer service at the forefront. ▪

Photo by Joe Guerriero

Photo by Dennis Keim

Two of the city's top tourist attractions— Omaha's Henry Doorly Zoo and Rosenblatt Stadium, the home of the Omaha Royals AAA baseball team and the NCAA Men's College World Series—and their close proximity to Interstate 80 are clear in this aerial view. Tourism has a significant financial impact on Greater Omaha. According to the Nebraska Department of Economic development and the Travel Industry Association, visitors pump more than $1 billion annually into the local economy. And they go away happy, too. **O!**

"*The Qwest Center Omaha placing among the top ten arenas in the world for ticket sales gives the city a tremendous opportunity when it comes to the concert scene. Paul McCartney, U2, the Rolling Stones, all styles of music, all big-name acts, they're all playing Omaha. That's fantastic.*"

Robert Fulkerson, university instructor

Photo by Eric Francis

Photo by Eric Francis

Every Sunday, voices raised in praise can be heard emanating from Salem Baptist Church in north Omaha. The church has enjoyed a wonderful history within the city, beginning with its founding in 1922, in a building known as Father Wagnor's Church. Over the years, Salem Baptist changed locations to accommodate a growing congregation. It has been led by some renowned pastors, including Reverend J. C. Wade Sr., who directed the church for more than forty years before his retirement in 1987. Salem Baptist offers worship services, midweek prayer meetings, community outreach programs, and leadership, volunteer, prison, and mentoring ministries. All are based out of a beautiful Lake Street church that boasts a thirteen-hundred-seat sanctuary, classrooms, a nursery, and a fellowship hall. Here, parishioners celebrate the Easter season with a glorious service and stirring gospel choir performance. **O!**

Photo by Eric Francis

Grow Into the Person You Were Destined to Become

College of
Saint Mary

In the classroom at CSM, students learn in a supportive atmosphere that is technology-rich and spiritually nourishing.

Founded on the belief that a society's most productive endeavor is the education of its women, College of Saint Mary (CSM) provides an environment for learning that calls forth potential and fosters leadership. A Catholic college for women, CSM offers an education that is based upon a solid academic foundation and complemented by several distinctive programs. Among these are an elementary education major that begins hands-on teaching exposure in the sophomore year; a Distinguished Scholars program for juniors and seniors that includes real-life research with faculty members; virtual-reality clinical experiences in nursing and occupational therapy; and a separate residence hall for single mothers and their children.

In the classroom at CSM, students learn in a supportive atmosphere that is technology-rich and spiritually nourishing. The college augments its quality undergraduate and graduate programs with studies in music, theatre, and art; team participation in competitive intercollegiate sports; leadership certificates and experiences; and a myriad of community service activities.

Meanwhile, beyond the classroom, Omaha's five locally based Fortune 500 companies and other interests provide for real-world learning through a host of internship and job opportunities.

Such a well-rounded education has, since 1923, produced intelligent, questioning women who achieve success in their careers and aspirations.

Like its alumnae, College of Saint Mary is always reaching for new goals—milestones that will enhance its mission of inspiring women to be valuable, productive leaders in our world. ■

Vala's Pumpkin Patch

Photo by Eric Francis

A favorite outing for area school groups is a visit to Vala's Pumpkin Patch west of Omaha in Gretna, one of the region's fastest-growing communities. Established in 1983 by Tim and Jan Vala this pick-your-own operation is a working farm and a family fun spot. From the end of September to October 31, visitors can enjoy hayrides and music shows; visit with animals in the petting corral, Bunnyville, and Storybook Barn; watch the Pumpkin-Eating Dragon Show; celebrate the Halloween season with a tour through several haunted attractions; and, of course, pick their own pumpkins. Vala's is a popular spot for birthday parties, special events, and corporate gatherings. **O!**

Photo by Dennis Keim

This outstanding sculpture memorial on display at Heartland of America Park honors World War II veterans and the people who worked on the home front for the war effort. The work of world-renowned Omaha sculptor John Lajba, it depicts three different views of service: a young boy considering the call, a father returning to the arms of his children, and parents receiving a folded flag for a child who paid the ultimate sacrifice. The memorial's dedication was on Veteran's Day, November 11, 1997. **O!**

Photo by Doug Henderson

An evening on the Fremont Dinner Train's WWII USO Show is a "Sentimental Journey" back to the Golden Age of the 1940s. A delicious five-course meal is but one of the treats of the evening. While chugging along fifteen miles of track between Fremont and Hooper, guests enjoy the tunes made famous by Glenn Miller, Peggy Lee, the Andrew Sisters, and, of course, Frank Sinatra. USO-style entertainers dressed in period costumes entice guests to sing along, participate in skits, and compete for prizes. It's a swell time for all! **O!**

Photo by Thomas S. England

Springtime at the Gene Leahy Mall is a perfect time to feed a swan or introduce your youngest to the downtown park. The colorful blossoms provide the ideal backdrop to the soothing waterfalls and paths that meander through the mall. Children love the twin slides and sandy play area on the south side near the Old Market. Here's a tip: bring along a sheet or two of wax paper. They add speed to the trip down the slide. **O!**

Photo by Thomas S. England

SilverStone
Group

In order to thrive in today's business and financial environment, it's imperative to have the support of a partner skilled in eliminating risk, managing resources, and enhancing growth. For more than two thousand businesses and thirty-five hundred individuals, SilverStone Group is that partner.

Since its establishment in 1945, SilverStone Group has grown to become an industry leader in risk management, property and casualty insurance, employee and executive benefits, investment services, and human resources consulting. By adhering to the fundamentals of a service organization, SilverStone Group is able to provide unparalleled customer service, offered by knowledgeable, innovative professionals who are supported by the latest in cutting-edge technology.

Integrating backgrounds in law, actuarial science, insurance underwriting, loss control, accounting, financial services, and human resources, SilverStone Group's highly trained team of 170 associates ensures client success by first identifying and evaluating risk and need, and then implementing effective solutions.

Dedicated to the well-being of their associates, SilverStone Group provides complimentary fresh fruit, healthy snacks, diet soda, and Crystal Light in their newly remodeled lounge. Additionally, they participate in SimplyWell, an online program that promotes a healthy lifestyle. ■

Photo by David Gibb

Photo by David Gibb

"It's imperative to have the support of a partner skilled in eliminating risk, managing resources, and enhancing growth."

SilverStone Group provides additional services designed specifically for individuals and families to help protect and enhance assets through estate planning, investment and retirement counseling, personal insurance, and even family office services that coordinate and manage the intricacies of financial planning for widows, retirees, and beneficiaries.

With client focus as a top priority, SilverStone Group provides up-to-date information on legislation, compliance, and industry trends through the *SilverLink* magazine, special bulletins, e-link, and client seminars. The firm has invested in one of the most sophisticated Web sites in the industry; www.silverstonegroup.com houses more than 250 downloadable documents, forms, and links with products, tools, and resources designed both for businesses and individuals. Additionally, their state-of-the-art teleconferencing capabilities allow consultants to communicate with clients more effectively and efficiently, no matter their location.

As a result of their industry leadership, SilverStone Group is consistently ranked as the top broker in Omaha by *The Midlands Business Journal*, and among the top brokers in the nation by *Business Insurance Magazine*. And thanks in part to SilverStone Group's assistance, many of the firm's clients are recognized as tops in their own fields, ranking on *Fortune* magazine's 100 Best Companies to Work For, *Training* magazine's Top 100, and *Working Mothers'* Top 100 List, and as recipients of *Workforce* magazine's Optimas Award.

SilverStone Group is committed to the success of its clients as well as their community. Besides the firm's monetary donations, they have several associates who volunteer their time to numerous causes and organizations. SilverStone Group and its associates are proud of their dedication to making Omaha a better place to live, both for today and for the future. ■

Photo by Eric Francis

Photo by Eric Francis

Photo by Eric Francis

Excitement begins to brew each May as the Nebraska School Activities Association welcomes varsity soccer teams from around the state to participate in the highly anticipated Boys and Girls State Soccer Championships. Eight top-ranked teams vie for titles in the Class A and Class B divisions over a two-day period during the finals, pictured here, which take place at Creighton University's renowned Michael G. Morrison, S.J. Soccer Stadium. The five-thousand-seat stadium features a unique turf that is a mixture of sand, rubber, and fibers, designed in Amsterdam especially for the sport. It incorporated more than sixty thousand used automobile tires. The facility is the only field in the country with the turf. **O!**

Photo by Eric Francis

Gondolas in Omaha? Only at the Heartland of America Park, where Heartland Gondolas take visitors on a relaxing (and sometimes romantic) tour of the fifteen-acre lake. Too relaxed? Try visiting one of the city's Internet cafes with your friends, where you can move at the speed of sight. Or be truly adventurous and try both. Just keep telling yourself. I'm on a gondola. In Omaha. Really. Ciao, baby! O!

RELAXIN'

You look good, you play better, right? With indoor facilities and outdoor courts throughout Omaha, tennis is a year-round sport where annually more than one thousand children ages five through eighteen learn to play a sport that often comes much easier for the young. The skills these children will learn from the on-site tennis pros will continue to improve each year. Who knows? Perhaps a future Wimbledon champion will be an Omahan. O!

Photo by David Gibb

Photo by Doug Henderson

The
FIRM

Brenda Banks is one of those people who can't help but help others. Whether through her position at The FIRM, a mortgage brokerage company with a ten-year reputation for integrity and extraordinary customer service, or through her volunteer work with Angels on Wheels, a ministry to assist the city's homeless, Banks is happiest serving others. And The FIRM's principals, Bruce and Anne McClatchey, wouldn't want it any other way.

"We told Brenda that if she wanted to minister first and be an employee second, we were open to that," Anne explains. Banks, who already had a relationship with the McClatcheys as their corporate banker, knew she'd found the perfect employer, not only allowing but also encouraging her to work a flexible schedule so she could pursue a degree in theology, as well as her volunteer outreach efforts.

The FIRM's Brenda Banks knows all about giving back to the community. The Angels on Wheels programs is just one of several ministries she's involved with. Angels on Wheels goes out on the streets and offers a meal, and a place to just sit and talk for those less fortunate who may also be homeless. "It's a chance for them to get away for a little while from their difficult circumstances," says Banks. ▪

Photo by Doug Henderson

Purchasing a home is one of the biggest decisions a person makes, and finding the right mortgage is part of the process. The FIRM's expertise in the mortgage industry, combined with a commitment to personal service, makes the process efficient and pleasant. ▪

The husband-and-wife team are mortgage-lending experts who understand far more than the ever-changing world of their industry.

That's the kind of people the McClatcheys are: people who draw on their faith to form the foundation for The FIRM. Following basic religious tenets—honesty and trust—the husband-and-wife team are mortgage-lending experts who understand far more than the ever-changing world of their industry. They understand that most people are unfamiliar with the myriad financing options and naturally depend on their mortgage brokers to guide them in the right direction. "Bruce and Anne always take the time to answer questions and make sure you understand," says client Jay West. "They simplify the process."

West adds, "The FIRM has a unique way of doing business. It's almost old-fashioned, in the sense that they are truly in business to serve the customer." For example, The FIRM's loan originators will often go to the borrower's home or office to assist with the loan application paperwork. In addition, many appointments are held in the evenings and on weekends when most people have more time to focus on the complexities of a mortgage decision. "When the kids are in bed, they can focus on what they're doing, and often a client is more relaxed in their own environment, able to think and assess the data more clearly," says Bruce. "They are trusting us to help them make the right decision, and we want them to be as educated as possible. We truly believe that it is optimal for the borrower to be active in the loan process," he adds.

As one of the original mortgage brokers in Omaha, The FIRM has stayed true to its acronym: First Independent Residential Mortgage. From construction loans to traditional thirty-year fixed loans, to creative lending products like nonconforming loans and adjustable-rate mortgages, The FIRM can tap into any number of options for borrowers because they are independent. As Bruce points out, "It's our responsibility to know what's out there, to get the best price and the best product for that customer. That's what sets us apart." ▪

O! Christmas Tree...

Photo by Eric Francis

Photo by Eric Francis

Few things light up a child's face with wonder like the sight of a gaily decorated Christmas tree. And there's no better— or bigger—yuletide evergreen in Omaha than the Great Christmas Tree at Durham Western Heritage Museum. Standing between forty and sixty feet tall, the live tree is adorned with thousands of twinkling lights and shiny ornaments. It is introduced to local residents during a special tree-lighting ceremony at the end of November, complete with holiday musical performances, kids' activities, a visit from Santa and Mrs. Claus, and a traditional countdown. Every weekend in December, live entertainment welcomes visitors as they stand in awe of the magnificent tree. **O!**

The numerous properties represented by Prudential Ambassador Real Estate are some of the most sought-after homes in Omaha. In fact, residences like the one pictured here not only boast stylish interiors and exteriors, but also provide exceptional locations for interested buyers. This well-built executive home is situated in a centrally located, established neighborhood close to all of the amenities Omaha has to offer. ■

Prudential Ambassador
Real Estate

For a real estate company to succeed, it must project a sense of professionalism, trust, aptitude, and genuine concern for its clients' well-being. For that company to rise to the next level and stand out in the marketplace, it must also be progressive—taking advantage of unique opportunities while staying on the cutting edge of the real estate business. Without a doubt, Prudential Ambassador Real Estate is a brokerage company that stands out.

Since its establishment in 1984, the family-owned company has served buyers and sellers throughout metropolitan Omaha with top-notch residential real estate services. The brainchild of Realtor Carol Leisey, it has grown steadily over the years, attracting over two hundred agents and an impressive inventory of both clients and home listings. Now helmed by Carol's son, Vince Leisey, the company has expanded to include some significant niches in the local market.

Photo by Doug Henderson

Photo by Doug Henderson

"We believe that Omaha is in its infant stages of urban revitalization, and we're on the forefront of that," explains Vince Leisey, president. Recognizing the outstanding potential for growth in downtown and midtown Omaha, Prudential Ambassador Real Estate embraced the condo and loft living market. With eleven initial projects, including the renovation of properties like the historic Beebe Runyan and Brandeis buildings, the company added more than five hundred units to its listings in a very short amount of time and has become the leading brokerage firm in this area.

Of course, Prudential Ambassador Real Estate has adopted other ventures as well. For Leisey, corporate relocation has become one of the company's principal services, thanks in part to Ambassador Real Estate's affiliation with Prudential in 1991. The corporate relocation department has been so successful, in fact, that Katie Adams, corporate relocation director, won Prudential's 2004 National Relocation Director of the Year award. "I think it's a great tribute to her efforts—and to our company and the time and energy that we spend on growing that business," Leisey observes.

Leisey also has praise for the company's skilled agents, for they are in the field every day supporting the company's goals. "We really see our agents as our clients," he asserts. "Our philosophy is that we need to be there to support our agents and give them the tools they need so they can be more successful." That's why the company maintains a close-knit single office location that boasts a casual atmosphere marked by high enthusiasm, as well as numerous educational and professional resources for its agents. Providing this enriching environment is important because, as Leisey says, "We believe that our agents need to have knowledge, give good service, and be supportive of buyers and sellers to help them accomplish their goals."

Continued on page 454

"We believe that Omaha is in its infant stages of urban revitalization, and we're on the forefront of that," explains Vince Leisey, president.

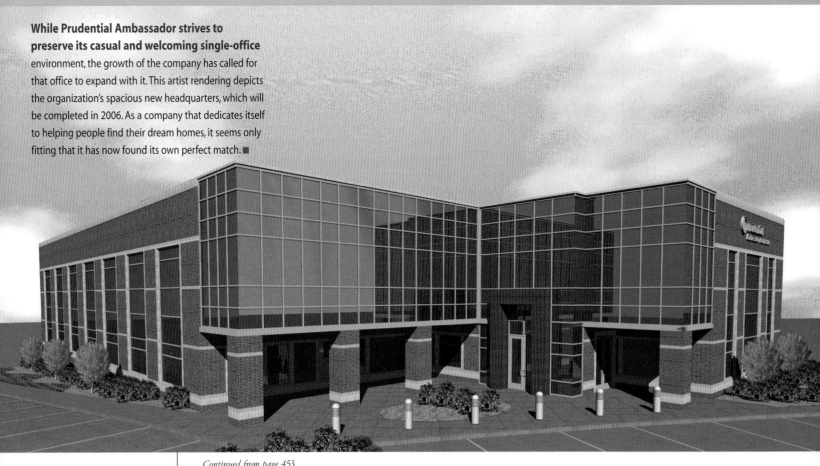

While Prudential Ambassador strives to preserve its casual and welcoming single-office environment, the growth of the company has called for that office to expand with it. This artist rendering depicts the organization's spacious new headquarters, which will be completed in 2006. As a company that dedicates itself to helping people find their dream homes, it seems only fitting that it has now found its own perfect match. ■

Continued from page 453

Supporting the local community also holds a special place in the hearts of everyone at Prudential Ambassador Real Estate. Once a month, Leisey and several agents serve food, clean dishes, and perform other tasks at the Open Door Mission homeless shelter. Additionally, the company participates in fundraising efforts for Sunshine Kids, an organization for children with cancer. The rewarding feeling Leisey and the agents receive from giving back rivals the excitement they sense when they consider Prudential Ambassador Real Estate's bright future, which includes a new thirty-two-thousand-square-foot office building for the team.

"My goal is not to be the biggest," Leisey admits, modestly. "My goal is to continue to slowly but steadily grow our business and give our agents all the support and help they need to make sure they will have successful transactions." ■

Vince Leisey and the Prudential Ambassador team host a fundraising event every eighteen months to benefit the Sunshine Kids, an organization that provides positive group activities for children with cancer. From putt-putt golf and a silent auction to a huge cookout, the function raises thousands of dollars for the organization, with 100 percent of the proceeds going directly to the Sunshine Kids. Here, Leisey, center, shares the day with two support nurses from Children's Hospital and four Sunshine Kids. ■

Photo by Eric Francis

Winter in Omaha inspired the staff-written, seasonal production of *Snow*, by the first-graders of Catlin Arts Magnet School. The cast included nearly fifty students who sang and danced for their fellow students—grades kindergarten through six—and their parents. At the end of the performance, they chose audience members to join in the fun. **O!**

Photo by Thomas S. England

Justin Hapner, dance captain for the Broadway touring company of *Fiddler on the Roof*, spends the day teaching Camp Orpheum students one of *Fiddler's* song-and-dance sequences. Developed as an educational arts program by Omaha Performing Arts in collaboration with local and touring theatrical professionals, Camp Orpheum provides high school students with four days of intensive instruction in all aspects of professional musical theater. Students qualify to attend this yearly program via letters of recommendation and an audition, after which they undergo a combination of lectures and instruction in song, dance, and acting. **O!**

Omaha is experiencing condo fever, and many of the buildings that have been converted into condominiums are managed by Prudential Ambassador Real Estate. From downtown units including those at the Beebe Runyan and Brandeis buildings, to the Park Plaza Condos at 31st and Dodge Streets, west to Belle Meade at 147th and Maple Streets, the living spaces provide convenience, elegant sophistication, and breathtaking views. Prudential Ambassador Real Estate and its agents throughout metropolitan Omaha and surrounding areas are dedicated to providing progressive real estate services, including residential sales. O

OLD PLACES,

Photo by Doug Henderson

Downtown living is hot, and when the living space is coupled with an entertainment venue and conference center, as it is at the Tip Top Apartments and inPlay at 16th and Cuming Streets in the north downtown mixed use development, the unique combination is tough to match. The apartments at the Tip Top, once a factory for the Ford Model T, offer incredible views of the downtown skyline. The inPlay entertainment center provides interactive games, a sports bar with full restaurant, billiards, rock-climbing wall, miniature bowling, and accommodations for large group meetings/parties. Throughout downtown, former warehouses and other buildings are being converted to suit the tastes of a growing population and lifestyle. O!

NEW SPACES

Photo by Doug Henderson

Omaha Public
Schools

Diversity meets academic excellence in Omaha Public Schools (OPS), and the result is a school system that is one of the country's few major urban districts to consistently maintain a coveted AA accreditation, the highest level of recognition awarded from the Nebraska Department of Education.

With test scores exceeding the national average, and many National Merit Scholars, the Omaha Public Schools' remarkable statistics are just part of the story.

"Our goal is to provide all students with the high-quality instruction needed to prepare for life in tomorrow's high-tech world," says John J. Mackiel, superintendent. Equally as important, OPS students gain another vital life skill: the ability to work, evolve, and maneuver in today's diverse world. Public education advocate Susie Buffett, whose children are fifth-generation students of OPS, puts it another way. "As the world gets smaller and smaller, the kids who graduate from Central High, or any other OPS high school, walk out into the world and find it's simply a bigger version of their high school."

OPS's programs are also diverse. To effectively meet the multifaceted needs of the students and the community it serves, OPS has fifteen magnet schools, the largest special education program in the state, a wide array of enrichment programs for and talented students, as well as a unique and productive partnership program with businesses and community organizations. ■

Photo by Doug Henderson

The Special Olympics Nebraska is special in many ways. More than fifteen thousand athletes from across the state participate in the nine-event Summer Games in Omaha. But the fun doesn't stop there. Special Olympics is a year-round program representing nineteen sports. Participants train and compete on a local and regional basis throughout the year. The fun isn't restricted to kids, either. Special Olympics is open to all ages from eight on up. In the Omaha area, 45 percent of those competing are adults. Special Olympics relies entirely on donations and the work of four thousand dedicated Nebraska volunteers. O!

The timeless sophistication, style, and grace of Apollo's Country French original design is second to none. For over thirty years, Apollo craftsmen, some of the best in Omaha, have been designing and building such magnificent structures. ∎

Apollo Building
Corporation

For more than thirty years, Apollo Building Corporation has been helping Omahans build the homes of their dreams. Today, the company—led by owner and founder Terry Ficenec—is proud to have designed and constructed more than eight hundred single-family homes and villas in twenty-seven communities across the metro area.

"We build relationships before we build homes" has been the driving philosophy behind Apollo throughout the years. It's more than just a saying: it's a commitment every member of the Apollo team makes well before they break ground on a new project. They take the time to get to know their homeowners as people, not just customers. They ask plenty of questions and listen carefully to the answers.

"Our company truly cares about the people who live in our homes," says Ficenec. "Above anything else, we want to make sure they're pleased with not only with the end result, but with the process along the way."

Mature, natural landscaping with the added security and privacy of a gated community are all indicative of an Apollo-designed and-built neighborhood. Legacy Villas also offers a seven-acre pond and 8.6 miles of walking trails. ■

Photo by Mark Romesser

Photo by Mark Romesser

"Above anything else, we want to make sure they're pleased with not only with the end result, but with the process along the way."

In an industry that's seen builders come and go, a philosophy built on relationships gives Apollo homes lasting value. In fact, on more than one occasion, Apollo customers have asked the company to build their next home, and their next. It's common for homeowners to recommend the builder to their neighbors and their children.

Quality Down to Every Detail

The Apollo team prides itself on the little things that go into every home they build. From design to execution, the company uses only time-tested materials and products from names like Lennox, Whirlpool, Jacuzzi, Kohler, Delta, and Pella. They implement construction details that go beyond the basic—such as waterproof poured foundations and structurally sound, reinforced I-beam joists. And they work only with craftsmen who share their same dedication to detail.

"Our long-term relationships extend not only to our homeowners, but to those who help build our homes," Ficenec says. "Many of our craftsmen have been with us since the beginning."

To ensure that every detail is attended to, every Apollo project is assigned an on-site supervisor, Joe Hermanek, who has worked for Apollo since 1974. He tracks each phase of the project and communicates with the homeowner regularly. In addition, the homeowner receives a personalized notebook prepared by Ed Ficenec, filled with information on their product choices, from appliances and fixtures, to hardware and cabinetry, to wall coverings and flooring.

Creating Homes for Life

A firm believer that a home is much more than four walls and a foundation, the Apollo team aims to create designs that match the homeowner's lifestyle. Their custom homes include ranch-style villas for the empty-nester or senior, as well as high-end single-family homes for growing families.

Continued on page 462

Photo by Mark Romesser

Continued from page 461

Dennis Scharp, a Realtor who coordinates sales through CBSHome real estate company, says, "Our homes reflect the nuances of our customers' personalities."

Helping to coordinate all of the interior design work for Apollo is Charlotte Dann and Deb Monro of The Interior Design Firm. Their professional abilities are second to none and help homeowners achieve the style and class that are required and expected.

The end result? A home that's not only welcoming and aesthetically pleasing, but one that will also stand the test of time architecturally and structurally—and one that the homeowner can proudly say is an extension of their own style.

It doesn't end there. When the project is complete, Apollo stays true to its commitment of building a relationship for life. The company offers a comprehensive warranty after the sale and takes the time to follow up and ensure that the homeowner is completely satisfied. Judging from the growing number of Omahans who've chosen an Apollo-built home, that's a promise the company continues to live up to. ■

Because the kitchen is the heart of every home, Apollo takes great pride in the design and build of this particular room. Beyond the design and build, Apollo pays special attention to every detail in the room's cabinet, countertop, and appliance selections. Only time-tested materials and products are used on every Apollo home. ■

The gentle curving of the water's edge is tastefully accented by the framing artistry in an Apollo home. Blending nature into the home's architecture is a feature of many Apollo designs. ■

Photo by Mark Romesser

PULL!

That's the call heard over and over
on the Harry A. Koch Trap and Skeet
Range in Omaha. The range is only one of
three in the country that is owned by a
municipality. It's here in early spring that
high school students from all across
Nebraska compete at a regional trap
shooting competition. With a history dating
back more than one hundred years, the sport
of marksmanship is gaining in popularity,
and Nebraska has the largest youth program
in the country. O!

Photo by Eric Francis

Every village must have leadership, and Boys Town, Nebraska, is no exception—but with a unique twist. Incorporated in 1936, Boys Town comprises nine hundred acres of land, with seventy residential homes, providing treatment and care to nearly one thousand boys and girls annually. Most importantly, it is the only village in North America where every adult's job is to help abused, abandoned, and neglected children achieve success. Boys Town has its own fire and police departments, churches, schools, a farm, and a U.S. Post Office. Each year, in a good old-fashioned political process, the boys and girls of Boys Town elect one of their own to represent them as mayor. The candidates must be high school juniors who are also demonstrated leaders and role models. The Boys Town mayor is a key voice for children and children's issues. It's a position of importance and achievement for the individual selected as mayor, and a lesson in self-governance for all. Every mayor takes his or her job seriously, and a few have even gone on to lead a life in public service in cities and states across the country. **O!**

Boys Town

"He ain't heavy,
he's my brother."

"I have yet to find a single boy who wants to be bad," said the Rev. Edward Flanagan, who founded Father Flanagan's Boys' Home in 1917. Today, through its national headquarters in Omaha and at nineteen sites in fifteen states and the District of Columbia, Girls and Boys Town is a leader in the treatment and care of abused, abandoned, and neglected children. The Hall of History Museum at the Village of Boys Town in Omaha contains many scenes and items of interest reflecting the organization's long history. One cherished item is the Oscar won by Spencer Tracy for his portrayal of Father Flanagan in the movie *Boys Town* (1938). Through their National Resource and Training Center, Girls and Boys Town continues to "Change the way America cares for her children and families." **O!**

Photo by Rod Reilly

As dusk falls on Creighton University's modern urban campus, the well-manicured, verdant environment begins to glow from the inside out. Running the length of the campus is a beautifully landscaped brick-paved mall—a welcoming and relaxing pathway that leads to much of Creighton's 130 acres. ■

Creighton University

Creighton University president, Rev. John P. Schlegel, S.J., chats with students Ashley Delisi and Jon Aquino on the Creighton campus. Along with the faculty and staff, Rev. Schlegel strives to offer students outstanding academics in a faith-based setting. He says, "Our students come to know and love the special character of Jesuit education. Our unique approach to forming women and men for and with others permeates every aspect of a student's experience at Creighton." ∎

Photo by Dennis Keim

For Reverend John P. Schlegel, S.J., president of Creighton University, "There is a difference between getting a degree and getting an education." Undoubtedly, students who attend this prominent institution receive an unparalleled education. That's because Creighton, one of the nation's twenty-eight Jesuit Catholic universities, "is devoted to educating the whole person—caring for the mind, body, and spirit of each student."

This philosophy has been in place since the school's founding in 1878. When Mary Lucretia Creighton, widow of Omaha pioneer Edward Creighton, reserved one hundred thousand dollars in her will to establish a college in her husband's honor, her brother-in-law, John Creighton, along with her executors, followed her wishes. After purchasing land and erecting a school building, they donated the complex to the bishop of Omaha, who asked the Jesuits to operate the university. More than a century later, the Jesuit tradition is the foundation upon which Creighton University's endeavors have been built.

"The Jesuit and Catholic identity of Creighton remains the primary focus of the university," explains Schlegel. "It is our *raison d'être*. Without it, Creighton is just another independent institution of higher learning at the crossroads of America. Our mission springs from our identity as Jesuit and Catholic, and this identity is our greatest asset."

As an institution that takes pride in its diversity, Creighton at the same time emphasizes the following core values across the full spectrum of campus life: the inalienable worth of each individual, respect for all of God's creation, a special concern for the poor, and the promotion of justice.

Today, Creighton is a national leader in preparing students for responsible leadership, professional distinction, and committed citizenship. Creighton's sixty-eight hundred students are studying in more than fifty undergraduate majors in arts and sciences, business administration, and nursing, as well as graduate, law, medical, dental, pharmacy, physical therapy, and occupational therapy programs.

Student life is equally important on the Creighton campus. The list of available activities, from service clubs to Greek life, is extensive. Through these activities, says Schlegel, "our campus becomes a classroom with a mission, to help our students work together, embrace differences, reach out to others with greater needs than their own, while owning values that can truly transform the world."

Creighton's unique offerings have placed the school among the top universities in the nation. The school is consistently ranked number one in the *U.S. News & World Report* listing of Midwest comprehensive universities and has been cited for its outstanding opportunities for undergraduate research in the sciences. Additionally, *U.S. News & World Report* named Creighton a "best value," an institution where students get the best return on their tuition investment, and Creighton's freshman academic profile places it among the top five private universities in the Midwest and the top ten Catholic universities in the nation.

Continued on page 468

Creighton, one of the nation's twenty-eight Jesuit Catholic universities, "is devoted to educating the whole person—caring for the mind, body, and spirit of each student."

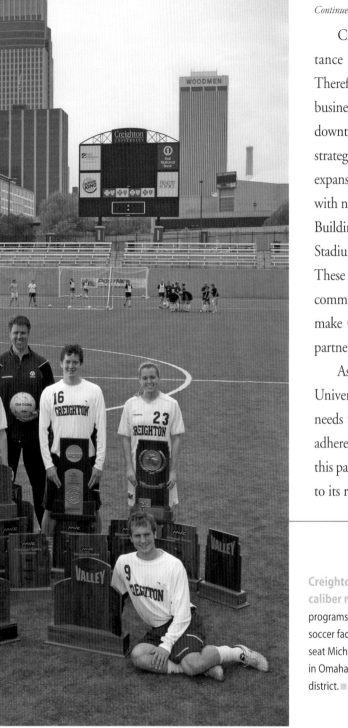

Continued from page 467

Creighton understands, as well, the importance of investing in Omaha's future. Therefore, the university has collaborated with business and community leaders to revitalize downtown Omaha. As part of Creighton's strategic plan, Project 125—the largest campus expansion in the university's history, complete with new facilities like the Hixson-Lied Science Building and the Michael G. Morrison, S.J. Stadium—is designed to enhance the city. These efforts, in addition to providing the community with a highly educated workforce, make Creighton one of Omaha's most valued partners.

As higher education evolves, Creighton University will continue meeting students' needs with academic excellence and a resolute adherence to its faith tradition. By following this path, the celebrated university will stay true to its roots as it heads boldly into the future. ■

Creighton University's championship-caliber men's and women's soccer programs play in one of the nation's top soccer facilities in the new five-thousand-seat Michael G. Morrison, S.J. Stadium, located in Omaha's vibrant, expanding downtown district. ■

Photo by Thomas S. England

Creighton professor and researcher Bernd Fritzsch, Ph.D., uses a special microscope to study the workings of the ear. Creighton scientists are looking to cure neurosensory hearing loss through the study of hair cells—the cells in the inner ear that perceive sound. ■

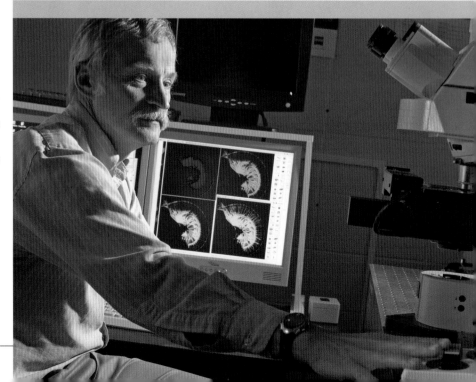

Photo by Mark Romesser

Visitors looking to enjoy a scenic adventure in the historic Old Market and along the riverfront should check into renting a quadracycle for the day from the River City Yacht Club at Miller's Landing. These unique covered bikes seat up to six people and provide an open-air ambience for touring the city. Here, the staff of the Greater Omaha Convention and Visitors Bureau swing by their own Visitors Information Center at 10th and Farnam Streets, where guests can pick up maps, ask directions, and receive information about Omaha's attractions, hotels, dining, and shopping destinations. **O!**

Greater Omaha Convention & Visitors Bureau executive director Dana Markel and Mayor Mike Fahey discuss the creative elements for a new advertising campaign. The strategy reinforces the need for members of the community to promote the city and help spur tourism and economic development in Omaha. **O!**

Photo by Eric Francis

Photo by Eric Francis

From fun interactive reading sessions, to finding a place to settle back with a good book or two, the nearly two dozen public libraries situated throughout Greater Omaha are a fine source for the latest in page-turning entertainment. Children and adults make great use of our local libraries and their collections of books, videos, and audio materials. How else could you travel from Alaska to Zanzibar and back in one day—and still be home in time for dinner? O!

O! What a Library

Photo by Eric Francis

Photo by Eric Francis

Making the most of nature's blueprint, the views outside are as much a part of the design of a Curt Hofer home as the features inside. The family's living environment can be as expansive as the landscape outside their windows. ■

Curt Hofer
Construction, Inc.

According to the song, "A dream is a wish your heart makes." Since 1990 Curt Hofer Construction, Inc., has been making heartfelt dreams come true. The company builds one-of-a-kind luxury homes, which begs the question, "How in the world do you continue to come up with one-of-a-kind ideas?"

President Curt Hofer instantly answers with a smile. "You just listen to the clients. Everybody's dream is different, so we let the client drive the process. Each person on our team pours their heart into designing and building these homes. However, in the end it's the client's wishes that matter, and when they see the final result, they immediately recognize their fingerprints all over it."

Of course, the basis of good construction is to build on a firm foundation. Hofer learned the business working in his father's construction company. Although he does not swing a hammer anymore—except on

Your dreams are worth having. Extraordinary attention contributes to the enjoyment of everyday living that is as lasting as the traditions a family will treasure for a lifetime. ▪

Photo by Dennis Keim

Photo by Dennis Keim

"Everybody's dream is different, so we let the client drive the process. Each person·on our team pours their heart into designing and building these homes."

a volunteer basis—he discovered he enjoyed every facet of construction. "I love seeing our team come together to create something that is bigger than any one of us. Each project is a total team effort."

Hofer introduced some of his key team members. "Marshall Wallman as director of design brings to life the dreams of the client with the creativity of our design team. He's got an amazing God-given talent." Craig Linnenbrink, vice president of construction, supervises all the day-to-day details, buffers issues for the client, and is responsible for the construction phase. "He makes it all happen for the client." Then there's vice president of operations Joshua Meyer. "He's the one behind the scenes who you may never meet, but you're glad he's there. He's the client's silent partner, and he adds a quiet sense of system and organization to an otherwise chaotic industry."

Stewardship is another vital part of the Curt Hofer way of doing business. "We build about fifteen homes a year in the half-a-million to six-million-dollar range. Needless to say, fiscal responsibility is important for our company and to our clients, who trust us in managing their money. We have a process that provides our clients with a clear understanding of the costs involved in building their home."

Management and accountability are extremely important. The company has a written system in place that acts as a safety net as well as creating a sense of well-being for their clients. "We consider our reputation and good name in the community a great honor and responsibility, so we're very protective of that."

When it comes to new products and new technologies, clients look to the Curt Hofer Construction team for advice on the best way to use what is being introduced to the market. "Often when a manufacturer wants to show off a new product for the high-end market, they come to us," explained Hofer. "We

Continued on page 474

Photo by Dennis Keim

Every person on the CHC team brings a unique set of skills. FRONT (l-r): Amy Hansen, Kristi Huber, Steve Huber, Curt Hofer, Joshua Meyer, Craig Linnenbrink. BACK (l-r): Tim Bialas, Jeff Hill, Marshall Wallman, Paul Logemann, Ron Schmidt, Nick Sila. ▪

Continued from page 473

have the ability to take the most recent innovations and newest products available to our clients and make them practical for everyday use."

This kind of constant attention to innovation balanced with a dedication to high standards has resulted in numerous awards. After a decade of head-to-head competition in the Omaha area, Curt Hofer Construction has quietly taken home the bulk of awards, ranging from People's Choice to Best Custom Builder to Best Overall. The company has also received significant recognition for its contribution to business by the Greater Omaha Chamber of Commerce.

Quality is a tangible feature. Although known for their use of the most recent innovations and newest products available, the Curt Hofer team is most proud of the centuries-old craftsmanship that produces a powerful impression that cannot be easily duplicated. ▪

Photo by Dennis Keim

Photo by Dennis Keim

At the heart of the company is a sense of responsibility, not only to their clients, but also to the community. Omaha Habitat for Humanity is a logical partner, according to Curt Hofer, with Nancy Hemesath, president and executive director. ■

"We are a relatively small company, and that's part of what keeps the work exciting. We're light on our feet, and we remain flexible so we can adapt readily to market conditions," Hofer explains.

A prime example is the creation of Castlewood Homes. "We knew there were people out there who thought, 'Gee, I wish I could afford a Curt Hofer home but . . . ,' so we created Castlewood Homes." The result is flexible plans and features in premium homes that Omaha previously has not enjoyed in the three-hundred-thousand-dollar-plus market. "We apply the same skill and expertise in Castlewood Homes that go into any Curt Hofer home." Clients can choose from featured plans, custom options, and architectural styles to make each home truly theirs.

It is not unusual to describe a construction company in terms of brick and mortar, but with Curt Hofer Construction the description would also have to include words like care, understanding, respect and responsibility. "This is a very personal business," said Hofer. "There's just no other way to approach it." ■

You're welcome. As warm and inviting as a home that has nurtured generations, Curt Hofer homes are noted for their welcoming entries that lead visitors into the heart of the home—made comfortable with all the conveniences of modern living. ■

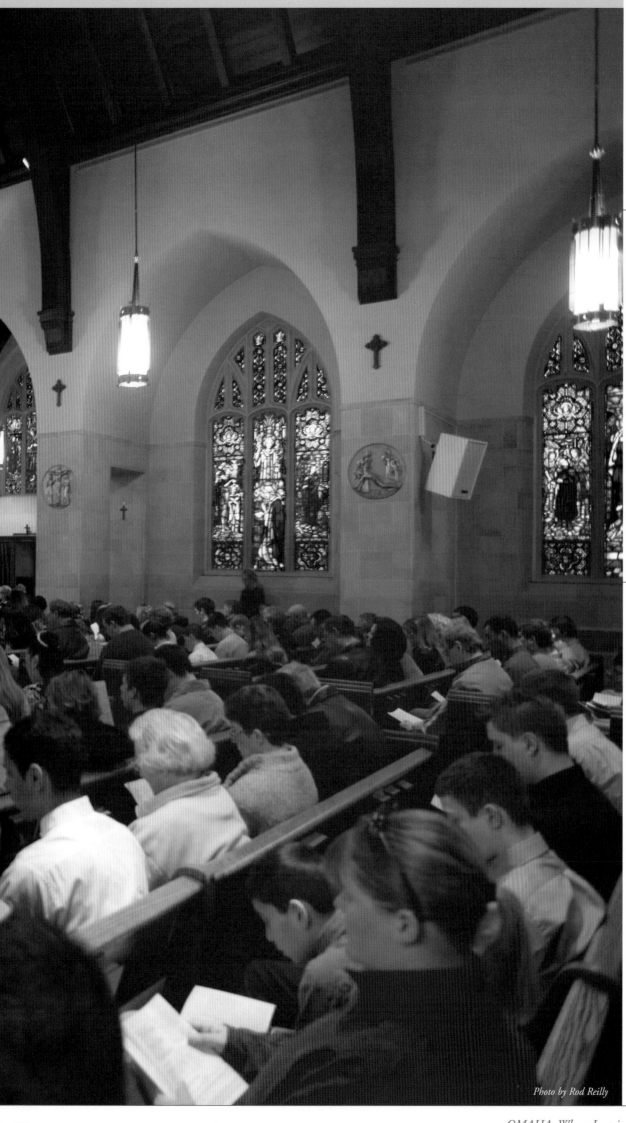

Photo by Rod Reilly

Spirituality is a way of life in the care of children at Girls and Boys Town. Two chapels, one Catholic (shown), and one Protestant, are part of the campus of the nonprofit, nonsectarian direct-care children's organization founded in 1917. Residential growth in west Omaha, in the areas surrounding Boys Town and beyond, has prompted the construction of many new churches, and the expansion of existing places of worship representing all faiths. **O!**

C&A Industries, Inc.

Aureus Medical Group, Aureus Group, AurStaff, Celebrity Staffing

People. They are the driving force in today's fast-paced, ever-changing business environment. To stay competitive, companies across all industries must identify, recruit, and employ the best people in the marketplace—people who are highly skilled and trained, people who have a strong work ethic and are as dependable as they are talented. Fortunately for corporations nationwide, there is a resource that specializes in finding these unique individuals: C&A Industries, Inc.

When Larry J. Courtnage founded C&A Industries in 1969 after receiving an engineering degree from the University of Nebraska–Lincoln, he wanted to create a recruitment firm that worked as a true extension of its customers' human resources departments and focused on specialization. Drawing on his educational background, Courtnage initially concentrated on helping firms throughout the Midwest locate knowledgeable and experienced engineers and architects. It did not take long, however, for this one-man executive search firm to grow by leaps and bounds, branching out into other areas of specialization.

Photo by Doug Henderson

The road to success. CEOs Larry Courtnage and Kathy Wolf-Courtnage believe in the power of people, a philosophy on which C&A Industries is based. They set a philanthropic tone through their involvement with the Shriners and other community organizations. ◼

Photo by Dennis Keim

Today, C&A Industries encompasses six divisions, with each one addressing a different industry. To start, **Aureus Medical Group**, which ranks among the top ten health-care staffing firms nationally, recruits and places health-care professionals in nursing and allied health positions at top hospitals nationwide. **Aureus Finance & Accounting** focuses on accounting and finance professionals, **Aureus Executive** provides interim and full-time executives, and **Aureus Systems** works with information systems and information technology professionals. **AurStaff** provides light industrial professionals, while **Celebrity Staffing** helps clients find administrative, office support, and managerial professionals. Nonstaffing areas include **AurTravel**, a full-service travel agency, and **AurHomes**, providing corporate housing services.

"Knowledge is power, and it provides consistent and quality service delivery. Our specialization enables us to effectively and efficiently train our internal employees so they are best able to interface with customers at their level," explains Courtnage.

Each internal employee hired by C&A Industries participates in an intense in-house training program through Aureus University, the company's state-of-the-art education and career development facility. Corporate clients appreciate this effort, as well as C&A Industries' flexible staffing options. In addition to project staffing, Direct-Hire, and Managed Services, the firm was the first to introduce Match Hire®, an innovative staffing solution in which contract employees work for a trial period before accepting full-time employment. And, thanks to Courtnage's dedication to staying on the technological cutting edge, C&A Industries was among the first Omaha-based companies to computerize in the early 1980s and continues to implement today's most sophisticated systems.

Continued on page 480

Photo by Thomas S. England

The Aureus Medical Plaza at Lakeside, built in 2002, houses Aureus Medical's Nursing branch, Celebrity Staffing, Aureus University, and Corporate Human Resources. C&A Industries is experiencing tremendous growth, particularly in the health-care staffing arena. ■

Continued from page 479

"We want every customer working with our firm to feel confident that we consistently provide the highest possible level of service. We're a company that's committed to our people—giving them the tools they need to succeed and to develop their careers with us. The stronger our employees are, the better they are able to deliver to our customers," Courtnage asserts.

With four hundred internal employees and more than four thousand contractors working in all fifty states, C&A Industries has proven the power of this philosophy. In fact, C&A Industries is among the top one hundred staffing firms in the nation and has twice been named to the Greater Omaha Chamber of Commerce's list of Fastest Growing Companies. Furthermore, the company received the Chamber's Sustained Excellence Award in 2003 and has been recognized for four consecutive years by *Inc.* magazine on its list of the nation's top five hundred fastest-growing privately held companies.

Photo by Thomas S. England

Monica Fuehrer of Celebrity Staffing meets with Jonathon White to discuss career opportunities available with a variety of clients. Celebrity Staffing is a leading provider of administrative, office support, and managerial personnel in Omaha. ■

This level of success has encouraged Courtnage and his team to give back to the community. Career Outreach, founded by Courtnage, is a nonprofit organization that provides counseling and seminars to individuals, including high school students, working to improve their employment situation as they strive to increase their skills and make a better life. The Kim Foundation, also founded by Courtnage, provides support to organizations that serve individuals with mental illnesses, their caregivers, and their families. The Kim Foundation works to break down the stigma associated with mental illness and provide valuable resources to mental health consumers and the community.

The company also supports organizations such as the United Way, the Multiple Sclerosis Society, the American Heart Association, Habitat for Humanity, local homeless shelters, and many more.

Courtnage proudly calls Omaha C&A Industries' corporate home. Yet he keeps his eye on the big picture and always looks for opportunities to expand and grow—to identify customers in new niches, introduce them to his firm's superior human capital management services, and let them relish the experience of finding the perfect employee to fit their needs.

He says, "Staffing is an investment. It is for any company or organization. Our customers want the assurance that they are receiving the best possible return, and we're consistently able to deliver that." ■

Photo by Doug Henderson

The company's philanthropic efforts through the Kim Foundation include support of Children's Respite Care Center and their new behavioral health program. CRCC provides specialized services for children with special needs, including therapy, education, and parental support. ■

C&A Industries is dedicated to giving their employees the tools they need to be successful. Each new corporate employee participates in an extensive training program and receives continued professional development through their in-house facility, Aureus University. ■

You may now kiss the bride—again! One of Omaha's many outdoor venues that are perfect for a wedding ceremony is Mt. Vernon Gardens, with its colorful flower gardens and formal rose garden. One of the most popular areas at Mt. Vernon Gardens for ceremonies, and for after-wedding photographs, is the long, narrow portico that overlooks the Missouri River. **O!**

Photo by Eric Francis

NP Dodge
Real Estate

NP Dodge is one of the oldest real estate companies in the United States. They have been in business since 1855. Today the company is led by the fourth generation of the Dodge family. The executive management team in the corporate conference room include Nate Dodge, Leslie Delperdang, N.P. Dodge Jr., Jan Kratky, and Kate Dodge, plus (standing), Mike Riedmann, Bill Morrison, Randy Wilson, and Rick Cooper. ■

Since its beginning in 1855, NP Dodge Company has never been without a Nathan Phillips Dodge at the helm. It is the nation's only real estate company to be led by the same family for over 150 years.

What began as a tiny land office is now one of the largest full-service real estate companies in the region, providing services in residential real estate, land development, insurance, employee benefits, commercial real estate, property management, global relocation services, and title services.

NP Dodge is proud to be based in Omaha. The company and its thriving home base have come a long way together. NP Dodge is poised to continue growing with, and supporting, the metro area. Five generations of Dodges have enthusiastically and generously served the community through a variety of civic and charitable organizations. NP Dodge is the classic American success story. It is a family-owned company that continues to succeed in the modern business world because it remains committed to principles established a century and a half ago: integrity, perseverance, innovation, and confidence in the future. ■

It is the nation's only real estate company to be led
by the same family for over 150 years.

Photo by Alan S. Weiner

When an addition to the Werner Enterprises corporate offices was being built, founder C. L. Werner wanted something unique for the entryway. His search led him to commission artist Tom Palmerton of Brownville, Nebraska, to produce a fabulous bronze sculpture titled, *Running Free*. The work is one-of-a-kind, as the mold was broken at completion of the project in 1999. The Werner construction department assisted in building the pond with the rocks and flowing fountain. Palmerton's work can also be enjoyed at the "Garden of the Senses" at Omaha's Henry Doorly Zoo. **O!**

Sitting atop one of Omaha's highest points, the twin spires of St. Cecilia Cathedral are a landmark by day and night. The beautiful edifice is the work of legendary American architect Thomas Rogers Kimball, who designed the church in the Spanish Renaissance Revival style, something not often seen in the United States when construction began on the cathedral in 1905. Upon its completion in 1916, the building was recognized as one of the ten largest cathedrals in the country at the time, standing 222 feet high.

Photo by David Gibb

St. Cecilia Cathedral serves as the "bishop's church" for the Archdiocese of Omaha and as a parish for more than sixteen hundred families who meet to worship and participate in many community-based programs. The parish includes St. Cecilia Cathedral Elementary School and a retreat center. In recent years, the century-old cathedral, which is listed on the National Register of Historic Places and is situated in a National Register Historic District, underwent an extensive restoration—a process that has brought the church back to its original glory, from the splendid Pasi organ to the stunning interior ceiling. **O!**

Photo by David Gibb

Photo by David Gibb

Metro Omaha
Builders Association

O maha is a vibrant city, a place where businesses thrive and where families enjoy friendly neighbor-hoods and quality, affordable housing. Amid this vitality is the Metro Omaha Builders Association (MOBA), an organization whose primary purpose is to make sure that productive growth continues in the area.

For a membership of close to seven hundred business firms that encompass builders, developers, remodelers, subcontractors, and suppliers, as well as people in banking and finance, MOBA proactively lobbies for affordable housing and less regulation in the industry. While seeing record home building numbers in recent years, escalating costs of materials, labor, and fees continue to threaten the industry. In this environment, MOBA works on local, state, and national levels to ensure that its members can continue to do business.

MOBA also provides value for its members through events that inform the public of the benefits, value, and availability of new home ownership. In addition, MOBA offers its members opportunities to enhance

Street of Dreams, held annually in July, showcases the premier builders in the Metro Omaha Builders Association and features a new development each year. The exciting event draws in excess of thirty thousand attendees who come to see the latest in architectural design, interiors, energy efficiency, and technology. ■

Photo by Eric Francis

MOBA proactively lobbies for affordable housing and less regulation in the industry.

Metro Omaha Builders Association hosts the "Omaha Home and Builders Show" each March, drawing over sixteen thousand attendees and more than five hundred exhibitors. This show attracts consumers from a five-state area who are looking to build, remodel, or improve an existing home. ■

Photo by David Gibb

their professionalism through ongoing communication as well as a host of programs and educational offerings.

Because MOBA knows that it takes more than quality homes to create a quality community, the organization contributes to the welfare of the public through a full scope of service-oriented projects.

For instance, in an effort to pave the way for new generations of industry professionals, MOBA places great emphasis on activities that encourage interest in future builders.

Among its work in this arena is the annual granting of numerous scholarships to metro-area high school students, a tradition that recently celebrated its half-century mark.

One of the scholarships awarded each year goes to an outstanding student from each school who participates in "Builders of the Future," another MOBA program, in which area high schoolers build playhouses within their classroom setting. MOBA and its members cover the cost of materials and mentor students through the construction of these structures, which are sold by the high school, for its own benefit, upon completion.

Reaching out to even younger generations, the MOBA Women's Council coordinates the "Homes of Our Own/Tommy Tree" program, in which volunteers deliver over twenty-six hundred trees annually and speak to third-grade students around the area about energy and resource conservation. This program, began in 1993, and has been adopted by the National Association of Home Builders.

Every year, residents enjoy showcases of the work of area builders through MOBA's springtime events—the Omaha Home and Builders Show, the Remodel Omaha Tour, and the Spring and Fall Parade of Homes—while summertime brings the organization's premier show, the Street of Dreams. All of these events are accompanied by beautiful four-color publications, among which is Distinctive Homes Magazine, winner of the Pinnacle Gold Award of Excellence for Communication in Small Business.

Like its community, the Metro Omaha Builders Association is a thriving entity, a group firmly fixed on building an even better tomorrow. ■

On May 25, 2005, as part of his historic tour of the United States, the president of Afghanistan, Hamid Karzai, visited the University of Nebraska at Omaha to receive an honorary doctorate degree bestowed upon him by UNO chancellor Nancy Belck in recognition of his national and international endeavors for peace and democracy. While in Nebraska, President Karzai visited the UNO Center for Afghan Studies and agricultural facilities in Cuming County. O!

Photo by Eric Francis

Forget home ec and shop class. Omaha's Westside Middle School students have life labs instead. Way more fun. In addition to the old standbys of cooking and woodworking, students can explore an array of activities including engineering, robotics, technology, and consumer science skills. The philosophy is for middle school to provide a nurturing place between elementary and high school, a place to help students develop new interests. **O!**

Photo by Eric Francis

Werner
Enterprises

They are some of the most prominent vehicles on America's highways: gleaming blue, state-of-the-art tractor-trailers with "Werner" emblazoned in gold lettering on their fronts and sides. And looking at them today, it's hard to believe that the company they represent started off as little more than a truck and a dream.

The truck and the dream both belonged to one man: Nebraska native C. L. Werner, who in 1956 at the age of nineteen left his family farm to strike out on his own in Omaha. Using his 1953 Mercury as down payment on a new Ford truck, Werner took his first steps toward creating a business that provides personal, high-quality service to customers needing to transport their goods across the country.

Today, Werner Enterprises operates a fleet of eighty-seven hundred tractors and over twenty-three thousand trailers that each day safely and efficiently transport America's commodities. Manned by some of the most skilled drivers in the industry, their extensive reach throughout the forty-eight contiguous states and

In 1999, Werner completed a 166,500-square-foot addition to its Omaha headquarters. The expansion provides the Werner family of employees with comfortable drivers' lounges, a five-thousand-square-foot computer center, a company store and a full-service cafeteria.

portions of Canada and Mexico makes Werner one of the largest carriers in the industry. In addition to its headquarters in Omaha, Werner also supports twelve service terminals located throughout the country, terminals that not only provide access for drivers and equipment but which also serve as vital local employment opportunities.

Six fleet services provide customers of all kinds with a diverse range of hauling options, including cross-country, regional, and intrastate transport; flatbed hauling of raw building materials direct to construction sites; and temperature-controlled units carrying frozen goods, produce, and pharmaceuticals. And when it absolutely has to be there tomorrow, expedited service is available through Team Werner, a fleet service composed of two-driver teams capable of transporting their loads up to one thousand miles a day.

Since C. L. Werner first climbed into his truck fifty years ago, he has worked to create partnerships with his clients. Says company president and COO Greg Werner of his father's philosophy: "A partner is someone who says 'yes' when 'no' is an option. That goes both ways. A customer says 'yes' to Werner even though there are plenty of other truck options. Werner says 'yes' to the customer even though, at the time, Werner had more profitable freight options. So we have a consistent customer base regardless of market conditions. They know we will stick with them, and they will stick with us."

And customers know that not only is the service timely and cost effective, it's also some of the safest in the industry. At Werner, the only place you'll find old trucks is in the company's museum. In fact, the average Werner tractor age is 1.5 years, which results in greater fuel efficiency, lower maintenance costs, and better on-time service. Likewise Werner employs some of the best drivers in the industry, providing them with frequent, ongoing, comprehensive training and equipping them with every technological advantage available.

Continued on page 494

Since C. L. Werner first climbed into his truck fifty years ago, he has worked to create partnerships with his clients.

Continued from page 151

"Innovation and the ability to respond quickly to changing market conditions have kept us on the leading edge in the transportation industry," says Greg Werner. "Often we have recognized situations in the market and have reacted with new programs before others have even perceived the change."

Certainly, this was the case when, in June 1998, Werner became the first truckload carrier authorized by the Federal Highway Administration to implement state-of-the-art paperless logging. With this system, drivers no longer manually record their hours and activities. Instead, this information is transmitted automatically from the trucks using a Qualcomm™ GPS system. Freed from this time-consuming task,

Werner's team, shown here at the company's Fleet Support and Customer Service Center, keeps the company running like a well-oiled machine. As part of their duties, each dispatcher is responsible for sixty-five drivers, providing them with daily instructions, tracking their monthly mileage, and ensuring they meet their delivery and pick-up schedules in a timely fashion.

Werner's drivers are better able to concentrate on driving. Likewise, Werner has taken advantage of the latest technologies to enhance operations in system scheduling, data processing, and route optimization.

But perhaps the company's greatest strength lies in its ability to consistently attract and retain great people. Today, each member of Werner's fourteen-thousand-person-strong workforce works towards fulfilling the company's mission to economically exceed their customers' expectations through continuous quality improvement. How does one get a workforce of this size to work so well together? Perhaps because C. L. Werner still promotes and maintains the tight-knit, familial feeling of his company's early years.

By staying true to his founding principles of customer service, technological advancement, and top-notch workforce recruitment, C. L. Werner has grown his one-man, one-machine operation into a nationwide trucking empire that every day benefits millions of people across North America. ▪

The 2005 Classic Freightliner as it heads out on a run on the I-680 overpass. A timeless workhorse, the Classic Freightliner is built for efficiency and comfort, with an advanced lightweight design, roomy interior, high horsepower, and state-of-the-art suspension for a cushioned ride. ▪

Photo by Doug Henderson

From placing flower baskets on the distinctive lampposts to preserving and enhancing the landscape and architecture, the Dundee-Memorial Park Neighborhood Association has been an active example of what it takes to create pride in a neighborhood. As is true for neighborhood associations throughout the city, members realize that neighbor helping neighbor is the only way to form community. It's this kind of attitude and effort that sets Omaha apart. Here, the flowering plants outside Dundee Hardware are watered. Owned since 1989 by Steve and Karen Schrader, the hardware store has been a Dundee fixture since the 1940s. O!

The brick path of the Old Market Passageway invites visitors to step down into a delightful mix of historic architecture and the modern offerings of its distinctive shops. The Passageway's restaurants, boutiques, sculptures, artwork, and fresh flowers awash in natural sunlight create a warm comfort unique to the Old Market. Each visit yields a new discovery, making every trip seem like the first. **O!**

"The sign of a vibrant arts community is when you have resident artists who come here to learn, stay, and do their art—a lot of which is pretty avant-garde and cutting edge."

Austin Riley, architect

Truck Mountain in Blair holds around fifty-five hundred new and used vehicles and has become a point of pride for Woodhouse. It's not uncommon to find people pulled over to the side of the road taking pictures of it. ∎

Woodhouse
Automotive Family

A phone call. That's what started the team that Bob Woodhouse describes as "magical." Together, Bob Woodhouse and Lance Pittack found the secret to success, which resulted in several growing dealerships across the Omaha metropolitan area. Annually, they serve more than twenty thousand customers nationwide, and that number continues to grow. Currently the Woodhouse Auto Family has Ford, Chrysler-Dodge-Jeep, Mazda, Lincoln-Mercury, Nissan, and Porsche. They will continue to grow the franchises as opportunities arise.

"I think the difference between our dealership and others is our people," says Woodhouse. "We hire for a lifetime. It makes us proud to watch an employee develop and grow with us."

"We want to instill in our people that they're the ones who made it happen . . . because they have," says Pittack.

As a sign of respect, a Woodhouse customer isn't allowed to open the door. We're here to serve and to take care of you! ∎

Photo by Dennis Keim

"We want to be able to find a product at the most reasonable price and provide it in a way so the experience is pleasurable," says Pittack.

With many of their own family members working at the dealerships, Woodhouse and Pittack hoped to grow the business not only for them, but also for their larger family: the employees. "We believe in family," says Woodhouse. "That's why we say Woodhouse Auto Family, we're all family here."

Woodhouse and Pittack teamed up in 1995, after both spending the first part of their careers at separate automobile dealerships. "Even though Lance and I are different, I've never met a man in principle where we're so aligned," says Woodhouse. Their first business, a Ford dealership in Blair, soon expanded and grew into the family of dealerships that Omaha-area residents know today.

Their success can be attributed to some of their trademark principles. For instance, as a sign of respect, a Woodhouse customer isn't allowed to open the door. "You come to any of our stores, and you will never have to open a door," says Woodhouse. "This sets the tone for the entire experience. We're here to serve you, to take care of you."

Other forms of service are maintenance plans offered at a 25 percent discount over the manufacturer's, workshops for diesel owners, child safety seat instructions, and a Woodhouse credit card—where money goes towards the purchase of a new car or maintenance.

With one of the largest inventory selections in the nation, customers should be able to find what they're looking for with ease. If they can't, Woodhouse will locate it and have it available within twenty-four hours. "We sincerely appreciate the business we receive," says Woodhouse. "We don't want to lose a customer just because they've chosen a vehicle we don't happen to have on the lot."

"We want to be able to find a product at the most reasonable price and provide it in a way so the experience is pleasurable," says Pittack.

Continued on page 500

Photo by Dennis Keim

Continued from page 499

Our award-winning service departments protect their old-fashioned values in a contemporary world. Among our franchises, you will find top-notch certified technicians to service all of your vehicle needs. ■

But the experience at Woodhouse is more than just the joy of buying a new car; it's the experience within itself that makes lifelong customers. From not having to open a door to discounted maintenance plans to just the average Sunday drive around town, Woodhouse strives to make each visit a memorable one.

"Anyone who's never been to Blair may have heard that there's a big dealership with a lot of cars," says Pittack. "But there's not many places in the world where you can see this much merchandise, let alone in a town of eighty-five hundred people." It is called Truck Mountain, and people all over the country simply can't believe it when they see it.

Woodhouse Auto Family's motto is simple and straightforward: "To provide an experience that exceeds your expectations." "Our objective is to completely satisfy the customer," says Woodhouse. With desires as honest as these, it's not hard to see why they're a leader in the automotive industry. ■

At the annual Woodhouse Family Picnic, you can expect a cozy atmosphere with potato salad but add a rock climbing wall, miniature golf, bingo, and over six hundred people. These highlights are just part of what makes the picnic second to none. ■

Woodhouse Auto Family
Mahoney State Park

The impressive ceramic sculptures, called "Dangos" which in Japanese means "rounded form," on display outside the Hilton Omaha are but one example of the impact internationally-acclaimed artist Jun Kaneko has made on his adopted hometown of Omaha. Kaneko has been a significant force in the Omaha artistic community since 1983. Moving here for the opportunity offered by the kilns at the Omaha Brickworks through the Bemis Alternative Worksite, he renovated a former Old Market warehouse into an impressive studio with living space. Today, Kaneko is establishing a $38 million cultural institution adjacent to his studio that will include a museum, gallery, and two sculpture gardens. The fifty-six-thousand-square-foot facility is to become operational in 2008. The artist plans to donate as many as two thousand pieces from his personal collection, including his work and that of other artists, to the institution. Kaneko's prolific roster of creations appears in numerous international solo and group exhibitions annually. His work is included in forty museum collections, and he has realized more than twenty-five public art commissions around the globe. With the world at his doorstep, Jun Kaneko has chosen to make his home—and his art—in Omaha. **O!**

> "*It was a Sunday afternoon, and I was leaving a function at the Hilton Omaha. Walking out the front door I saw a large group of visitors to our city crowding around the Kaneko sculpture for a group photo. Their portrait of Omaha was our public art, and it reinforced to me how important this is to our community.*"
>
> *Pete Festersen, Greater Omaha Chamber of Commerce*

Darkness falls on the historic 10th Street bridge and the Durham Western Heritage Museum as residents and visitors gather at one of the city's many outdoor celebrations. Both the bridge, redesigned by HDR in 2002, and the museum are fine examples of the rewards that come from the community's active preservation programs. No longer a passenger-filled railroad terminal, the museum brings people together for a variety of other reasons. No longer a route for horse-drawn carriages or streetcars, the bridge still carries people to and from work, and home, and play. The picture is quite symbolic. Omahans are eagerly moving toward an exciting, dynamic future, yet we are mindful not to forget our past along the way. O!

Omaha Featured Companies

Alegent Health

1010 North 96th Street, Suite 200
Omaha, Nebraska 68114-2995
P: 1.800.ALEGENT
F: 402.398.6032
W: www.alegent.com

Health Care (pp. 412–414)

Alegent Health a nonprofit, faith-based health system, the largest in Nebraska, with a network of nine acute hospitals serving more than 320,000 people annually. It is sponsored by Catholic Health Initiatives and Immanuel Health Systems and founded on the traditions of the Sisters of Mercy, Regional Community of Omaha, and the Evangelical Lutheran Church of America, Nebraska Synod.

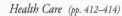

American National Bank

8990 West Dodge Road
Omaha, Nebraska 68114
P: 402.399.5042
F: 402.399.5057
W: www.anbank.com

Financial Institution—Bank (pp. 230–231)

American National Bank offers commercial banking, cash management, premiere banking, mortgage and construction lending, and other services in over twenty communities in Nebraska and Iowa.

Anderson Partners

1650 Farnam Street, Suite 1010
Omaha, Nebraska 68102
P: 402.341.4807
F: 402.341.2846
W: www.andersonpartners.com

Consulting Firm—Public Relations, Marketing & Advertising (p. 46)

Anderson Partners is a full-service advertising, public relations, and marketing consulting company based in Omaha, Nebraska, which serves a broad range of national and local clients in the health care, food, and retail industries.

Apollo Building Corporation

3102 South 169th Plaza
Omaha, Nebraska 68130
P: 402.502.7411
F: 402.502.7414
W: www.apollohomes.com

Construction—Home Builders (pp. 460–462)

Apollo Building Corporation has a thirty-year record of building top-quality homes, townhomes, and villas in the Omaha area.

Aquila-Metro Omaha Operations

501 West Sixth
Papillon, Nebraska 68046
P: 800.303.0752
F: 402.437.1736
W: www.aquiladevelopment.com

Utility (p. 272)

Based in Kansas City, Missouri, Aquila, Inc. (NYSE: ILA), operates electricity and natural gas distribution networks, serving customers in seven states. In Nebraska, Aquila delivers safe, reliable natural gas service to more than 110 communities in the eastern third of the state.

Arc of Omaha at the Ollie Webb Center, Inc., The

1941 South 42nd Street
Suite 122
Omaha, Nebraska 68105
P: 402.346.5220
W: www.olliewebb.org

Nonprofit—Disabilities (p. 352)

Since the 1950s, The Arc of Omaha at the Ollie Webb Center, Inc. has discovered untapped abilities, improved the quality of life, changed perceptions, and influenced the legislature for families and people with developmental disabilities.

Bass & Associates, Inc.

2027 Dodge Street, Suite 500
Omaha, Nebraska 68102
P: 402.346.1505
F: 402.346.6454
W: www.bass-inc.com

Consulting Firm—Technology (p. 200)

Bass & Associates, Inc., is one of Omaha's most prominent information technology consulting firms. Featuring a comprehensive array of business and technical services, the company offers clients customized, high-quality business solutions for any number of complex issues.

Blackwell Sanders Peper Martin, LLP

1620 Dodge Street, Suite 2100
Omaha, Nebraska 68102
P: 402.964.5000
F: 402.964.5050
W: www.blackwellsanders.com

Law Firm *(pp. 206–208)*

With offices in Nebraska, Missouri, Washington, D.C., and London, Blackwell Sanders Peper Martin distinguishes itself by offering its commercial clients exemplary transactional and litigation services no matter the location, jurisdiction, or international borders.

Bland & Associates, P.C.

8712 West Dodge Road, Suite 200
Omaha, Nebraska 68114
P: 402.397.8822
F: 402.397.8649
W: www.blandcpa.com

CPA *(pp. 260–261)*

Bland & Associates, P.C., is a public accounting firm that strives to achieve excellence through the personal attentiveness shown to its clients. With expertise in accounting and auditing, taxation, business valuation, forensic accounting, cost segregation, and management consulting, the firm works with numbers and people every day. Discerning their differences is what sets the firm apart from others.

Blue Cross and Blue Shield of Nebraska

7261 Mercy Road
Omaha, Nebraska 68180
P: 402.390.1800
W: www.bcbsne.com

Insurance—Health Care *(pp. 218–220)*

Blue Cross and Blue Shield of Nebraska is a mutual insurance company providing affordable health-care coverage to Nebraskans. Founded in 1939, Blue Cross and Blue Shield's commitment to service is evidenced by the company's relationship with its members, and its contracted physicians, hospitals, and other health-care providers. Blue Cross and Blue Shield of Nebraska is an independent licensee of the Blue Cross and Blue Shield Association.

Borsheim's Fine Jewelry and Gifts

120 Regency Parkway
Omaha, Nebraska 68114
P: 800.642.GIFT
F: 402.391.2762
W: www.borsheims.com

Retail—Jewelry *(pp. 54–55)*

Since 1870, Borsheim's Fine Jewelry and Gifts has earned a legendary international reputation for expertise, selection, and customer service. With over one hundred thousand pieces of inventory, Borsheim's is proud to offer a stunning selection of spectacular diamond and gemstone jewelry, fine watches, elegant tableware, and exceptional gifts.

Brownell-Talbot School

400 North Happy Hollow Boulevard
Omaha, Nebraska 68132
P: 402.556.3772
F: 402.553.2994
W: www.brownell.edu

School—Private

Brownell-Talbot is Nebraska's only independent, coeducational private college preparatory school. Serving a diverse student body of approximately 450 individuals from preschool to twelfth grade, Brownell-Talbot is recognized for its focus on excellence in scholarship and personal growth.

C&A Industries, Inc.

11825 Q Street
Omaha, Nebraska 68137-3503
P: 402.891.0009
F: 402.891.9461
W: www.ca-industries.com

Staffing Firm *(pp. 478–481)*

C&A Industries, Inc. is a multifaceted staffing firm that specializes in a variety of industries, from the medical and information technology fields to the financial and administrative industries. The company comprises six staffing divisions: Aureus Medical Group, Aureus Finance & Accounting, Aureus Executive, Aureus Systems, AurStaff, and Celebrity Staffing, as well as two nonstaffing divisions: AurTravel and AurHomes.

Certified Transmission

1801 South 54th Street
Omaha, Nebraska 68106
P: 402.558.2117
F: 402.558.2202
W: www.certifiedtransmission.com

Remanufacturing Company—Transmissions *(pp. 234–237)*

Certified Transmission utilizes a centralized remanufacturing procedure to bring together quality, price, and speed into one convenient package. By living up to its motto, "The Job Done Right . . . at the Right Price," Certified Transmission has become the largest transmission remanufacturer in the Midwest and earned the National Torch Award for Marketplace Ethics.

Children's Hospital

8200 Dodge Street
Omaha, Nebraska 68114
P: 402.955.6951
F: 402.955.6959
W: www.chsomaha.org

Health Care—Hospital *(pp. 364–365)*

Children's Hospital is a 142-bed, nonprofit, pediatric health-care facility drawing patients from around the region for conditions ranging from primary to critical to specialized care.

City of Omaha
1819 Farnam Street
Office of the Mayor
Omaha, Nebraska 68183
P: 402.444.5000
F: 402.444.6059
W: www.ci.omaha.ne.us

Government—City (pp. 34–37)
Distinguished by over 150 years of progressive city leadership, Omaha has developed into one of the Midwest's most prosperous and livable cities.

Coldwell Banker Commercial World Group
780 North 114th Street
Omaha, Nebraska 68154
P: 402.697.8899
F: 402.697.8585
W: www.worldgroupllc.com

Real Estate—Commercial (p. 136)
Coldwell Banker Commercial World Group is a full-service commercial real estate firm that offers seller and landlord representation, buyer and tenant representation, property management services, and more.

College of Saint Mary
1901 South 72nd Street
Omaha, Nebraska 68124
P: 402.399.2400 or 800.926.5534
F: 402.399.2341
W: www.csm.edu

School—College (p. 438)
College of Saint Mary is a Catholic college dedicated to the education of women in an environment that calls forth potential and fosters leadership.

Commercial Federal Bank
13220 California Street
Omaha, Nebraska 68154
P: 402.514.5306
F: 402.514.5486
W: www.comfedbank.com

Financial Institution—Bank (pp. 286–289)
With locations in seven states, including its headquarters in Omaha, Commercial Federal Bank is not only one of the largest financial institutions in the central United States, but also one of the most innovative and community-minded.

ConAgra Foods
One ConAgra Drive
Omaha, Nebraska 68102
P: 402.595.5129
F: 402.595.4707
W: www.conagrafoods.com

Manufacturing Company—Food Products (pp. 210–213)
With a history in Nebraska that goes back to 1867, ConAgra Foods is as committed as ever to producing the foods that consumers love and the expertise that customers value, while remaining a company that cares for the land and its communities.

Cornerstone Mansion, The
140 North 39th Street
Omaha, Nebraska 68131
P: 402.558.7600 or 888.883.7745
F: 402.551.6598
W: www.cornerstonemansion.com

Hotel—Inn (pp. 138–139)
The Cornerstone Mansion is an elegant guest inn located in Omaha's historic Gold Coast district. Built in 1894, the Gothic Revival–style manor offers seven distinctive guest rooms, a living room, library, and formal dining room surrounding an elegant foyer and grand staircase. It also serves as a special-event facility, hosting corporate meetings, weddings, and luncheons, among other occasions.

Creighton University
2500 California Plaza
Omaha, Nebraska 68178
P: 402.280.2700
F: 402.280.2549
W: www.creighton.edu

School—University (pp. 466–468)
Creighton University is one of twenty-eight Jesuit colleges in the nation. The school has been listed as number one in the *U.S. News & World Report* rankings of Midwest comprehensive universities seven times and is considered one of the top ten Catholic universities in the country. Offering fifty majors in a wide array of subject areas, Creighton serves more than sixty-five hundred students annually.

Creighton University Medical Center
601 North 30th Street
Omaha, Nebraska 68131
P: 402.449.4000
F: 402.449.4428
W: www.creightonhospital.com

Health Care—Medical Center (pp. 340–343)
Creighton University Medical Center is the one of the region's premier academic medical centers, serving patients throughout eastern Nebraska and western Iowa. The organization comprises St. Joseph Hospital; the Creighton University Schools of Medicine, Nursing, Dentistry, Pharmacy, and Health Professions; Creighton University Medical Laboratories; the Center for Health Policy and Ethics; and Creighton University Medical Associates.

Crowne Plaza Hotel Omaha–Old Mill

655 North 108th Avenue
Omaha, Nebraska 68154
P: 402.496.0850
F: 402.493.8848
W: www.ichotelsgroup.com

Hotel (pp. 90–92)

The Crowne Plaza Hotel Omaha–Old Mill, conveniently located in West Omaha, prides itself on being every guest's home away from home. The deluxe property offers 223 guest rooms, including 11 guest suites, and a wide variety of superior amenities, including the Crowne Plaza Sleep Advantage, complimentary high-speed Internet access, an oversized swimming pool, Jacuzzi, business center, and much more.

Curt Hofer Construction, Inc.

2332 Bob Boozer Drive
Omaha, Nebraska 68130
P: 402.758.0440
F: 402.758.0443
W: www.curthofer.com

Construction—General Contractor (pp. 472–475)

Since 1990, Curt Hofer Construction, Inc. has been building one-of-a-kind luxury homes. After a decade of head-to-head competition in the Omaha area, the firm has taken home the bulk of awards, ranging from People's Choice to Best Custom Builder to Best Overall.

Destination Midtown

1301 Harney Street
Omaha, Nebraska 68102
P: 402.233.7142
F: 402.346.7050
W: www.destinationmidtown.org

Non-Profit—Community Development (pp. 354–355)

Destination Midtown is an unprecedented coalition working on a comprehensive plan for the city's urban district that is designed to enhance the area and make it a destination of choice in Omaha.

DLR Group

400 Essex Court
Omaha, Nebraska 68114
P: 402.393.4100
W: www.dlrgroup.com

Architect (pp. 162–164)

DLR Group is a firm that people look to for innovation and the design resources to produce premier facilities that have unique design characteristics. The Peter Kiewit Institute, Qwest Center Omaha, Creighton University soccer stadium, and Tecumseh State Correctional Institution are four prime examples.

Durham Western Heritage Museum

801 South 10th Street
Omaha, Nebraska 68108
P: 402.444.5071
W: www.dwhm.org

Museum—History (pp. 68–71)

At the Durham Western Heritage Museum, visitors can explore history in a hands-on atmosphere, enjoy countless opportunities to discover Omaha's history, and remember the lives of the people who traveled through the former Union Station during the 1930s, 1940s, and 1950s.

Famous Dave's

locations:
7051 Ames Street
1101 Harney Street
17330 West Center Street
2015 Pratt Avenue (Highway 370 and Cornhusker Road)
Omaha, Nebraska
W: www.famousdaves.com

Restaurant (pp. 42–43)

The best barbecue, side dishes, desserts, and good family fun are found at any of the four Famous Dave's restaurants in Omaha.

FIRM, The

8025 Maple Street
Omaha, Nebraska 68134
P: 402.493.7760
F: 402.493.8275
W: www.thefirminc-ne.com

Financial Institution—Mortgage Company (pp. 448–449)

The FIRM, First Independent Residential Mortgage, is a personal mortgage lending company. Founded in 1995 and guided by principles of the Christian faith, The FIRM has earned a reputation for extraordinary customer service.

First Data Corporation

6902 Pine Street, PS20
Omaha, Nebraska 68106
P: 402.222.8195
F: 402.222.8554
W: www.firstdatacorp.com

Technology—Credit (pp. 252–253)

First Data Corporation is a leader in electronic commerce and payment services. With global headquarters in Denver and key operations in Omaha, First Data serves millions of merchants and consumers, making it easy, fast, and secure for people and businesses to buy goods and services, using virtually any form of payment: credit, debit, smart card, stored-value card, or check at the point-of-sale, over the Internet or by money transfer.

First National Bank

1620 Dodge Street
Omaha, Nebraska 68197
P: 402.341.0500
W: www.firstnational.com

Financial Institution—Bank (pp. 306–309)
First National Bank has provided personalized attention and innovative products to the people of Omaha and the Midwest since 1857.

First Westroads Bank

10855 West Dodge Road
Omaha, Nebraska 68154-2666
P: 402.778.1307
F: 402.778.1397
W: www.fwrb.com

Financial Institution—Bank (pp. 202–203)
Since its founding fifty years ago, the locally owned and operated First Westroads Bank has remained committed to serving the personalized needs of its personal, business, and entrepreneurial customers.

Fraser Stryker

500 Energy Plaza
409 South 17th Street
Omaha, Nebraska 68102
P: 402.341.6000
F: 402.341.8290
W: www.fraserstryker.com

Law Firm (pp. 248–249)
Fraser Stryker is a century-old firm with roots that extend far beyond Omaha through an innovative approach to law.

Gallup Organization, The

1001 Gallup Drive
Omaha, Nebraska 68102-4222
P: 402.938.6195
F: 402.938.5917
W: www.gallup.com

Consulting Firm—Information (pp. 256–257)
The Gallup Organization has studied human nature and behavior for more than seventy years. Gallup employs many of the world's leading scientists in management, economics, psychology, and sociology. Gallup's two thousand professionals deliver services at client organizations, through the Web, at Gallup University's campuses, and in forty offices around the world.

Great Western Bank

9290 West Dodge Road
Omaha, Nebraska 68114
P: 402.952.6000
F: 402.393.6819
W: www.greatwesternbank.com

Financial Institution—Bank (p. 292)
Great Western Bank is an independently owned community bank with nineteen local branches, online capabilities, and the full scope of products and services for retail and commercial customers.

Greater Omaha Chamber of Commerce

1301 Harney Street
Omaha, Nebraska 68102
P: 402.346.5000
F: 402.346.7050
W: www.omahachamber.org &
www.accessomaha.com

Chamber of Commerce (pp. 50–51)
The Chamber is the catalyst organization that ensures Greater Omaha is a vibrant place to do business, work, and live by encouraging new and existing commercial growth, providing a unifying voice for the business community and serving as a facilitator for business resources.

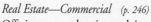

Greater Omaha Convention & Visitors Bureau

1001 Farnam-on-the-Mall, Suite 200
Omaha, Nebraska 68104
P: 402.444.4660 or 866.YES.OMAHA
W: www.visitomaha.com

Visitors Bureau (pp. 64–65)
The Greater Omaha Convention & Visitors Bureau, a division of the City of Omaha, promotes the Omaha area as an exciting destination for those planning business conventions and meetings, group tours, and family reunions.

Grubb & Ellis/Pacific Realty

1905 Harney Street
Omaha, Nebraska 68102
P: 402.345.5866
F: 402.345.0422
W: www.gepacificrealty.com

Real Estate—Commercial (p. 246)
Offering comprehensive and integrated real estate advisory services, Grubb & Ellis/Pacific Realty has grown to become one of the most successful regional commercial real estate firms serving Nebraska and Iowa.

HDR
8404 Indian Hills Drive
Omaha, Nebraska 68114
P: 402.399.1474
W: www.hdrinc.com

Engineering Firm *(pp. 108–111)*
HDR, Inc. is an architectural, engineering, and consulting firm providing out-of-the-ordinary solutions, which is one reason they have major projects in all fifty states and several countries.

Hilton Omaha
1001 Cass Street
Omaha, Nebraska 68102
P: 402.998.3400
F: 402.998.4242
W: www.omaha.hilton.com

Hotel *(pp. 150–153)*
The Hilton Omaha is a new property in the city's downtown area that is connected to the convention center and that offers premier accommodations, dining, and amenities.

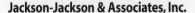

Home Instead Senior Care
13330 California Street
Suite 200
Omaha, Nebraska 68124
P: 402.498.4466
W: www.homeinstead.com

Home Care *(p. 362)*
Home Instead Senior Care, which is the world's largest provider of nonmedical companionship and home-care services, was founded in 1994 by Omaha natives Paul and Lori Hogan. In addition to offices in Omaha, Bellevue, and Fremont, it has locally owned franchise offices in Canada, Japan, Portugal, Australia, and Ireland.

Jackson-Jackson & Associates, Inc.
1905 North 81st Street
Omaha, Nebraska 68114
P: 402.391.3999
F: 402.391.3583
W: www.jackson-jacksonassociates.com

Architect *(pp. 170–171)*
Clients throughout Nebraska and the Midwest depend on architectural innovator Jackson-Jackson & Associates, Inc., to create beautiful and functional buildings that improve the quality of life for people and their communities.

John A. Gentleman Mortuaries
14151 Pacific Street
Omaha, Nebraska 68134
P: 402.391.1664
W: www.johnagentleman.com

Mortuary *(pp. 302–303)*
The motto of John A. Gentleman is "Service Beyond the Service," which means they do whatever a family needs to help them during their healing process.

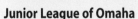

Junior League of Omaha
608 North 108 Court
Omaha, Nebraska 68154
P: 402.493.8818
F: 402.493.5823
W: www.juniorleagueomaha.org

Volunteer *(pp. 76–77)*
The Junior League of Omaha reaches out to women of all races, religions, and national origins who demonstrate a commitment to volunteerism, empowering them with the training and support to make positive changes in their communities.

Knights of Ak-Sar-Ben Foundation, (The)
302 South 36th Street, Suite 800
Omaha, Nebraska 68131
P: 402.554.9600
F: 402.554.9609
W: www.aksarben.org

Nonprofit—Philanthropic *(pp. 80–81)*
Since 1895, this civic and philanthropic organization has—through scholarships, volunteerism awards, and community partnerships—upheld its mission: "To build a more prosperous Heartland, where communities can flourish and every child can succeed."

Koley Jessen P.C.,
A Limited Liability Organization
One Pacific Place, Suite 800
1125 South 103rd Street
Omaha, Nebraska 68124
P: 402.390.9500
F: 402.390.9005
W: www.koleyjessen.com

Law Firm *(pp. 224–225)*
The law firm of Koley Jessen represents businesses and individuals in a full spectrum of practice areas. Since its founding in 1988, the firm has been guided by its belief in placing the interests of clients first, providing quality and diverse legal services and a commitment to its community.

Kutak Rock LLP
1650 Farnam Street
Omaha, Nebraska 68102
P: 402.346.6000
F: 402.346.1148
W: www.kutakrock.com

Law Firm (p. 216)
From a network of sixteen offices, Kutak Rock LLP provides legal services to a wide variety of clients across a broad spectrum of businesses.

Lauritzen Gardens, Omaha's Botanical Center
100 Bancroft Street
Omaha, Nebraska 68108
P: 402.346.4002
F: 402.346.8948
W: www.omahabotanicalgardens.org

Botanical Gardens (p. 26 - 27)
Lauritzen Gardens, Omaha's Botanical Center, is a one-hundred-acre living plant museum located near the banks of the Missouri River. Boasting a wide array of botanical displays, a thirty-two-thousand-square-foot visitor and education center, annual festivals, and more, the venue has become one of the city's must-see destinations, attracting more than one hundred thousand visitors per year.

LEO A DALY
8600 Indian Hills Drive
Omaha, Nebraska 68114
P: 402.391.8111
F: 402.391.8564
W: www.leoadaly.com

Architects (pp. 114–116)
With nearly a century of experience and a staff of over one thousand multidisciplined professionals, this world-renowned architecture, planning, engineering, and interior design firm is committed to providing clients with nothing less than the broadest range of services and the highest possible level of expertise.

Lovgren Marketing Group
120 Regency Parkway, Suite 280
Omaha, Nebraska 68114
P: 402.397.7158
F: 402.397.0354
W: www.lovgren.com

Marketing Firm (pp. 158–159)
Lovgren Marketing Group is a strategic-based hands-on marketing communications and public relations firm. Lovgren Marketing Group has been bringing business-building ideas to clients since 1978.

Lund Company, The
120 Regency Parkway
Omaha, Nebraska 68114
P: 402.393.8811
F: 402.393.2402
W: www.lundco.com

Real Estate—Commercial & Investment (pp. 282–283)
The Lund Company is a commercial and investment real estate firm managing and marketing some 5.1 million square feet of retail, office, and industrial space as well as multifamily properties valued at over $500 million.

McGrath North Mullin & Kratz, PC LLO
First National Tower, Suite 3700
1601 Dodge Street
Omaha, Nebraska 68102
P: 402.341.3070
F: 402.341.0216
W: www.mnmk.com

Law Firm (pp. 314–315)
McGrath North Mullin & Kratz, PC LLO, the second largest law firm in Nebraska, is an Omaha-based law firm founded in 1959 that offers a comprehensive, nationwide legal practice with the personal attention and reasonable cost of a mid-sized midwestern firm.

Methodist Health System
8511 West Dodge Road
Omaha, Nebraska 68114
P: 402.354.4800
F: 402.354.4819
W: www.bestcare.org

Health Care—Medical Center (pp. 394–396)
Methodist Health System is a regionally recognized leader in the delivery of quality health-care services. A nonprofit entity, it is composed of seven affiliates, including Nebraska Methodist Hospital; Physicians Clinic, Inc.; Jennie Edmundson Memorial Hospital; Jennie Edmundson Memorial Hospital Foundation; Nebraska Methodist College; Nebraska Methodist Hospital Foundation; and Shared Services System.

Metro Omaha Builders Association
11421 Davenport Street
Omaha, Nebraska 68154
P: 402.333.2000
F: 402.333.2002
W: www.moba.com

Association—Builder (pp. 488–489)
The Metro Omaha Builders Association is an organization of individuals, firms, and related industries involved in the building and development of residential and light commercial properties. For its members the organization creates value, and for the community as a whole it promotes quality housing and a favorable building climate.

Metropolitan Community College
PO Box 3777
Omaha, Nebraska 68103-0777
P: 402.457.2400
F: 402.457.2413
W: www.mccneb.edu

School—College (pp. 400–402)
Metropolitan Community College serves students with more than one hundred one- and two-year associate degree, certificate, and specialized diploma programs that are designed to provide outstanding career training and preparation. The school was established in 1974 and today offers a wide array of classes at three main campuses and three educational centers throughout the metropolitan area.

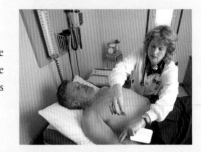

Midwest Minor Medical
5310 South 84th Street
Suite 100
Omaha, Nebraska 68127
P: 402.827.6510
W: www.midwestminormedical.com

Health Care—Medical Center (pp. 346–347)
Midwest Minor Medical was the first urgent-care center in Omaha, and their three clinics have been providing quality care and convenience seven days a week since 1982. Their mission is to provide families with prompt treatment for minor injuries and illnesses, and to offer businesses a variety of occupational health services.

Mutual of Omaha
3300 Mutual of Omaha Plaza
Omaha, Nebraska 68175-0002
P: 402.351.2889
F: 402.351.2404
W: www.mutualofomaha.com

Insurance & Financial Institution (pp. 240–243)
For nearly one hundred years, Mutual of Omaha has distinguished itself by providing insurance and financial services that allow its clients to care for the present and plan for the future.

Nebraska Wesleyan University
11815 M Street, Suite 100
Omaha, Nebraska 68137
P: 402.827.3555
F: 402.827.3647
W: www.wesleyanadvantage.com

School—University (pp. 328–329)
Nebraska Wesleyan University is an independent liberal arts institution founded in 1887 by the Nebraska Methodists. Students can select from more than fifty-one traditional undergraduate majors on the Lincoln campus. Three disciplines are available to nontraditional students through the accelerated Wesleyan Advantage program on both the Lincoln and Omaha campuses: business, social work (Lincoln only), and nursing.

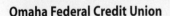

NP Dodge Real Estate
12002 Pacific Street
Omaha, Nebraska 68154
P: 402.938.5008
W: www.npdodge.com

Real Estate—Commercial (p. 484)
NP Dodge is one of the largest full-service real estate companies in the region, providing services in residential real estate, land development, insurance, employee benefits, commercial real estate, property management, global relocation services, and title services.

Omaha Federal Credit Union
3001 South 82nd Avenue
Omaha, Nebraska 68124
P: 402.399.9001
F: 402.399.0129
W: www.omahafcu.org

Financial Institution—Credit Union (pp. 274–275)
Omaha Federal Credit Union operates seven branches in the four-county area and has more than $50 million in assets. As a federally chartered credit union, OFCU is organized under strict regulatory laws that are monitored and enforced by the National Credit Union Administration (an agency of the U.S. government).

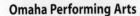

Omaha Hearing School for Children, Inc., The
1110 North 66th Street
Omaha, Nebraska 68132
P: 877.672.5332
W: www.oraldeafed.org

School—Hearing Impaired (p. 370)
The mission of the Omaha Hearing School is to serve children who are deaf or hard-of-hearing, their families, and the community by providing auditory oral education that teaches children to listen and talk . . . so choices will be available to them in the talking and hearing world.

Omaha Performing Arts
1314 Douglas-on-the-Mall, 15th Floor
Omaha, Nebraska 68102
P: 402.345.0202
F: 402.345.0222
W: www.omahaperformingarts.org

Nonprofit—Performing Arts (pp. 146–147)
Omaha Performing Arts is a nonprofit organization that serves as steward and manager of the Orpheum Theater and Holland Performing Arts Center, as a presenter of national and international touring artists, and as an arts educational and community involvement program provider.

Omaha Print
4700 F Street
Omaha, Nebraska 68117
P: 402.734.4400
F: 402.734.7492
W: www.omahaprint.com

Commercial Printer (pp. 184–186)
Building on a proud history of over one hundred years of service, today Omaha Press produces full-color catalogs, magazines, booklets and marketing brochures, statement stuffers, newspaper inserts, and direct marketing materials.

Omaha Public Power District
444 South 16th Street Mall
Omaha, Nebraska 68102-2247
W: www.oppd.com

Utility (pp. 432–434)
Omaha Public Power District, established in 1946, is a public utility owned by the people it serves in thirteen southeast Nebraska counties. The largest electrical utility in Nebraska, OPPD has also maintained rates well below the national average, and continually ranks as a national leader in customer satisfaction.

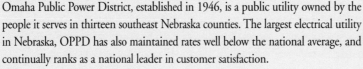

Omaha Public Schools
3215 Cuming Street
Omaha, Nebraska 68131
P: 402.557.2222
F: 402.557.2079
W: www.ops.org

School—Public System (p. 458)
Omaha Public Schools, which enrolls approximately forty-six thousand students annually in eighty-three schools, is one of the country's few major urban school districts to maintain state AA accreditation. Its mission is to provide educational opportunities that enable all students to achieve their highest potential.

Omaha's Henry Doorly Zoo
3701 S. Tenth Street
Omaha, Nebraska 68107-2200
P: 402.733.8401
F: 402.738.2083
W: www.omahazoo.com

Attraction—Zoo (pp. 104–106)
This first-class entertainment facility is more than just a zoo; it's a world-renowned center for conservation, research, and education, whose professionals and interns work both on-site and in the field to help protect and enhance the world's wild animal and plant populations.

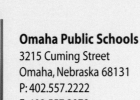

Oriental Trading Company, Inc.
4206 South 108th Street
Omaha, NE 68137
P: 402.596.2401
F: 402.331.9017
W: www.orientaltrading.com

Import/Export—Novelty Wholesaler (pp. 130–133)
Oriental Trading Company, Inc. is one of the nation's leading direct marketers of value-priced novelties, toys, party supplies, crafts, imported gift items, and more through the Internet, catalogs, and a direct sales force. The company is recognized as one of the country's top 100 Internet retailers and one of Omaha's 25 Fastest Growing Companies.

Papio–Missouri River Natural Resources District
8901 South 154th Street
Omaha, Nebraska 68138
P: 402.444.6222
W: www:papionrd.org

Nonprofit—Environmental (pp. 96–97)
Papio–Missouri River Natural Resources District creates multipurpose projects that combine sound resources management with recreation and other quality-of-life benefits.

Peter Kiewit Institute/Scott Technology Center
1110 S. 67th Street
Omaha, Nebraska 68182
P: 402.554.3333
W: www.pki.nebraska.edu & www.scott-technology.com

School—Technical Institute (pp. 404–407)
Peter Kiewit Institute works with the University of Nebraska–Lincoln's College of Engineering and Technology, the University of Nebraska at Omaha's College of Information Science and Technology, and business leaders working with real-world applications. The Scott Technology Center is a direct outgrowth of PKI.

Prudential Ambassador Real Estate
1045 North 115th Street, Suite 208
Omaha, Nebraska 68154
P: 402.493.4663
F: 402.932.1703
W: www.paomaha.com

Real Estate—Residential (pp. 452–454)
Prudential Ambassador Real Estate, with almost two hundred agents, serves the metropolitan Omaha market with numerous residential real estate services, including buying, listing, and corporate relocation. With downtown Omaha's urban revitalization, the company also now specializes in the condo and loft living market sector.

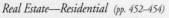

Qwest
1314 Douglas Street
Omaha, Nebraska 68102
P: 800.899.7780
F: 303.896.8515
W: www.qwest.com

Telecommunications Company (pp. 422–424)
As a leading provider of telecommunications and wireless services in the West and Midwest, Qwest's Spirit of Service in Action™ is going strong in Omaha, where it continues a 125-year legacy of providing exemplary products, services, and community action.

Qwest Center Omaha
455 North 10th Street
Omaha, Nebraska 68102
P: 402.341.1500
F: 402.991.1501
W: www.qwestcenteromaha.com

Convention Center (pp. 124–125)
Qwest Center Omaha is a state-of-the art, $291 million convention center and arena in the heart of the revitalized historic downtown and riverfront area. Qwest Center Omaha attracts businesses and organizations from across the country because of its affordability, accessibility, and overall appeal.

Rossi Clothiers
11032 Elm Street
Omaha, Nebraska 68144
P: 402.397.3608
F: 402.397.9695

Retail—Apparel (p. 74)
Since 1991, Rossi Clothiers has provided Omaha's professional men with access to some of the finest clothing lines from around the world. In addition to excellent merchandise, this leading men's specialty store also prides itself on offering unparalleled customer service in a genuinely welcoming environment.

Rotella's Italian Bakery, Inc.
6949 South 108th Street
LaVista, Nebraska 68128
P: 402.592.6600
W: www.rotellasbakery.com

Bakery (pp. 84–87)
Rotella's Italian Bakery, Inc., specializes in breads and rolls made in their state-of-the-art production facility from ingredients that ensure products superior in appearance and nutrition.

SAC Federal Credit Union
11515 South 39th Street
Omaha, Nebraska 68123
P: 402.292.8000
F: 402.293.9074
W: www.sacfcu.com

Financial Institution—Credit Union (pp. 318–320)
As a not-for-profit, full-service financial cooperative owned by its members and serving Douglas, Sarpy, Cass, and Pottawattamie counties, SAC Federal Credit Union provides a host of benefits to its membership, not the least of which is responsive, personalized service and the latest in financial services technologies.

Security National Bank of Omaha
1120 South 101st Street
Omaha, Nebraska 68124
P: 402.344.7300
F: 402.449.0977
W: www.snbconnect.com

Financial Institution—Bank (pp. 298–299)
Established in 1964, Security National Bank is one of Omaha,s preeminent community banks. With personal and business banking, loan services, an investment company, a trust division, and an extensive branch and ATM network, the organization boasts more than $470 million in assets and is one of the city,s most distinguished full-service community financial institutions. Member FDIC.

SilverStone Group
11516 Miracle Hills Drive
Omaha, Nebraska 68154
P: 800.288.5501
F: 402.964.5454
W: www.ssgi.com

Insurance & Financial Institution (pp. 442–443)
Since 1945, SilverStone Group has provided business and individual clients with the insurance, human resources, investment, and benefit services that help eliminate risk, manage assets, and grow wealth.

SITEL Corporation
7277 World Communications Drive
Omaha, Nebraska 68122
P: 800.257.4835
F: 402.963.3097
W: www.sitel.com

Outsourcing Company (pp. 264–266)
Since 1985, SITEL Corporation has helped some of the world's leading industries grow their businesses by providing customer support as well as operational and information technology services that achieve the highest levels of customer satisfaction, retention, and loyalty.

U.S. Bank
1700 Farnam Street
Omaha, Nebraska 68102
P: 402.348.2921
W: www.usbank.com

Financial Institution—Bank (pp. 278–279)
With the backing of U.S. Bancorp's $195 billion in assets, Omaha's U.S. Bank provides a wide range of high-tech services locally, nationally, and internationally.

UltraAir, LLC
3737 Orville Plaza
Omaha, Nebraska 68110
P: 402.345.7372
F: 402.345.7371
W: www.ultraaircharter.com

Aircraft Charter Service (pp. 120–121)
UltraAir operates the area's highest-quality aircraft charter service for clients traveling throughout North and South America and the Caribbean.

Union Pacific Corporation
1400 Douglas Avenue
Omaha, Nebraska 68179
P: 402.544.4250
W: www.up.com

Transportation—Railroad (pp. 194–197)
Maintaining a legacy of innovation and efficiency that goes back over 140 years, as a transportation company, Union Pacific continues to move the goods, services, and people that help build America.

United Way of the Midlands
1805 Harney Street
Omaha, Nebraska 68102
P: 402.342.8232
F: 402.522.7995
W: www.uwmidlands.org

Nonprofit—Community Service (pp. 418–419)
Since 1923, United Way of the Midlands has raised funds for human care programs in the three-county metropolitan area. The organization offers community service information by phone (Dial 211) and over the Web, and recruits volunteers of all ages.

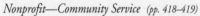

University of Nebraska at Omaha
6001 Dodge Street
Omaha, Nebraska 68182-0286
P: 402.554.2800
F: 402.554.2789
W: www.unomaha.edu

School—University (pp. 386–389)
The University of Nebraska at Omaha (UNO) is an urban-based university located in midtown Omaha. With a strategic mission to place students first, strive for academic excellence, and engage with the community, UNO serves more than fifteen thousand students with a truly unique and award-winning educational experience.

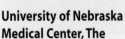

University of Nebraska Medical Center, The
987400 Nebraska Medical Center
Omaha, Nebraska 68198
P: 402.559.2000
F: 402.595.1091
W: www.nebraskamed.com

Health Care—Hospital (pp. 376–381)
Formed in 1997 with the merger of Clarkson Hospital and University Hospital, the Nebraska Medical Center is a 689-bed not-for-profit hospital known for its excellence and innovation in medicine. As the primary teaching hospital for its partner, the University of Nebraska Medical Center, the hospital is a respected leader in transplantation, neuroscience, and cancer and cardiac care.

University of Nebraska Foundation
8712 West Dodge Road, Suite 100
Omaha, Nebraska 68114
P: 402.595.2302
F: 402.595.2239
W: www.nufoundation.org

Nonprofit—Scholarships (pp. 374, 382, 390)
The University of Nebraska Foundation is a nonprofit corporation supplementing support for students, faculty, facilities, and programs at the University of Nebraska's four campuses through gifts from alumni, friends, corporations, and other foundations since 1936.

Visiting Nurse Association
1941 South 42nd Street, Suite 225
Omaha, Nebraska 68105
P: 402.342.5566
F: 402.342.0034
W: www.vnam.org

Health Care Agency (pp. 358–359)
Helping patients learn independence and self-care while providing home health-care services has been the mission of this nonprofit independent health-care agency for over one hundred years.

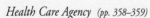

Werner Enterprises, Inc.
PO Box 45308
Omaha, Nebraska 68145-0308
P: 402.894.3000
F: 402.894.3736
W: www.werner.com

Transportation—Trucking *(pp. 492–495)*
Moving goods safely, efficiently, and economically across much of North America is the goal of Werner Enterprises, today one of the largest motor carriers of general commodities in interstate and intrastate commerce.

West Corporation
11808 Miracle Hills Drive
Omaha, Nebraska 68154
P: 800.841.9000
F: 402.963.1603
W: www.west.com

Outsourcing Company *(p. 228)*
From customer acquisition, retention, and care to technical support, conferencing, and receivables management, West Corporation provides the powerful and effective customer contact solutions that ensure success for some of the nation's premier Fortune 1000 companies.

Westin Foods
11808 West Center Road
Omaha, Nebraska 68144-4397
P: 402.691.8800
W: www.westinfoods.com

Food Industry *(pp.176–178)*
Westin Foods, the parent company and corporate headquarters for Mario® Olives and Feaster Foods, is proud to offer innovative services and the best-quality products within the industry.

Westside Community Schools
909 South 76th Street
Omaha, Nebraska 68114
P: 402.390.2100
F: 402.390.2120
W: www.westside66.org

School—PreK-12 *(pp. 428–429)*
Westside Community Schools provides preK-12 education that is steeped in community support and innovative programs.

Woodhouse Automotive Family
Blair- Highways 133 & 30
Omaha- 66th & L Street
Bellevue- Fort Crook Road North
P: 800.889.1893
F: 402.504.1503
W: www.woodhouse.com

Car Dealership *(pp. 498–501)*
This "family" of auto dealerships has developed a formula for success, resulting in nothing less than the most satisfying car buying experience nationwide.

Woodmen of the World/Omaha Woodmen Life Insurance Society
Woodmen Tower
1700 Farnam Street
Omaha, Nebraska 68102
P: 402.271.7211
W: www.woodmen.com

Insurance & Financial Institution *(pp. 294–295)*
Woodmen of the World/Omaha Woodmen Life Insurance Society is one of the nation's largest and oldest fraternal benefit organizations. In addition to a wide array of insurance and financial products and services, the society provides value-added benefits and numerous community service opportunities for its more than eight hundred thousand members nationwide.

Thank you for supporting our community!

Omaha's Editorial Team

Rena Distasio, Senior Writer, Tijeras, New Mexico. Freelance writer Rena Distasio contributes articles and reviews on a variety of subjects to regional and national publications. In her spare time she and her husband and three dogs enjoy the great outdoors from their home in the mountains east of Albuquerque.

Grace Hawthorne, Writer, Atlanta, Georgia. Starting as a reporter, she has written everything from advertising for septic tanks to the libretto for an opera. While in New York, she worked for Time-Life Books and wrote for *Sesame Street.* As a performer, she has appeared at the Carter Presidential Center, Callanwolde Fine Arts Center, and at various corporate functions. Her latest project is a two-woman show called *Pushy Broads and Proper Southern Ladies.*

Amy Meadows, Writer, Canton, Georgia. Meadows is an accomplished feature writer who has been published in a wide variety of local, regional, and national consumer and trade publications since launching her freelance writing career in 2000. She also specializes in producing corporate marketing literature for companies large and small and holds a master of arts degree in professional writing from Kennesaw State University.

Kimberly Fox DeMeza, Writer, Roswell, Georgia. Combining business insight with creative flair, DeMeza writes to engage the audience as well as communicate the nuances of the subject matter. While officially beginning her career in public relations in 1980 with a degree in journalism, and following in 1990 with a master's in health management, writing has always been central to her professional experience. From speechwriting to corporate brochures to business magazine feature writing, DeMeza enjoys the process of crafting the message. Delving into the topic is simply one of the benefits, as she believes every writing opportunity is an opportunity to continue to learn.

Regina Roths, Writer, Andover, Kansas. Roths has written extensively about business since launching her journalism career in the early 1990s. Her prose can be found in corporate coffee-table books nationwide as well as on regionally produced Web sites, and in print and online magazines, newspapers, and publications. Her love of industry, history, and research gives her a keen insight into writing and communicating a message.

Nick Schinker, Writer, Omaha, Nebraska. Since his first newspaper byline nearly thirty years ago, Schinker's work has been published in more than two dozen newspapers and magazines. As a freelance writer, the Omaha native has built a national market for his feature articles, Web site text, and advertising copy. In addition to his regular clients, he serves as writer-in-residence at the University of Nebraska at Omaha's College of Information Science & Technology.

Thomas S. England, Photographer, Decatur, Georgia. England grew up internationally, graduated from Northwestern University, and began photography as a newspaper photographer in the Chicago area. He began freelancing for *People* magazine in 1974. Since then he has taken assignments from national magazines and corporations, specializing in photographing people on location. He lives in Decatur, Georgia, with Nancy Foster, a home renovator, and their little dog Chessey. More of his photographs may be viewed online at www.englandphoto.com.

Eric Francis, Photographer, Omaha, Nebraska. Francis was born and raised in Nebraska. Early on, he honed his skills freelancing for local newspapers, magazines, and commercial clients. Francis now also works regularly for some of the nation's largest and best-known magazines, newspapers, and wire services, covering news, features, and sports. He continues to make his home in Omaha with his son Mitch, his girlfriend Michelle, and her children.

David Gibb, Photographer, Jacksonville, Oregon. David was raised and educated in Rochester, New York. He now operates his studio out of the historic town of Jacksonville, Oregon. David has photographed for many local and national clients including Harry and David, Jackson & Perkins, Roper U.S.A., Weyerhauser, Eastman Kodak, and Meredith Corporation. David can be reached at www.dgibbphoto.com.

Joe Guerriero, Photographer, Newton, New Jersey. A professional photographer for more than two decades, Joe operates a commercial studio out of his home in rural New Jersey with clients that include Barnes & Noble, Ames Rubber, Zurich North America, Poland Spring, and Samsung, among others. His first love, however, is travel/documentary photography. His work has appeared in many publications including *Sports Illustrated*, *Photo District News*, and *Studio Photography and Design*. Recently, Joe has completed international photo projects in Pakistan, Turkey, and Cuba. In addition to being a member of Black Star photo agency, his work has been featured at several national galleries; his work was most recently accepted into a major traveling exhibition from Lehigh University entitled *Viajeros: North American Photographers/Artists Images of Cuba*. His Web site is www.joeg.com.

Douglas Henderson, Photographer, Tulsa, Oklahoma. Doug is a commercial photographer and graphic designer. As a professional photographer his work has appeared in *The New York Times*, *Newsweek*, *Newsweek Japan*, the *National Enquirer*, and others. He has worked in the United States, Mexico, South Africa, Ghana, and Côte D'Ivoire. He is the author of several textbooks on digital photography and Adobe Photoshop. See more of his work online at www.douglashenderson.com.

Jackson Hill, Photographer, New Orleans, Louisiana. Hill is a New Orleans–based location shooter with extensive assignment experience worldwide. Jackson began his career as a photojournalist for daily newspapers in the American South. He now shoots annual reports as well as industrial and editorial assignments from the Canadian Rockies to the Gulf of Thailand. Jackson frequently shows his personal work, and samples can be seen at his studio's Web site, www.southernlights.com.

Scott Indermaur, Photographer, Lawrence, Kansas. Indermaur received a degree in journalism with an emphasis on photography at Northern Arizona University. Scott then moved to Kansas in 1992 to start his independent career, combining photography with his enthusiasm and knowledge of computers and programming to keep up to date on the latest advances in technology. Having enjoyed the fast-paced atmosphere of journalistic photography, as well as developing environmental portraiture, he decided to turn his focus to environmental portraiture for corporate annual reports, editorial magazines, and advertising. Scott lives with his wife, children, dogs, and a cat in Lawrence, Kansas, where he is also a fine food and wine enthusiast. He is an accomplished sailor and snowboarder and contributes his time to speak to and mentor students of photography. You can find more information about Scott at www.siphotography.com.

Dennis Keim, Photographer, Huntsville, Alabama. Keim is a local photographer with over twenty-five years of experience producing creative imagery for the editorial, advertising, and corporate communities. His editorial work has been featured in regional, national, and international publications. Notable in his professional career was his employment as an Aerospace Photojournalist by NASA (National Aeronautics and Space Administration) from 1976 to 2000 at the Marshall Space Flight Center. Dennis is a member of ASMP and currently maintains a commercial studio specializing in corporate, editorial, and stock photography. In addition he is an exhibited and published fine arts photographer. You can view more of his work at www.dk-studio.com.

Rod Reilly, Photographer, Atlanta, Georgia. Since 1979 Rod has used his training at Carnegie Mellon School of Design and Rochester Institute of Technology to create compelling environmental portraits on location of people as they live and work. His clients include Home Depot, Coca-Cola USA, United Parcel Service, Cox Communications, and McGraw Hill. Starting his career as a staff shooter for Georgia Pacific, Rod has owned his own studio, Reilly Arts & Letters, for the last eleven years, and travels often on assignment. He is a member of ASMP and the father of three.

Mark Romesser, Photographer, Bellevue, Nebraska. Romesser was born in Warsaw, New York, and grew up in Indiana. He graduated from Brigham Young University in 1980, and started his career as a manager of a small photography shop in Crawfordsville, Indiana. He worked for commercial photography studios in Indianapolis, Indiana; Columbus, Ohio; and Omaha, Nebraska, before starting his own photography business in 2001. He lives in Bellevue, Nebraska, with his wife Paula and their children. A sample of Mark's work can be viewed at www.markromesser.com.

Alan S. Weiner, Photographer, Portland, Oregon. Weiner travels extensively both in the United States and abroad. Over the last twenty-three years his work has appeared regularly in *The New York Times*. In addition, his pictures have been published in *USA Today* and in *Time, Newsweek, Life,* and *People* magazines. He has shot corporate work for IBM, Pepsi, UPS, and other companies large and small. He is also the cofounder of The Wedding Bureau (www .weddingbureau.com). Alan has worked throughout the Pacific Northwest and the Carolinas on books. His strengths are in photojournalism.

Greater Omaha Chamber of Commerce president and CEO
David G. Brown and the Chamber's dedicated staff, shown here in the Storz Fountain Court at Joslyn Art Museum, thank the sponsors, photographers, writers, production staff, and fellow Omahans who helped create *Omaha—Where Imagination Meets Opportunity.* O!

Magnolia trees blossom in springtime on the grounds of the Joslyn Castle, one of the many landmarks and historic places that enrich the Destination Midtown area of Omaha. Every season and every neighborhood affords exceptional beauty, making Greater Omaha a place to be treasured by its residents—and eagerly shared with the rest of the world.

About the Publisher

OMAHA–*Where Imagination Meets Opportunity* was published by Bookhouse Group, Inc., under its imprint of Riverbend Books. What many people don't realize is that in addition to picture books on American communities, we also develop and publish institutional histories, commemorative books of all types, contemporary books, and others for clients across the country.

Bookhouse has developed various types of books for prep schools from Utah to Florida, colleges and universities, country clubs, a phone company in Vermont, a church in Atlanta, hospitals, banks, and many other entities. We've also published an art collection for a gallery in Texas, a picture book for a worldwide Christian ministry, and a book on a priceless collection of art and antiques for the Atlanta History Center.

These beautiful and treasured tabletop books are developed by our staff as turnkey projects, thus making life easier for the client. If your company has an interest in our publishing services, do not hesitate to contact us.

Founded in 1989, Bookhouse Group is headquartered in a renovated 1920s tobacco warehouse in downtown Atlanta. If you're ever in town, we'd be delighted if you looked us up. Thank you for making possible the publication of OMAHA–*Where Imagination Meets Opportunity.* ∎

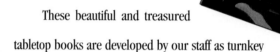

BOOKHOUSE
GROUP, INC.

Banks ∎ Prep Schools ∎ Hospitals ∎ Insurance Companies ∎ Art Galleries ∎ Museums ∎ Utilities ∎
Country Clubs ∎ Colleges ∎ Churches ∎ Military Academies ∎ Associations